The New European I

M000275077

The years since the global financial crisis have seen something of a renaissance in the manufacturing industry. The United States has launched its Advanced Manufacturing Partnership, and China owes much of its spectacular economic boom in the last decades to it being the 'world's factory'. Is there room for the EU in this landscape?

This timely new book explores Europe's role in this evolving environment. It argues that on the one hand, in terms of sheer numbers, the role of the manufacturing industry in the EU is on a par with other major global economies. However, the book also states that Europe falls short of its global competitors (the USA in particular) in terms of its involvement in the most innovative manufacturing sectors. The volume therefore argues that this creates the opportunity for a new European industrial policy.

Exploring the development of current EU policy, the book puts forward suggestions as to how the EU can improve in terms of the competitiveness of its technology policy. Placing the EU's position in the context of the industrial structures of the USA, Japan and the BRICs, this book blends theoretical models and practical examples in order to offer a state of the art look at the current and future direction of Europe's industrial policy. This book will be of relevance to all those with an interest in European economics, industrial economics, public policy, European politics and European studies.

Franco Mosconi is Associate Professor of Industrial Economics at the University of Parma, where since 2003 he has held the 'Jean Monnet Chair'.

Routledge Studies in the European Economy

The New European Industrial Policy

Global competitiveness and the manufacturing renaissance

Franco Mosconi

LONDON AND NEW YORK

First published 2015 by Routledge

2 Park Square, Milton Park, Abingdon, Oxfordshire OX14 4RN
52 Vanderbilt Avenue, New York, NY 10017

Routledge is an imprint of the Taylor & Francis Group, an informa business

First issued in paperback 2020

British Library Cataloguing in Publication Data
A catalogue record for this book is available from the British Library

Library of Congress Cataloging in Publication Data
Mosconi, Franco
The new European industrial policy: global competitiveness and the
manufacturing renaissance / Franco Mosconi.
   pages cm. – (Routledge studies in the european economy)
   1. Manufacturing industries–Europe. 2. Industrial policy–Europe–
History–21st century. I. Title.
   HD9735.A2M67 2015
   338.94–dc23   2014048163

ISBN: 978-1-138-79282-1 (hbk)
ISBN: 978-0-367-59910-2 (pbk)

Typeset in Times New Roman
by Wearset Ltd, Boldon, Tyne and Wear

To my parents

Contents

Figures

Tables

Acknowledgements

It was at the end of 2004 that I published a book under the title *Le Nuove politiche industriali dell'Europa allargata* through the publishing house of my university – Monte Parma Università Editore. The book that is currently in your hands is the evolution of that earlier project; an outgrowth, I would like to think.

The research project that ran alongside these books was initially funded by a grant from the European Commission that I received in 2003 upon being named the 'Jean Monnet Professor, Chair in *The Economics of European Industry*' at the University of Parma – a position I still hold today. This project was later funded by UniCredit and, more recently, by PGlobal – Global Advisory and Training Services Ltd, whose funding will also allow us to carry out more research on new industrial policies in the years to come. I would like to express my thanks to the European Commission, to UniCredit and to PGlobal for their generous support.

In these more than ten years, the evolution of manufacturing and industrial policy have remained my primary areas of scientific interest, to which I have dedicated both my research activities and the majority of my teaching. I have taught both at the University of Parma (in the Department of Economics and in the School of Political Science) and at the European College of Parma (a post-graduate school for European Affairs). In each of these, I have gained much from the interaction and exchange of ideas with my students, with whom I worked out some of the early forms of these analyses on various subjects.

I have been quite fortunate during these ten years to have had the opportunity to discuss portions of this research project with distinguished colleagues at national and international conferences. Of primary importance were the conferences organized annually in Italy by the academic journal *L'Industria: Rivista di Economia e Politica Industriale* – published by Il Mulino – at which I presented papers during various editions: Parma (27th edition, 2003), Ancona (28th, 2004), Foggia (31st, 2007) and Trieste (35th, 2011).

I was also honoured to discuss preliminary results of my work at the tenth edition of the EUNIP (European Network on Industrial Policy) International Conference (Florence, 2007); at the conferences organized by the University of Wroclaw under the guidance of Dr Jaroslaw Kundera on topics such as 'Economic integration in the EU enlarged' (Wroclaw, 2008), and 'Globalization, European integration and economic crisis' (Wroclaw, 2010); and, finally, at the important international symposium at the Istanbul Commerce University on 'Smart economic planning and industrial policy' (Istanbul, 2014) organized by that university in cooperation with the University of Virginia, the National University of Singapore and my own university. I am grateful to have had these opportunities, and thankful to all the organizers and participants from whom I received a constant and constructive flow of criticism and suggestions.

I give especial thanks to Giacomo Degli Antoni (Università di Parma), Sandrine Labory (Università di Ferrara), Hiroshi Nakazato (Boston College), Dani Rodrik (Institute for Advanced Studies, School of Social Science, Princeton, and previously at the John F. Kennedy School of Government, Harvard University), André Sapir (Université Libre de Bruxelles and Bruegel), Dario Velo (Università di Pavia) and Murat Yülek (Istanbul Commerce University) for the many useful comments that they provided on individual chapters of this work. I owe a particular debt to the anonymous referees who led me to expand and improve this book.

I would also like to thank those people who helped me through different stages of this work: Gabriele Roberto Maranza and Davide Paini – both graduates of our School of Political Science – for their research into certain relevant data on M&As and new EU programmes such as Horizon; Rosangela De Simone and Alessandra Lorenzano – both members of the academic coordination unit at the European College of Parma – for bringing into focus some of the important features of the *acquis communautaire*; Douglas Heise, who revised and improved the manuscript, and who also translated – from the language of Dante into that of Shakespeare – the excerpts from Italian scholars that deserved, in my opinion, to be cited herein.

Sentiments of friendship and gratitude that transcend the limits of our academic discipline of Industrial Economics go out to two people in particular: Fabio Gobbo and Romano Prodi. Fabio is sadly no longer with us. It was with him that I began my research activity more than 25 years ago at the University of Bologna (Centro di Economia e Politica Industriale), and in the intervening years, the path that I have tried to follow was often influenced by his wisdom. Romano Prodi gave me the great privilege of working with him during his first Italian Cabinet – the 'Euro Government' of 1996–1998 – and during the first years of his term as the head of the European Commission of Brussels (1999–2001). I learned great lessons from these two institutional experiences: the real possibility – not merely theoretical – of trying to help the common good; and the necessity, in the world of the twenty-first century, of a stronger Europe. Today, we share an interest in promoting empirical research as a means for making informed, intelligent decisions about policy; in this, Fabio would have been, once again, a wonderful travel companion.

In this first book with Routledge I am indebted to the Editorial Staff and, above all, to my Editor Emily Kindleysides and Editorial Assistant Laura Johnson.

My greatest debts are to my family: to Marialuisa and to my children Francesca and Filippo, for their unwavering encouragement during the period of writing this book, and for their patience with me during all these years of work and study. Without this encouragement and without this patience, I never would have made it to the finish line.

Prologue

In two acts

Something has truly changed in the world of economics over the past few years. I feel that the best proof of this change lies in two *Economist* debates from 2010 and 2011, where the positions expressed by both the managerial class and public opinion have shifted radically on a subject which, in the pursuit of simplicity, we will call the Manufacturing Renaissance/New Industrial Policy binomial.

In its long-standing practice of stimulating economic debate, the London *Economist* launches discussion on a wide range of topics between two prestigious economists (or other relevant experts) on its website. This is how it works: first of all, the two participants must have diametrically opposed ideas on the motion being debated; second, they ask the readers of the British weekly from all over the world to vote for their respective thesis via the Internet, the result of which dictates the winner of the debate.

Taking the two debates that interest us here in chronological order, we will dedicate Act I of this Prologue to *Industrial Policy*, and Act II to the importance of *Manufacturing*.

In the first case, *The Economist*'s thesis – a position that went against industrial policy – was roundly defeated by the votes cast by readers. In the second case, though, the magazine's proposal – one which was firmly in favour of manufacturing – was widely supported by readers.

The sum of these results, as we suggest, marks a new point of view after years (and decades) of the hegemony of finance, and comes in the midst of the severe economic crisis that was set off by the Lehman Brothers' collapse six years ago. We can even go so far as to say that the winds of change have come, especially in the 'Anglo-Saxon Capitalist' nations, which are now rediscovering the virtues of manufacturing that the nations of 'Rhine Capitalism' have ably conserved as one of their strong points. Yet both styles of capitalism must face the challenges and opportunities that are presented, now more than ever, by the ceaseless march of technological innovation and the rise of the newly industrialized and developing nations (in particular, but not exclusively, the BRIC). This theme takes on a unique characteristic for the nations of the European Union (EU), which during its 60-plus-year history has formed the world's largest Single Market.

The following chapters will be dedicated to each of these themes. First, though, it is necessary to take a brief step backwards and look at the substance of the two debates engendered by *The Economist* during the summers of 2010 and 2011.

Act I

Have *The Economist* readers suddenly become nostalgic for some form of planned economy? Do they somehow miss the notorious five-year plans? We don't think so, and we hope that no one will judge the result of the recent debate on *Industrial policy* promoted by the British weekly through the lenses of the past. No, there is no nostalgia in the minds of the 71 per cent of the readers who, on Saturday 17 July 2010, at the end of an engaging week of debate (clash) between two opposite theses, have defeated the following motion of *The Economist*: 'This house believes that industrial policy always fails'.

Looking at what is happening around the world, starting from the United States, is it really true that 'industrial policy always fails', asked Dani Rodrik in his counterargument. Rodrik, who at that time was professor of the John Kennedy School of Government (Harvard University),[1] was indeed given the hard task of opposing the motion of the magazine, which was defended by another distinguished professor of Harvard University, Josh Lerner (Harvard Business School).

It is almost impossible, in this short Act I, to recount how rich the debate was. As if it was a real trial, it was divided in three phases (opening remarks, rebuttal of the proofs of evidence, final declarations) that went on throughout an entire week (12–17 July) and were moderated by a journalist of *The Economist*, Tamzin Booth. All this was enriched by dozens and dozens of online comments by the readers, as well as by two special guests.[2] But we must make two fundamental notes: one regarding the method, the other the substance of the debate.

The first regards the profile of the two opponents invited by the weekly to animate the debate: two champions, to use a sports' term. Each of them with his own history, as clearly emerged during all stages of the debate, which at times has been a brawl and at others a fencing match. Josh Lerner teaches 'Investment Banking' and is the author of the celebrated book *Boulevard of Broken Dreams* (Lerner 2009). The title recalls that of a famous Green Day song and is an accurate comparative analysis of 'why public efforts to boost entrepreneurship and venture capital have failed – and what to do about it', as stated by the book's subtitle.

No wonder that the motion of *The Economist* was entrusted to the author of such a book. On the other side, Dani Rodrik, professor of 'International Political Economy' and the author of two seminal papers, 'Industrial Policy for the Twenty-First Century' (Rodrik 2004) and 'Normalizing Industrial Policy' (Rodrik 2008), which in the past decade reopened the debate on industrial policy in international economic literature. His basic thesis is that normalization means considering this public policy like any other policy. Do governments deal with education, health and taxes, facing in each of these fields the interests of advocacy groups and lobbies? Obviously the answer is yes, but this cannot prevent them from intervening. Indeed, everybody – governments and scholars – discusses how best to offer these public services to citizens. The same – says Rodrik – needs to be done with industrial policy without being scared off by genuine problems, such as 'regulatory capture' and the fine-tuning of incentives for the implementation and assessment of aid schemes for enterprises.

By describing the profile of the two Harvard professors, we have passed smoothly from our first note on method to the second concerning the substance of the debate. This, summarizing at best, can be found in this statement made by Rodrik (first phase of the debate, 12 July):

> The essence of economic development is structural transformation, the rise of new industries replacing traditional ones. But this is not an easy or automatic process. It requires a mix of market forces and government support. If the government is too heavy-handed, it kills private entrepreneurship. If it is too standoffish, markets keep doing what they know how to do best, confining the country to its specialization in traditional products and low-productivity sectors.

In the face of such great challenges, which remind us of Schumpeter, the question is not so much to ask ourselves 'whether' there should be an industrial policy, as to ask 'how' to organize it, manage it and assess its outcomes. Three-quarters of the voters (71 per cent against 29 per cent) agreed with Rodrik, as the moderator of the debate declared in her *Winner announcement.*

However, Lerner does not agree, or at least not completely, because in his final remarks there is a timid partial opening to Rodrik's thesis (promptly underlined by the latter): with Industrial Policy there are both unresolved conceptual problems and some downright 'failures in its implementation', but something can be done. And the counter-evidence comes straight from Lerner's book – cited and recommended by Rodrik himself – where it talks about the historically important role played by the Department of Defense in the growth of Silicon Valley.

Two notes, we said. Actually, following the debate from a European perspective, there is also a third note, which is the one I made in my contribution to the debate on 13 July (Comments from the floor, 9/58).[3] It is thanks to the European Commission, at the time headed by Romano Prodi with the Finnish commissioner Erkki Liikanen in charge of the dossier, that industrial policy has gone back to the top of the European agenda, first with the Communication of December 2002, 'Industrial Policy in an Enlarged Europe' (European Commission 2002) and then with the others that followed as we will see in Chapter 1.

Besides, isn't the New Industrial Policy supposed to be the (right) mix of market forces and public intervention?

Given its traditions, Europe has much to say and do in all these matters.

One thing that we cannot afford to do is waste this fleeting moment. If there is a place in the world where it is worth re-examining and putting into practice industrial policy – the 'normalized' kind, to quote Rodrik – well, that place looks very much like the EU.

Act II

When a poll of any type ends with 76 per cent voting yes and 24 per cent voting no, then we can easily say that it has ended with an overwhelming majority (what else could we call three-quarters of a pie?).

Well, this is exactly what happened in the first days of July 2011 in the very authoritative house of the London *Economist*. The motion, for the week of June 28 to 6 July, was the following: 'The Economist believes that an economy cannot succeed without a big manufacturing base'.[4] The defence of the *Economist*'s motion was entrusted to Ha-Joon Chang, a young professor of Economics at Cambridge University and a well-known author on these kinds of topics (e.g. Chang 1996), while against it was one of the *éminences grises* of American academia, Jagdish Bhagwati, professor of Economics and Law at Columbia University.

When the readers began to vote on the very first day of debate, the overwhelming majority we mentioned above emerged immediately. Initially, it was indeed 80 per cent against 20 per cent. Then Bhagwati succeeded in reducing the gap a little, but not enough, as Patrick Lane, the journalist at *The Economist* who was chosen to moderate this debate, commented in conclusion.

I wonder how this debate would have ended some years ago, when the 'Washington Consensus' held sway along with what the late Edmondo Berselli (2012) in his last touching essay – *L'economia giusta* – called 'l'imbroglio liberista', i.e. the 'free-market machine fraud'.[5] What is certain is the radical meaning of this debate – that is, the fact that *The Economist* launched it in exactly these terms – and its final results.

It is definitely a sign of the times.

But what are the key elements of the reasoning of Ha-Joon Chang that turned out to be so convincing? For brevity's sake, without claiming to be complete (Chang made three very dense and penetrating interventions) we can highlight the following:

i   It is in manufacturing that you find the highest levels of productivity growth and it is the latter, in turn, that leads to higher living standards.
ii   Manufacturing activities are more open to international trade and this makes it essential for a country to perform relatively better than others. In the author's words: 'If a country's manufacturing sector has slower productivity growth than its counterparts abroad, it will become internationally uncompetitive, leading to balance-of-payments problems in the short run and falling standards of living in the long run.'
iii In many service activities it is really difficult to increase productivity due to intrinsic reasons, says Chang: it ensues that 'services are becoming ever more expensive in relative terms' (given the faster productivity growth in manufacturing) and this explains why 'it may appear that people in rich countries are consuming ever more services'.
iv   However, there is a subset of service activities (such as finance, telecommunications and transport) where in recent years there has been substantial

productivity growth. Not accidentally, argues Chang, since these are 'trada-ble' services and therefore are basically ' "producer services", for which the main customers are manufacturing firms, so their growth is in large part dependent on the vitality of the manufacturing sector'.

v   The last key point relates to the nature of the productive process itself, since in his first intervention (*Opening remarks*), Bhagwati had questioned the primacy of the so-called advanced (or high-tech) manufacturing industries comparing the 'chips' (of the semiconductors) to 'potato chips'. Indeed, he points out, the visitor of the factory where the famous Pringles are produced would find a perfectly automatized production that has nothing to envy to that of semiconductors. In fact, quite the opposite: in his second intervention (*Rebuttal remarks*), Chang replies to this argument of Bhagwati by pointing out how the process he describes refers only to the last and the least sophist-icated part of semiconductor manufacturing, i.e. the 'packaging', while what is really relevant is the 'fabrication process', which requires using high-purity materials as well as very complex and expensive production pro-cesses. In other words, Chang observes, 'what matters is not what you make, but how you make it'.

We could go on reporting the exchange of opinions between Chang and Bhag-wati, which at times resembled a skirmish, with the two of them resorting to the pillars of economic science, and at times a full-out battle. However, we think that the key points we have outlined here, especially from the remarks of the professor who represented the thesis of *The Economist*, suffice to give you an idea of what was at stake. The readers, as we said, largely agreed with the argu-ment that without a solid manufacturing base there is no chance to succeed in modern economy.

Now, if this message comes from the heart of Anglo-Saxon capitalism, it would be a serious mistake not to take it into consideration in a country like Italy, a country that, thanks to the efforts of its enterprises, has fortunately not lost its manufacturing tradition, but that today needs to find a way to make it evolve in a changing world.

Here the situation becomes – if possible – even more complicated, first of all from the intellectual point of view, considering the lack of popularity of this policy area among economists and many politicians. However, things are chang-ing also in this view, and maybe a new spirit of the time is emerging. In his *Opening statement* in defence of his motion Ha-Joon Chang (*The Economist* 2011) writes:

There is truth in the argument that above a certain level of development, countries become 'post-industrial', or 'deindustrialised'. But this is only in terms of employment – the falling proportion of the workforce is engaged in manufacturing. Even the richest economies have not really become post-industrial in terms of their production and consumption. From expenditure data in current (rather than constant) prices, it may appear that people in rich countries are consuming even more services, but this is mainly because services are becoming even more expensive in relative terms, thanks to structurally faster productivity growth in manufacturing.

The results of these two debates give us a clear sense of the path that must be taken: in order to grow, we need both manufacturing and a new industrial policy to be instrumental in promoting necessary *structural changes* – what Joseph A. Schumpeter (1950, 83) called 'Creative Destruction', one of the most famous concepts in economics.[6]

It is a major shift from the times, not too long ago, of the 'paper castles'.

The plan of this book

This monograph is organized according to the themes laid out in this Prologue.

Chapter 1 sheds light on the 'new' European industrial policy that has been coming to the fore – in great part thanks to the efforts of the Brussels Commission – since the beginning of the twenty-first century. The new approach that has evolved has become known as the 'integrated' approach, due to its emphasis on integrating some of the fundamental 'vertical applications' within the traditional 'horizontal approach'. In so doing, the crucial development lies in the EU's *technology policy* (R&D, human capital): a policy that should be given the same importance, on an EU-wide level, that is already afforded to *competition policy* and *trade policy*.

Chapter 2 enters into the theme of 'European Champions', those big players that have capitalized on the opportunities provided by the Single Market, especially as it has expanded into Central-Eastern European nations. Compared to the 'National Champions' of decades that are now long-gone, 'European Champions' reflect a much larger change than just a simple variation in adjectives: the entire nature of the species has evolved. No longer do these enterprises come into existence at the will of the Prince; rather, it is now market operations (i.e. cross-border mergers and acquisitions (M&As)) that determine their form. These big players, especially those from certain industrial sectors (and/or technological fields), can and must play a relevant role in increasing research and development (R&D) investments, an area in which the EU still lags significantly behind the US, not to mention the tremendous growth in China in this regard. This analysis of large companies has no intention, naturally, of ignoring the fact that the structure of European industry is made up predominately of small- and medium-sized enterprises (SMEs). Nor should we forget that there often exist very tight links between one and the other type of firm within value chains. For these reasons, Chapter 2 concludes with the two Boxes (2.1 and 2.2) dedicated to: a look at SMEs from a European perspective; and the situation of Italian industry – Europe's second-largest industrial power after Germany and a particularly relevant case study.

After the analysis of Chapter 2, which identified the Big European Players (who they are, what they produce, which growth strategies they have adopted),

Chapter 3 continues with an in-depth analysis of the industrial specializations of the EU. This is examined from the perspective of contrasting 'models of capitalism'. Two (if not more) models – the 'neo-American' and the 'Rhine' – entered vigorously into debate immediately following the fall of the Berlin Wall, and the crux of the discussion often revolved around the question of finance (or rather, on the modalities for financing enterprises: Bank versus Stock Exchange). But the story does not end here, since the literature on the subject – also referred to as 'varieties of capitalism' – has greatly widened the range of institutions of political economy that each 'model' is based upon. The roadmap that each nation gives to these institutions will determine both the (relative) strength of manufacturing and industrial specialization (USA vs Germany is the textbook example). From here, the chapter attempts a description of the most comprehensive 'model of capitalism' possible; afterwards, it tries to focus in on which institutions and policies in today's context of a *manufacturing revival* can buttress the vision of a new industrial policy. Can this policy, we ask in conclusion, represent the Elysian Fields where a happy reconciliation between the 'models of capitalism' may take place? At least, we hope, within the confines of Europe?

The next chapter takes up and expands upon the very issue that we left at the end of the former: how to strengthen the third side of the industrial policy triangle, a side that we have come to call *technology policy* (in the broad sense). In so doing, Chapter 4 narrates two 'storylines' that – at first glance – seem to run parallel to one another. The first tries to reconstruct the European path towards economic reforms, from the Delors Commission White Paper on 'Growth, Competitiveness, Employment' (European Commission 1993), through the Lisbon Strategy, and up to today's new EU strategy: 'Europe 2020' (European Commission 2010), where we find the crucial Research Framework Programme 'Horizon 2020'. The second storyline is that which, following our initial analysis of the importance of European manufacturing in Chapter 1, goes into greater detail on the strength of the European productive system, examining it through the lens of three international rankings. And the final section of the chapter will attempt to demonstrate – through a more intense analysis – why these two separate but parallel storylines can and must merge into a single narrative. European manufacturing, in fact, will be shown to have two main characteristics: on one side, it is still highly fragmented between the 28 Member States; on the other, these national manufacturing systems are still capable, by and large, of turning out good (if not great) performances in a global context. European manufacturing could thus benefit enormously from a truly supranational research and innovation (R&I) policy.

Chapter 5 looks to further broaden our horizons to include the entire European integration process, which goes well beyond the field of economics. Almost seven years after the crash of September 2008, the time is ripe, we believe, for a re-reading of the reactions by the EU (and, on some salient points, by the euro area countries) to the crisis. At the end of 2008 through the beginning of 2009, it became popular to make reference to Jean-Baptiste Colbert – the legendary Minister of Finances to Louis XIV – and to call for the practice of a kind of 'neo-Colbertism'. But is this the real state of things? Looking at the situation from a genuinely EU perspective, we must delineate between its four cohesive but different dimensions: State and Market (or better, the respective roles of each), and Member States and Supranational Government (as before, their respective duties and responsibilities). The events of the second half of the twentieth century – there's no need to go further back – teach that the pendulum rarely stands still: it is always shifting from one extreme to another according to different phases of history. The wisdom of politics – here and now – lies in finding a new and proper balance between State and Market, but also, and at the same time, between the responsibilities of Member States and EU institutions. An arduous task, but one that is indispensable for the Europe of our times.

An Epilogue concludes the text with a few brief observations. We will return to the thesis that we have been defending from the very beginning, that *something has truly changed in the world of economics*: the 'rebirth of manufacturing' and the 'new industrial policy' represent – in our opinion – a more than sufficient case study for testing the validity of this thesis. Based on the analysis that we have performed throughout this book, we will see how these themes have already begun to take their rightful place in the economic literature, and continue to do so in growing fashion.

Under the influence of new theories, our hope is that the world of economy will change as well. At this point, it is the case study of the European Union that becomes particularly important because it provides us with one of the most complete international economic integration schemes of our times, though one which still needs to find the political will to throw off the chains of the status quo *ex ante* in which it appears to be mired. One area – we will argue – where the EU must give a strong signal of its resolve to strengthen its supranational role is that of a new industrial policy, seen as part and parcel of broader structural reforms. The EU of the twenty-first century cannot allow its reforms to be limited to the range of macroeconomics, however important that may be. The evolution of the Treaties has begun to show glimpses of a growing role of microeconomic policies, and the time to strike the hammer is now.

Notes

1 As of 1 July 2013, Dani Rodrik is the Albert O. Hirschman Professor of Social Science at the Institute for Advanced Study in Princeton.
2 See: www.economist.com/debate/overview/177.
3 I posted a comment while voting 'No' to *The Economist*'s thesis: see the abovementioned website.
4 See: www.economist.com/debate/overview/207.
5 Here, we mention only the chapter (no. 9) which Berselli, in his book, devoted entirely to a focus on the 'Social Market Economy', where he wrote:

> There are two fundamental principles that support the structure of *soziale Markt-twirtschaft*: a) Economic dynamics are based on the market, which must be guaranteed the greatest possible freedom, particularly with regard to prices and salaries. b) The functioning of the market cannot by itself regulate the entirety of

social life. It demands factors of external equilibrium, it must be balanced by elements of social policy that are determined *a priori*, and that are protected by the State.

(Berselli 2012, 55–59)

6 In Schumpeter's words (1942, 83, emphasis added):

> The opening up of new markets, foreign or domestic, and the organizational development from the craft shop to such concerns as U.S. Steel illustrate the same process of industrial mutation – if I may use that biological term – that incessantly revolutionizes the *economic structure* from within, incessantly destroying the old one, incessantly creating a new one. This process of Creative Destruction is the essential fact about capitalism.

References

Berselli E. (2012) *L'economia giusta*, 2nd ed., Preface by Romano Prodi, Torino, Einaudi.

Chang H-J. (1996) *The Political Economy of Industrial Policy*, London, Macmillan.

Economist, The (2010) Industrial Policy: This House Believes that Industrial Policy Always Fails, 'Economist Debates', July.

Economist, The (2011) Manufacturing: This House Believes that an Economy Cannot Succeed without a Big Manufacturing Base, 'Economist Debates', June/July.

European Commission (1993) Growth, Competitiveness, Employment: The Challenges and Ways Forward into the 21st Century, (COM (1993) 700), Brussels, 5 December.

European Commission (2002) Industrial Policy in an Enlarged Europe, (COM (2002) 714), Brussels, 11 December.

European Commission (2010) Europe 2020: A Strategy for Smart, Sustainable and Inclusive Growth, (COM (2010) 2020), Brussels, 3 March.

Lerner J. (2009) *Boulevard of Broken Dreams: Why Public Efforts to Boost Entrepreneurship and Venture Capital Have Failed – and What to Do About It*, Princeton, NJ, Princeton University Press.

Rodrik D. (2004) Industrial Policy for the Twenty-First Century, John F. Kennedy School of Government, Harvard University, September (www.sss.ias.edu).

Rodrik D. (2008) Normalizing Industrial Policy, Commission on Growth and Development (International Bank for Reconstruction and Development/World Bank), Working Paper No. 3 (www.sss.ias.edu).

Schumpeter J. A. (1950) *Capitalism, Socialism, and Democracy*, 3rd edn (first edn 1942), New York, Harper & Brothers.

1 The new European industrial policy*

An overview

The primary richness of the most advanced nations was represented by its reserves of human capital, which is the same as saying by the relatively high number and quality of their entrepreneurs and craftsmen. This capital was at the same time the result of and a factor in development, and throughout the Medieval and Renaissance periods, authorities and administrators kept a (watchful) eye not only on the import and export of foodstuffs and precious metals, but also on the immigration and emigration of technicians and craftsmen.

(Cipolla 1967)

Introduction

What should the term *industrial policy* mean to us today?

The Prologue has already offered, we believe, useful indications about how to establish an intellectual methodology that takes into account both new directions in economic theory, and empirical evidence of what is actually taking place in the real world of policy decisions.

With Chapter 1 we begin our journey, one which will have Europe – from an international perspective, of course, for no man is an island – as its primary destination. This European focus – as we will see along the road – will prove itself to be highly apropos to our attempts to answer the question we posed at the very beginning. We know, in fact, that in determining the dynamics of economic growth, *history* counts as much as *institutions*: the EU of our days is the outcome of a solid process of integration that has lasted more than 60 years.

The purpose of this first chapter is to provide an *overview*; in so doing we will find that the concept of 'knowledge-based investments' will be our principle travelling companion.

It is thanks to certain distinguished contemporary economists, whom we will read in the pages of this book, that we recognize the full importance of these investments – an essential part of the new endogenous growth theory – to the evolution that industrial policy must undergo here and now. But there's more. Looking backwards in time, we truly understand that 'history is life's teacher' (*Historia Magistra Vitae*): the epigraph to this chapter, in which the great economic historian was referring to a Europe of many centuries ago, still today manifests extraordinary prescience, and can still offer great insights into the reforms Europe must undertake.

And so, let us return to the European Union (EU) of our times.

An extensive report by the Conseil d'Analyse Économique (CAE), commissioned by the French Prime Minister's Office (Cohen and Lorenzi 2000), noted how industrial policy – in the European tradition – is the result of a triangle formed by *competition policy, commercial (trade) policy* and *technology policy*.[1] European competition policy has paved the way towards the so-called level playing field where firms may meet and compete on equal footing. Meanwhile, Europe's commercial policy for international trade must continue to contribute to a growing openness of the global economy and inclusion of new players, thus overcoming forms of closure that are chiefly damaging to developing countries.

Today's core issue, more than in the past, is how to envisage new policies for the competitiveness of European industry in this period of new technological revolutions (information and communication technologies (ICT), of course, but also biotechnologies and life sciences) and the expansion of international markets in which to compete (the 'Asian miracle' and an 'enlarged Europe'); policies that here in Europe call into play R&D investment, innovation and human capital. In a word: the third side of the aforementioned 'triangle'.

A suitable path to reform should be – to our mind – that the new industrial policy we are beginning to glimpse in the EU must lean towards a definite reinforcement of the triangle's third side ('technology policy') at a pan-European level, without weakening the other two sides ('competition' and 'commercial' policies). The main purpose of this chapter is to shed light on this reinforcement through the lens of the recent *manufacturing renaissance*. In fact, the rebirth of manufacturing is one of the most distinctive characteristics of the twenty-first century; the Western world – Anglo-Saxon capitalism, above all – has rediscovered manufacturing's fundamental role in promoting economic growth. The objective of this chapter is to chart a course for maximizing the economic and social potential of a new industrial policy in order to make the most of this renaissance.

After this Introduction, the first chapter will have the following structure. The second section goes back to the very beginning of the twenty-first century when in Brussels the European Commission (2002) unveiled its first new Communication on Industrial Policy. The third section sets the groundwork by providing an overview of the main EU industrial policy-related documents and studies which now cover the entire decade (2002–2012), splitting them into two groups with the aim of highlighting the 'integrated approach'. Is this approach (and especially the proposed 'vertical applications') consistent with the technological revolution that is taking place worldwide? A look to the US and, within the EU, Germany provides some proofs, while – in the same vein – the fourth section provides a theoretical background to the debate by drawing from the insights of two prominent scholars, Alexis Jacquemin and Dani Rodrik, who both advocate a strategic industrial policy. The two sections following this, which respectively deal with the European manufacturing base and innovation landscape, describe what is happening on the ground, as an attempt to bridge the gap between theory and practice. The final section concludes by once again drawing attention to the fact that in the European context, industrial policy should be seen as the result of the 'triangle' formed by *competition policy, trade policy* and *technology policy*. The reasonable conclusion is that the new industrial policy in the EU must move towards a definite reinforcement – at the pan-European level – of the *triangle's third side*, without weakening the other two. Today it is vital to attain this balance with a fully fledged European technology policy that fosters an industrial policy which focuses on 'knowledge-based investments' (i.e. R&D, human capital and ICT).

The re-launch of industrial policy in Brussels

During the 1990s European industrial policy did not have the same impact on the political agenda as it has over the last decade. At that time, the European Commission presented a Communication entitled 'Industrial Policy in an Open and Competitive Environment: Guidelines for a Community Approach' (European Commission 1990). However in December 2002 – here we are in the present days – the Commission issued a new paper entitled 'Industrial Policy in an Enlarged Europe' (European Commission 2002). This was the first of a long series of new Community reports that we will discuss further. The original 'Bangemann' Communication of 1990 – named after the Commissioner who was responsible for the dossier at that time – was followed by others throughout the decade.[2] Nevertheless, at least in the context of industrial policy, there was the distinct impression of unfinished business.

Europe was making headway in completing the two great, and ultimately successful, ideas of a *Single Market* (the 'four freedoms' of circulation) and the *European Monetary Union* (the convergence towards the 'Maastricht criteria'). Despite the necessary integrations and improvements required, these achievements contributed to building the European economic structure we know today. In addition, it was at the turn of the twenty-first century that the fundamental steps were being taken for what was to become the third great historical success for the EU: its *enlargement towards the east* (the 'unification of Europe').

What remains to be understood, however, is what caused the sort of 'suspension' of industrial policy we referred to and which lasted at least ten years. Was it because in those years united Europe was busy completing the fulfilment of three of its great ideas, as we just described? Or did it depend more on the fact that for much of the 1990s, competition policy, liberalization and privatization were considered to be the best tools for public intervention in the economy?

If we take the first theory as valid, it is not surprising that we have to make a leap from 1990 – following our simple reconstruction – to 2002 to discover a decisive drive by Community institutions towards a (new) industrial policy: in the previous decade, united Europe had other priorities ('one market, one currency'), and other achievements. On the other hand, if we are to evaluate the second theory, we need to undertake a patient investigation of how the European integration process came about: the ideas that influenced its progress, the institutions called upon to generate its growth. This chapter is an initial attempt in the latter direction.

Theories aside, there is in any case another key factor: the economic context was different, at least in the early 1990s. The revolution of information and communication technologies (ICT) and America's new economic boom (The White House 2001) were just getting started. The affirmation of new major global economic players – China in particular, but more in general all of the 'BRIC countries' (Brazil, Russia, India, China) (Goldman Sachs 2003) – could certainly be glimpsed on the horizon but had not yet fully produced their explosive effects. We do know that all these phenomena completed their growth curve between the end of the 1990s and the beginning of the new century, thus fully revealing their effects. So, driven by this dual revolution (the New Economy and the Asian miracle), the European economy – starting with the manufacturing industry – found itself dealing with quite serious long-term challenges that it had not seen for some time.

As we mentioned, another big challenge was forming on home turf via the EU policy to embrace, between 2004 and 2007, ten Central-Eastern European countries, as well as Cyprus and Malta.[3] By simplifying a great deal, we can narrow down eastward enlargement to its economic dimension alone, without neglecting the enormous importance it had in political, historical, cultural and institutional terms. Yet, if we consider the economic implications of enlargement – especially against a backdrop of literature that has become quite boundless (European Commission 2001) – we will see that above all, this has represented a further extension of the Single Market, which has always been (from the Treaty of Rome onwards) the driving force behind European integration and the growth of wealth in a united Europe.

The analysis of the links between 'growth effects' and 'European integration' was at the heart of the well-known textbook by Richard Baldwin and Charles Wyplosz (2004). Building on the new theoretical foundations offered by endogenous growth models, the authors tried to demonstrate how international economic integration – and European integration is an excellent example – stimulates economic growth 'by changing the rate at which new factors of production – mainly capital – are accumulated, hence the name "accumulation effects"'. In turn, the creation of new 'capital' must be considered as part of three categories: 'physical capital (machines, etc.), human capital (skills, training, experience, etc.) and knowledge capital (technology)'. All three categories contribute to economic growth. What changes is their relative importance in the medium and long term: certainly, the accumulation of investments in physical capital is a significant growth factor. Nevertheless, as such investments face diminishing returns to scale – the argument goes – 'long-run growth effects typically refer to the rate accumulation of knowledge capital, i.e. technological progress'. In the same perspective we could include the OECD (2003) works published in the context of their extensive research project, *The Sources of Economic Growth in OECD Countries.*[4]

To sum up these initial points, we might say that the challenge the EU faced at the turn of the century was twofold: first, the renewed American challenge, whose core is in high-tech production, and, second, the new Asian challenge, consisting initially of large volumes and low costs, but also in growing technolo-gical improvement of production. In addition, the EU was dealing with the chal-lenge – which is exclusively European – of Eastern enlargement, i.e. a bigger Single Market. According to André Sapir (2005), this should be seen as a great opportunity – and not as a burden – for 'a pan-European industrial reorganisa-tion', provided that Europe is able to transform

> the enlarged European Union of 27+ members into a genuine Single Market, where goods, services, capital and labour are allowed to freely circulate … Giving countries the opportunity to exploit their full comparative advantage and companies the chance to restructure their activity on a pan-European scale would much improve the attractiveness of Europe as a place to create wealth and employment.

The sources of new European industrial policy

By the beginning of the 1990s, the substantial changes occurring in the inter-national economy brought about the need to reformulate the EU approach to industrial policy, making a shift from the policies of the 1960s, 1970s and 1980s in terms of both the aims and the instruments used.

In addition, two other fundamental factors were also pushing for a new indus-trial policy approach. The first were the new insights gained by economic liter-ature in fields such as endogenous growth theory, determinants of market structure, clusters evolution and production networks, etc. (for comprehensive reviews see De Bandt 1999; Navarro 2003). The second factor regards the insti-tutional changes occurring at policy level, involving complementary competen-cies between the Member States, on the one hand, and the EU, on the other. Especially worthy of attention are the inclusion into the Treaties – since the middle of the 1980s – of several provisions concerning 'Research and technolo-gical development' (European Single Act 1986) and the 'Competitiveness of the Community's Industry' (the famous ex-Article 130 of the 1992 Maastricht Treaty, then Article 157 and now 173). All these competencies trace back to a microeconomic perspective.

A more detailed examination of these three factors, only briefly outlined here, would make us stray away from the focus of this chapter. Here it suffices simply to note that their combined effect was to redefine the aims of industrial policy away from blanket attempts to rescue declining firms (or sectors) through state subsidies, and from a policy of 'picking winners' by means of planning methods and financial incentives. The result was the birth of a new industrial policy approach, which had two crucial aims: first, to address *economic restructuring*; second, to encourage *innovation* and the creation of a *knowledge-driven economy*.

It should be observed that in Europe the rediscovery of industrial policy at the beginning of the 2000s – after more than a decade of silence on the subject – has been accompanied by a new urgency in the academic studies in this field. In a literature that has become relevant again, we would like to mention, by way of example, the seminal paper of Rodrik (2004), and the works of Bianchi and Labory (2006), Pelkmans (2006), Budzincki and Schmidt (2006), Lin and Chang (2009), Aghion *et al.* (2011), Owen (2012), Aiginger (2012, 2013), OECD (2013), Török *et al.* (2013) and O'Sullivan *et al.* (2013) up to the most recent of Stiglitz and Lin (2013) and Yülek (2015a); a re-evaluation of the role of the state in the most advanced economies is the subject in the incisive and influential book by Mariana Mazzucato (2014).

In the Introduction to their *Handbook*, Bianchi and Labory (2006a, xv) significantly write:

> The meaning of the term 'industrial policy' has changed a lot over time. Until the 1980s, the term meant the direct intervention of the state in the economy, the direct control by the government of large parts of the production apparatus and a set of public actions aimed at limiting the extent of the market and at conditioning productive organization. Nowadays, the term 'industrial policy' indicates instead a variety of policies which are implemented by various institutional subjects in order to stimulate firm creation, to favour their agglomeration and promote innovation and competitive development in the context of an open economy.

Starting from a general definition of industrial policy ('we mean government policies directed at affecting the economic structure of the economy'), Stiglitz, Lin and Monga shed light on technological innovation, industrial upgrading and economic diversification in the light of modern economic growth theories where *technology* – and not *factor accumulation* – is the main engine to increase per capita income. They write: 'If improvements in standards of living mainly come from diffusion of knowledge, learning strategies must be at the heart of the development strategies' (Stiglitz *et al.* 2013, 7). In the same vein, they argue that 'this new theoretical perspective focuses on the reasons that markets, by themselves, are not likely to produce sufficient growth enhancing investments, such as those associated with learning, knowledge accumulation, and research' (Stiglitz *et al.* 2013, 7–8).

The viewpoint encompassing economic planning and industrial policy has been taken by Yülek, who – looking to the future – writes: 'industrial policies, including new generation or newer versions of what went before, are likely to be part of economic planning efforts'. In fact, he points out:

> more recently, 'traditional' industrial policies that target the development of selected sectors have given way to a new generation of industrial policies based on innovation, R&D, technology and entrepreneurship. It could be argued that, for the developed economies in Western Europe, the USA and Japan, where stronger and relatively competitive industrial structures have been put in place ... these newer policy frameworks are appropriate.

(Yülek 2015b, 22–23)

Bearing in mind this literature, the EU's documents are useful for distinguishing what can be called *new* European Industrial Policy from what the nation-states and the European Economic Community (EEC) were implementing throughout the early decades of the post-Second World War period. Considering these, we will first make reference to fundamental documents beginning in December 2002; then we will discuss what approach emerges, on what principles it is founded and what nuances can be extrapolated.

The heading 'Industrial Policy'[5] currently covers many European Commission Communications, all presented in the 2002–2014 period. We can divide this decade into two periods for our purposes: by first focusing on the 2002–2006 Communications, we will try to clear up the approach to the new industrial policy, which, although it is mainly horizontal, also has some vertical applications (i.e. specific sectors); then we will focus on the 2006–2014 Commission Communications, also making a comparison between the European approach and the one which has in the meantime emerged in the US.

Towards an 'integrated' approach (2002–2006)

Let us start by briefly recalling the initial documents:

i   the first, already identified as the opening sally of this new episode, was that dated December 2002 (European Commission 2002);
ii   the second arrived in November 2003: 'Some Key Issues in Europe's Competitiveness: Towards an Integrated Approach' (European Commission 2003);
iii whilst the third was dated April 2004: 'Fostering Structural Change: An Industrial Policy for an Enlarged Europe' (Euroepan Commission 2004a);
iv   the fourth issued in October 2005 by the new Barroso Commission: 'Implementing the Community Lisbon Programme: A Policy Framework to Strengthen Manufacturing. Towards a More Integrated Approach for Industrial Policy' (European Commission 2005b), which 'includes new horizontal initiatives and tailor-made initiatives for specific sectors'.

All the Communications are supported by many extensive research projects that include ad hoc studies and presentation conferences – the first dated January 2003 – including speeches by the then President Prodi and Commissioner Liikanen. Even though this is already quite an extensive selection of studies and analyses, the set of documents worth reviewing in the light of new industrial policy does not end here. A useful integration certainly involves the annual *European Competitiveness Report*, a series inaugurated in 1999.

In the background there are also two main points of reference, the 'Lisbon Agenda' and the 'Sapir Report':

1   The 'Lisbon Agenda' was a farsighted ten-year strategy (2000–2010) for the modernization of the European economic and social model(s), but at the same

time an agenda showing countless significant methodological problems (European Commission 2004c, 2005a). A large body of economic literature has discussed European R&D policies in the broader context of this strategy (Pisani-Ferry 2005; Pisani-Ferry and Sapir 2006; Aghion 2006; Cassi *et al.* 2008): one of the main insights gained from this work is that the more an economy approaches the world technological frontier, the more crucial it becomes for it to invest in R&D and to coordinate its technology policies. The Lisbon Agenda's aim for Europe to invest 3 per cent of its GDP in R&D by 2010 was not met,[6] and this is still a worrying lacuna that needs rectifying by the implementation of the new EU strategy, 'Europa 2020' (Chapter 4 will be devoted to these strategies, starting from the White Paper on 'Growth, Competitiveness, Employment' (European Commission 1993)).

2 The 'Sapir Report' ('An Agenda for a Growing Europe')[7] was an excellent attempt to update what the report by Tommaso Padoa-Schioppa (*Efficiency, Stability and Equity*)[8] had laid down 15 years earlier, i.e. 'the intellectual foundation for the construction of a coherent economic edifice resting on three pillars: the Single Market, to improve economic efficiency; an effective monetary arrangement, to ensure monetary stability; and an expanded Community budget, to foster cohesion'. In short, 'Europe's growth problem' (Table 1.1(a) and (b)) was at the heart of the new Report, and as a consequence 'growth must become Europe's number one economic

Table 1.1a 'Europe's growth problem': a historical perspective

	1950–1973 'The Golden Age'	1973–1993 'The Fall'	1993–2000 'The Stabilisation'
Growth	4.6%	2.4%	2.4%
Cohesion:			
• unemployment	2%	8%	9%
• public spending (% GDP)	<35%	37% → 51%	51% → 46%
Stability:			
• inflation	4%	8%	3%
• public deficit	<2%	0% → 6%	6% → 0%

Source: Sapir (2003).

Table 1.1b 'Europe's growth problem': the last 15 years (real GDP, % change)

	2000–2004 (5 year average)	2005–2009 (5 year average)	2010	2011	2012	2013	2014	2015 (forecast)	2016 (forecast)
EU area	1.9	0.7	2.0	1.6	−0.7	−0.5	0.8	1.1	1.7
EU	2.3	0.9	2.1	1.7	−0.4	0.0	1.3	1.5	2.0
USA	2.7	0.9	2.5	1.6	2.3	2.2	2.2	3.1	3.2

Source: European Commission (2014).

priority'. Figures indicated in table 1.1a show the decreasing trend of growth in the EU from the creation of the first European Community until the very beginning of the 2000s, while figures in table 1.1b show the even more disappointing growth performance during the last fifteen years – before and after the big crash of 2008. Overall, this is in stark contrast to the US growth path.

In 2003 the 'Sapir Report' – a six-point *agenda* – demonstrated the importance of encouraging 'knowledge investments'. More specifically, the 'Sapir Report' argued that Europe needs 'to boost investment in knowledge' because nowadays 'innovation is the driver of economic growth'.[9] It further argued that Europe should reach this objective by: (i) substantially increasing 'government and EU spending for research and postgraduate education, but at the same time putting the main emphasis on excellence when allocating the new additional funds'; (ii) creating an 'independent Agency for Science and Research (EASR), functioning on the model of the US National Science Foundation (but also the Nordic and British research councils) ... Like the NSF, the EASR should focus on financing bottom-up academic research.'

All in all, as will be argued further in this chapter, there was growing evidence that Europe's relative weakness in the technological race had been – and still is – the key factor behind its main economic malaise of recent years, that is, its low productivity growth and level. Thus, helping both science and business to catch up in this race is most desirable. Moreover, it is possible: following Dosi *et al.* (2005), 're-discovering the use of industrial policies as a device to foster a stronger, more innovative, European industry' is a suitable proposal, especially 'in order to strengthen the European presence in the most promising technological paradigms'.

As mentioned above, for the sake of simplicity we have focused thus far on the 2002–2006 period in which the new European industrial policy – with the so-called 'integrated' approach – took shape in Brussels. How did the EU envisage this (new) approach to industrial policy, one that is more consistent with the most important underlying trends in the global economy (technological change and globalization)? Once again, we ought to take a step back.

The origins of industrial policy at the EU level closely mirrored the then-accepted practices at the Member State level: during much of the 1970s and 1980s, the EU (at the time, the EC) fostered a policy of actively and directly aiding certain industrial sectors in their process of structural adjustment, with the primary goals being political and social rather than economic in nature. The clearest example was the assistance given to the steel industry through the ECSC Treaty, which provided the legal basis for the EC to set up a crisis cartel during the period 1980–1985 that established a system of production quotas, minimum prices and voluntary export arrangements with foreign exporters (Maicent and Navarro 2006).

However, by the beginning of the 1990s, with the Single Market Programme well under way, it was felt that the sectoral approach to industrial policy had run its course. With competition becoming increasingly more intense and global, policy emphasis shifted towards creating framework conditions for all EU businesses to thrive and develop in, without governments playing a direct role in picking and promoting specific firms or sectors.

The 1990 Commission Communication entitled 'Industrial Policy in an Open and Competitive Environment: Guidelines for a Community Approach', laid the foundations for the new industrial policy approach of the EU. The central idea was 'the need to concentrate on the creation of the right business environment … [through] a positive, open and subsidiarity-oriented approach' (European Commission 1990, 5). EC industrial policy was to 'promote permanent adaptation to industrial change in an open and competitive market … based on the principle of free trade and on the competitive functioning of markets around long-term industrial and technological perspectives' (European Commission 1990, 21). This Communication criticized the sector-oriented industrial policy of the past, arguing that 'sectoral approaches to industry policy can work during a period, but they entail inevitably the risk of delaying structural adjustments and thereby creating job losses in the future' (European Commission 1990, 5). Moreover, it felt that 'most "sectoral" policies in practice have been directed more towards social objectives', and have 'led to grave misallocation of resources and exacerbated problems of budgetary imbalances' (European Commission 1990, 19). The Commission felt that 'the role of public authorities is above all as a catalyst and path-breaker for innovation … [and] the main responsibility for industrial competitiveness must lie with firms themselves' (European Commission 1990, 1).

The Commission recognized that issues affecting specific sectors may have to be tackled at the EC level from time to time, especially in 'areas that can play a key role for the development of the European industry … such as telecommunications, information technology, aeronautics, and maritime industry'. However, it would remain 'essential that policies aimed at specific sectors are fully consistent with the general principles of industrial policy', namely, that a competitive environment is applied to all of them on the same basis (European Commission 1990, 19).

The policy path set out by the 1990 Communication on industrial policy remained more or less unchanged for over a decade.[10] However, by 2002 there was a change in the line of thinking of the Commission, which began re-emphasizing 'sectoral applications' of industrial policy, alongside the creation of 'framework conditions' for businesses. Although it did not involve a complete paradigm shift as in the 1990s, this change in policy focus was substantial enough to warrant our further attention.

To be sure, the policy direction set by the 2002 Communication, entitled 'Industrial Policy in an Enlarged Europe' (European Commission 2002), did not advocate a return to the 1970s to 1980s approach of subsidizing or protecting specific industrial sectors or firms. Rather, it was a far more subtle policy that aimed to 'take into account the specific needs and characteristics of individual sectors' when applying the broader horizontal policy that 'aims at securing framework conditions favourable to industrial competitiveness'; the central tenet of the Commission's new policy approach was that an 'industrial policy... inevitably brings together a horizontal basis and sectoral applications' (European Commission 2002, 3).

The question that naturally arises at this point is: what warranted this realignment of the Commission's industrial policy focus? Could the upcoming massive project of the EU – the enlargement to the East – have been a cause for the Commission's concern? A quick reading of the 2002 Communication gives a resounding 'No' to that question. The Commission believed that, overall, enlargement was going to be highly beneficial for EU industry, both old and new, although some localized problems were likely to occur, for example restructuring of the steel sector in the 'new' Member States, or increased competition in labour-intensive sectors in the border regions of 'old' Member States. Moreover, it felt that although 'sizeable differences still exist between the structure of the manufacturing industry in the existing and in future Member States ... [there was] growing evidence of catching up and gradual convergence with the industrial patterns prevailing in the EU'. Essentially, the Commission believed that 'given the increased heterogeneity of wage structures and technological skills in the enlarged EU', this process would offer industry new opportunities for 'competitive organisation' (European Commission 2002, 14).

In fact, at the heart of the Commission's initiative for a new realigned industrial policy was the belief that, although 'European industry is modern and, in many respects, successful ... its slow productivity growth is a serious cause for concern', particularly given the future challenges of enlargement. In particular, Table 1.2 (see table 4.1 from O'Mahony and van Ark 2003)

> shows levels in the EU-14 relative to the US for 26 sectors within manufacturing for the same time periods. Many sectors currently show the EU-14 either ahead or at US productivity levels. However, the US is ahead in sectors that have the highest value added per head, in particular in computers, semiconductors and the telecommunication equipment sectors. These sectors show a significant deterioration in the EU relative position compared to the early 1980s.

The Commission feared that unless something was done to reverse these trends, the ambitious goals set by the Lisbon Strategy in 2000 – 'to make the EU the most competitive and dynamic knowledge-based economy in the world' by 2010 – would not be met.

The Communication identified insufficient innovative activity and weak diffusion of ICT as key determinants of Europe's under-performance in productivity growth. In fact, drawing from the above-mentioned study by O'Mahony and Van Ark, in 2003 the Commission further specified that:

> Developments in EU industry competitiveness in recent years show considerable diversity. Productivity growth in manufacturing began to decelerate in the mid-1990s and it has since fallen behind the US. The sectors that have contributed to the widening of the productivity gap are

Table 1.2 Labour productivity in EU-14 manufacturing industries relative to the US (US=100)

	ISIC rev. 3	1979–1981	1994–1996	1999–2001
Food, drink and tobacco	15–16	64.5	79.7	100.6
Textiles	17	103.4	99.1	100.8
Wearing apparel	18	66.1	67.7	61.0
Leather	19	95.2	88.0	89.9
Wood products	20	63.0	86.8	101.3
Pulp and paper products	21	76.8	104.9	120.0
Printing and publishing	22	67.0	120.3	134.5
Chemicals	24	54.7	70.5	78.4
Rubber and plastics	25	180.2	145.8	127.0
Non-metallic mineral products	26	121.2	142.6	148.8
Basic metals	27	65.1	109.1	107.8
Fabricated metal	28	108.9	108.5	111.4
Machinery	29	66.5	97.4	110.8
Computers	30	133.3	89.8	71.9
Insulated wire	313	87.3	93.7	77.6
Other electrical machinery	31–313	79.7	91.3	112.1
Semiconductors	321	47.8	31.8	41.6
Telecommunication equipment	322	71.9	63.9	65.7
Radio and television receivers	323	44.0	62.8	63.1
Scientific instruments	331	114.4	106.9	103.2
Other instruments	33–331	42.8	49.2	47.3
Motor vehicles	34	30.0	44.9	43.7
Ships and boats	351	59.2	95.8	88.7
Aircraft and spacecraft	353	46.7	71.1	71.8
Railroad and other transport	352+359	68.8	76.4	80.4
Furniture, miscellaneous manufacturing	36–37	110.5	100.8	94.4
Total manufacturing	*15–37*	*84.6*	*88.0*	*80.3*

Source: O'Mahony van Ark (2003).

mainly high-tech sectors. However, European ICT-producing manufacturing and services have performed extremely well, but productivity growth in ICT-using sectors has not accelerated as in the US. It is clear that ICT has been a key factor in sectoral productivity performance.

(European Commission 2003)

In fact, the Commission had earlier noted that:

[the] EU tends to specialise in medium-high technology and mature capital-intensive industries ... [and if it is to] keep the strengths in these sectors, which represent a higher share of total output and employment, the EU should seek to reinforce its position in enabling technologies such as ICT, electronics, biotechnology or nanotechnology, where it is often lagging behind its main competitors.

(European Commission 2002, 11)

Hence, although the bulk of the 2002 Communication focused on refining the horizontal approach and improving the framework conditions, it already provided a first glimpse of the sectors that were to gain increasing attention in the coming years due to their importance in promoting productivity and economic growth.

By 2005, the Commission's industrial policy that combined a horizontal approach with sectoral applications was especially clear that:

> for industrial policy to be effective, account needs to be taken of the specific context of individual sectors. Policies need to be combined in a tailor-made manner on the basis of the concrete characteristics of sectors and the particular opportunities and challenges that they face. This inevitably has as a consequence that *whilst all policies are important, in the EU today some policies have greater importance for some sectors than others*.
> (European Commission 2005a, 3–4, emphasis added)

In light of this, the Commission undertook a screening exercise to assess the competitiveness of 27 individual sectors of the manufacturing and construction industries. The policy areas chosen for screening were those deemed to be particularly important for sectoral productivity growth and international competitiveness.[11] The individual sectors were grouped into four broad categories: (a) food and life science industries (food, drink, pharmaceuticals, biotech etc.); (b) machinery and system industries (ICT, mechanical engineering); (c) fashion and design industries (textiles, footwear); and (d) basic and intermediate product industries (chemicals, steel, pulp, paper). The result was the establishment of seven major cross-sectoral policy initiatives and a number of new sector-specific initiatives, as summarized in Table 1.3.

Table 1.3 A new 'integrated' (horizontal and vertical) industrial policy

Seven major cross-sectoral policy initiatives	*Seven new sector-specific initiatives*
1 An intellectual property right (IPR) and counterfeiting (2006)	1 New pharmaceuticals forum (first meeting in 2006)
2 A high-level group on competitiveness, energy and the environment (end 2005)	2 Mid-term review of life sciences and biotechnology strategy (2006–2007)
3 External aspects of competitiveness and market access (spring 2006)	3 New high-level groups on chemicals and the defence industry (2007)
4 New legislative simplification programme (October 2005)	4 European space programme
5 Improving sectoral skills (2006)	5 Taskforce ICT competitiveness (2005/2006)
6 Managing structural change in manufacturing (end 2005)	6 Mechanical engineering policy dialogue (2005/2006)
7 An integrated European approach to industry and innovation (2005)	7 A series of competitiveness studies, including ICT, food, and fashion and design industries

Source: European Commission (2005b).

What is immediately evident from the list(s) in Table 1.3 is the special attention dedicated to certain high value-added and high-tech sectors, such as pharmaceuticals, biotechnology or the defence industry, which are considered important to ensure the future competitiveness of EU industry in the knowledge-based economy. Indeed, these and other similar sectors are mentioned in a number of other Commission documents that do not directly address industrial policy, but which nevertheless have important implications for it. For example, the report of the independent expert group on R&D and innovation – the so-called 'Aho Report' entitled 'Creating an Innovative Europe' – argues that Europe must develop an 'innovation-friendly market for businesses' that 'should be focused on large-scale strategic actions ... [in sectors such as]: e-Health, Pharmaceuticals, Energy, Environment, Transport and Logistics, Security, and Digital Content'. The group believed that 'public policy can have a significant role (in these key areas), as they have for past successes as GSM and Airbus' (European Commission 2006).

The importance attached to high-technology sectors is not a new feature of EU industrial policy. In fact, over time, the EU supported a number of major projects designed to enhance the technological base of European industry, of which Airbus and GSM are some of the most famous and successful examples.

These years, however, have seen a revitalization of efforts to support technology and innovation projects, with an important – if not exclusive – impact on European industry as Box 1.1 tries to show.

Box 1.1 Technology policy and its mechanisms (mid-2000s)

As we already know, the impetus for a knowledge-based economy came from the Lisbon Strategy, especially after its mid-term review, which put greater emphasis on growth and employment. As the Spring European Council of 2005 put it: 'it is important to develop research, education and all forms of innovation insofar as they make it possible to turn knowledge into an added value and create more and better jobs' (Council of the EU 2005). The Union felt that in order to realize this ambitious goal, a stronger link between research and industry was particularly important.

These sorts of goals and mechanisms will be dealt with in detail throughout the book, particularly in Chapter 4. In this Box, let us focus specifically on what was going on during the decade of the Lisbon Strategy.

For analytical purposes, the tools used by the EU during that time for what is broadly termed 'technology policy' can be divided roughly into two categories. On the one hand, there are the tools whose primary goal was to facilitate communication and cooperation among stakeholders and to provide general institutional support. The European Technology Platforms (ETPs) and the European Research Area (ERA) are prime examples of this kind of initiative. On the other hand, there are policy tools that focused on providing financial support and incentives for technology and innovation. The seventh Framework Programme for Research (FP7) and the Joint Technology Initiatives (JTIs) are most important in this respect. Of course, there is natural overlap among these policy tools, and there are initiatives that combine both the institutional and the funding aspects, for example, the

European Research Council (ERC) (already part of FP7) and the European Institute of Technology (EIT).

ETPs are forums that bring together industry representatives – both from large and small firms – public authorities and private capital as well as other stakeholders such as consumer groups, with a view to defining research and development priorities, timeframes and action plans for a number of industries and fields. They are not research ventures themselves, but aim to facilitate cooperation among various stakeholders on strategically important issues that are dependent on major research and technological advances. At the beginning of 2007, there were 31 ETPs up and running, spanning a wide range of technologies, from aeronautics, software development and construction technology to nanoelectronics, textiles and clothing (European Commission 2007).

The ETPs were quite important to the early development of the ERA – an initiative that combined three related and complementary concepts: (a) 'the creation of an "internal market" in research, an area of free movement of knowledge, researchers and technology'; (b) 'a restructuring of the European research fabric, in particular by improved coordination of national research activities and policies'; (c) 'the development of a European research policy which not only addresses the funding of research activities, but also takes account of all relevant aspects of other EU and national policies'.

These institutional support measures were later coupled with a significantly increased financial support programme. The FP7, the main EU instrument for funding research in Europe, was worth around €55 billion to be spent between 2007 and 2013. This represents a 63 per cent increase in the budget allocated during FP6 (2002–2006), which was only €17.6 billion. From the point of view of Europe's industrial policy, of major importance is the focus of the bulk of the funding (€32.4 billion) on ten major research themes, the majority of which resonate strongly within the sectors identified by the 2002 Commission Communication by former President Prodi, and by the 'Aho Report': health, biotechnology, ICT, nanosciences and new production technologies, energy, environment, transport (including aeronautics), space and security. Also very important is the funding dedicated to the ERC, 'the first pan-European funding body set up to support investigator-driven frontier research'. It aims to stimulate scientific excellence by supporting the best creative scientists, engineers and scholars so that they can take risks in their research, and hopes to offer further institutional support through peer review and the setting up of international benchmarks of success. On the economic side, the ERC hopes 'to nurture science-based industry and create a greater impetus for the establishment of research-based spin-offs'.

For areas where very significant resources must be invested over a longer timeframe than the FP7 could offer, and where there is a need for public–private partnerships, the Commission proposed launching JTIs, identifying six potential JTIs based on strict criteria: the strategic importance of the sector and the presence of a clear deliverable; existence of market failure, such as externalities or very high-level risk; concrete evidence of Community value added; evidence of substantial, long-term industry commitment; and inadequacy of existing Community instruments. The possible JTIs identified were in the fields of hydrogen and fuel cells, aeronautics and air transport, innovative medicines, nanoelectronic technologies, embedded computing systems, and global monitoring for environment and security – again similar to the other EU documents mentioned above.

As we have already argued, the development of a strong EU-level 'technology' policy is a *sine qua non* of a modern industrial policy that aims to support businesses in the knowledge-based society. The range and variety of tools the Commission has developed in order to promote research, innovation, excellence and human capital have put the EU on the right track. The increases in funding for both the FP7 (2007–2013) and then 'Horizon 2020' (2014–2020) are also highly commendable (see the analysis in Chapter 4). However, as will be argued in the following chapter, in order for true 'European Champions' to develop in the high-technology sectors, an even more robust common 'technology' policy – one that further overcomes the segmentation of the 'technology' policies of Member States – is required.

Bringing together all the various insights and policy advice that have been put out by the Commission in various documents on industrial policy's third side (i.e. research and technology policy), we can see which sectors have gained the greatest prominence in the last few years: ICT, energy, defence, space, biotechnology and pharmaceuticals (see Table 1.4).

The core businesses of firms in these sectors are all very high-tech and R&D intensive. In order for European companies to develop a leading edge in such sectors, two factors are absolutely crucial: first, they must have access to a high level of financial resources in order to conduct R&D at the required plane; second, they must be able to hire excellent researchers, engineers and managers – human capital – who have the right skills and knowledge to come up with new and innovative production, organizational and management outputs. As a result, developing strong European research, technology and education policies, as well as overcoming the segmentation of policies of individual national governments, is the main path for innovation and growth.

Meanwhile, in between the first and second period of revival of industrial policy that we have plotted here (2002–2006 and 2007–2014), the economic and financial crisis in which the industries of Western European countries are still struggling would explode, due to the bankruptcy in September 2008 of Lehman Brothers. In addition, Europe is facing increasing global competition, especially from emerging Asian and Latin American economies. A remarkable change in attitude has been emerging in the ruling classes, including – and perhaps above all – those managing 'Anglo-Saxon capitalisms': it is now customary to speak of a 'manufacturing renaissance', meaning that manufacturing is recovering its rightful place in the economy as a springboard to growth. Europe needs its industry but industry needs Europe as well. It is essential to increase productivity in manufacturing and related services to underpin the recovery of growth and jobs. 'This house believes' – wrote *The Economist* launching its Debate of June/July 2011 – 'that an economy cannot succeed without a big manufacturing base': as argued in the Prologue, from the way the thesis is formulated, we think we can say that a change of attitude has emerged as compared to previous years. Here the topic of manufacturing is tackled positively, whereas the issue of industrial policy was dealt via a negative approach ('Industrial policy always fails'), as we have also seen in the Prologue. While in 2010 the readers defeated the

Table 1.4 A summary of Commission documents on the new industrial policy (vertical applications)

European background documents	Sectors identified												
	Biotech[1]	ICT[2]	Energy[3]	Defence[4]	Space[5]	Pharma[6]	Mech[7]	Health[8]	Environment[9]	Transports[10]	Digital[11]	Nano[12]	Socio-economic[13]
EC Communication Industrial Policy (2002)	✓	✓	✓	✓	✓	–	–	–	–	–	–	–	–
EC Communication Industrial Policy (2005)	✓	✓	–	✓	✓	✓	✓	–	–	–	–	–	–
'Aho Report' (2006)	–	✓	✓	–	✓	✓	–	✓	✓	✓	✓	–	–
Joint Tech Initiatives (2006)	–	✓	✓	✓	✓	✓	–	–	✓	–	–	✓	–
Competitiveness Report (2006)	–	–	–	✓	–	–	–	✓	✓	✓	–	–	–
Seventh FP (2007–2013)[14]	✓	✓	✓	✓	✓	–	–	✓	✓	✓	–	✓	✓

Source: author's elaboration based on European commission documents.

Notes
1 Life sciences and biotechnology.
2 Including embedded computing systems.
3 Including renewable forms of energy (e.g. hydrogen and fuel cells).
4 As far as FP7 is concerned, global monitoring for security.
5 Including aerospace industry, the European space programme, aeronautics.
6 Pharmaceutical industry, including innovative medicines.
7 Mechanical engineering.
8 Including e-Health.
9 Including climate change; as far as FP7 is concerned, global monitoring for environment.
10 Transportation and logistics, and in the 7th FP including aeronautics.
11 Digital security and content.
12 Nanoelectronics technologies, nanosciences, materials and new production technologies.
13 Socio-economic sciences and the humanities.
14 The European Research Council's Work Programme identifies three main research domains: (i) physical science and engineering; (ii) life science; (iii) social science and humanities.

thesis of *The Economist*, in 2011 they approved it – again with a large majority (76 per cent against 24 per cent) – thus giving consistency to the two results, which can be summarized as follows: manufacturing matters, and in order to make it grow, a far-sighted industrial policy is needed.

Identifying new European industries (2007–2014)

Europe is a world leader in many strategic sectors such as automotive, aeronautics, engineering, space, chemicals and pharmaceuticals. When at the beginning of the twenty-first century the European Commission began speaking of 'European Champions' – early 2003, right after the first Communication on new industrial policy (European Commission 2002) – it simultaneously identified a sort of proper playing field. In his speech, the then President of the European Commission Romano Prodi provided an initial list, as follows:[12]

i   '*biotechnologies and life sciences*';
ii   '*information and communications technology sector*, where our leadership in mobile telecommunications runs heavy risks in a new standards battle';
iii 'the so-called "*hydrogen economy*", as the alternative means for accumulating and transferring energy';
iv   '*defence industry*, still fragmented in the absence of the intention to build a truly integrated European defence system';
v   '*our aerospace*', 'still undecided between civilian and safety applications'.

Alongside some unequivocal strengths in European industry, which have been outlined above, we do meet some weaknesses that constitute the *raison d'être* for renewing industrial policy at the European level. As far as competitiveness of European industry is concerned, the performance is not entirely positive 'in some of the highest value-added segments of the economy' (e.g. electronics and office machinery and computer industries). In other words, the EU 'tends to specialise in medium-high-technology and mature capital-intensive industries. If it is essential to keep the strengths in these sectors … the EU should seek to reinforce its position in enabling technologies such as ICT, electronics, biotechnology or nanotechnology' (European Commission 2002).

The 'integrated' approach, with an emphasis on high-tech sectors, will be consolidated in Brussels year after year, as evidenced clearly by the Communication approved by the European Commission, just ten years after the first, which marked the revival of industrial policy:

> *Europe needs to reverse the declining role of industry in Europe for the 21st century....* To achieve this, a comprehensive vision is needed, focusing on investment and on innovation, but also mobilising all the levers available at EU level, notably the single market, trade policy, SME policy, competition policy, environmental and research policy in favour of European companies. *This Communication proposes a partnership between the EU, its Member*

States and industry to dramatically step up investment into new technologies and give Europe a competitive lead in the new industrial revolution.

(European Commission 2012)

Between 2005 and 2006 (the time of mid-term review) and this Communication of 2012 there will be numerous other documents approved and/or published on the subject (the full list is published in Appendix I to this book), especially in view of the fact that industrial policy – as it will be explained in Chapter 4 – had become part of the wider economic reform strategy, named 'Europe 2020' (European Commission 2010), which in 2010 replaced the 'Lisbon Strategy'. Summing up, *an industrial policy for the globalization era* represents one of the so-called 'Europe 2020 Flagship Initiatives' since the Commission 'will draw up a framework for a modern industrial policy, to support entrepreneurship ... to promote the competitiveness of Europe's primary, manufacturing and service industries and help them seize the opportunities of globalisation and of green economy' (European Commission 2010).

Drawing our attention to the 'six priority action lines' expressly mentioned in the 2012 Communication, we find the evidence that had already emerged in the early 2000s (see Table 1.2); namely, the idea of focusing public–private joint investment on general purpose technologies rather than on individual industrial sectors, narrowly defined (the old-fashioned 'picking the winners' approach) as happened in the 1970s and 1980s.

The trend seems to be more general. Two other important experiences are currently underway: the first in the United States, promoted in 2011 at the behest of the Obama Administration (www.manufacturing.gov/welcome.html); the second within the EU industrial powerhouse, Germany (Federal Ministry of Education and Research 2010). Table 1.5 gives an account of these three initiatives, which together with some specificity share a common thread.

As a whole, Table 1.5 reveals the many existing similarities – both from the point of view of the method (moving the technological frontier forward) and from the point of view of substance (technology development) – among these three initiatives. The 'national' differences, so to speak, reside – in our opinion – more on theoretical aspects. For example, while the European Commission speaks specifically of 'Industrial Policy' because 'The word is no longer taboo' (Monti 2010),[13] the federal government of the United States describes its solutions in great detail but omits the explicit expression. However, at a time when President Obama launched, with a speech at Carnegie Mellon University (24 June 2011), the Advanced Manufacturing Partnership (AMP), the official website of the White House explained that:

The U.S. Government has had a long history of partnership with companies and universities in developing and commercializing the new technologies that have been the foundation of our economic success – from the telephone, to the microwave, to the jet engine, to the internet. The AMP will provide the platform for similar breakthroughs in the next decade.[14]

Table 1.5 Science-based industries and blending technologies: a summary of initiatives

	Year/country		
	2010/Germany	2012/EU	2011/USA
Institution(s)	Federal Ministry of Education and Research	European Commission	White House
Title	'Ideas. Innovation. Prosperity: High-Tech Strategy 2020 for Germany'	'A Stronger European Industry for Growth and Economic Recovery'	'Advanced Manufacturing Partnership'[1]
Contents	*5 key technologies:* climate/energy; health/nutrition; mobility; security; communication	*6 priority action lines:* advanced manufacturing technologies; key enabling technologies; bio-based products; sustainable industrial and construction policy and raw materials; clean vehicles; smart grids	*4 key steps:* capabilities in critical national security industries; advanced materials; next-generation robotics; energy-efficient manufacturing processes

Source: author's elaboration based on official documents.

Note
1 According to the Council of Advisors on Science and Technology, 'Advanced manufacturing is a family of activities that (a) depend on the use and coordination of information, automation, computation, software, sensing, and networking, and/or (b) make use of cutting edge materials and emerging capabilities enabled by the physical and biological sciences, for example nanotechnology, chemistry, and biology' (see: *Advanced Manufacturing Portal*, www.manufacturing.gov).

Returning to Europe's landscape we can see that even the federal government of Germany is very cautious to use the expression 'industrial policy', preferring to speak about 'High-Tech Strategy 2020'.[15] Through the pages of this document, however, once again we find the *fil rouge* which binds the other two initiatives (EU and USA): 'The aim of the High-Tech Strategy is to make Germany a leader when it comes to solving these global challenges' (see the above-mentioned 'five key technologies', Table 1.5).

> This will not just improve people's lives and standard of living; it will also offer new value creation potential for the private sector, create high-level jobs in Germany and help us make better use of talents here in Germany. For this reason, the Federal Government's innovation policy activities area geared towards these five fields of action, with the aim of tapping emerging markets.
> (Federal Ministry of Education and Research 2010, 5)

The three programmes laid out in Table 1.5, important as they may be, cannot be seen as exhaustive of everything that is taking place all over the world in the field of the new industrial policy. The same European Commission, after that of 2012, published another important Communication (European Commission 2014) two years later, with the intention of reinforcing the decision to locate this policy area within the larger context of the Europe 2020 agenda. It is for this reason that, while speaking of 'completing the integration of networks' (in the sense of 'integrated infrastructure') it cites those in 'information, energy, transport, space and communication' (p. 5); when speaking of 'industrial modernisation' and 'stimulating investment in innovation and new technologies', the Commission once again mentions the priorities that should be aspired to: 'Advanced manufacturing', 'Key Enabling Technologies', 'Bio-based products', 'Clean Vehicles and Vessels', 'Sustainable construction and raw materials', 'Smart Grids and Digital Infrastructures' (pp. 10–11).

We should here recall *The Entrepreneurial State*, in which Mazzucato (2014) shows how in the most advanced economies, the most dynamic engine behind sectors like the green economy, telecommunications, nanotechnology and pharmaceuticals is precisely that of the state, which shoulders the risks of initial investment at the origins of new technologies. Numerous examples are drawn from the American experience.

Again: Stiglitz *et al.* (2013) in the above-cited text (Stiglitz and Lin 2013) call attention in their Introduction not only to the experiences of the US and the EU, but also to those of the United Kingdom and Japan. For the former, in particular, the reference is to the initiative launched by Minister Vince Cable, with Prime Minster David Cameron's support;[16] for the latter, to the initiative of Prime Minister Shinzo Abe to create various 'Economic Revitalisation Headquarters'.[17] The authors then mention a series of

> emerging economies such as China, Russia, Brazil, India, Indonesia, or Nigeria ... where policymakers are also eager to encourage new thinking on

the various ways in which smart industrial policy can help sustain growth and open up new possibilities for employment creation,

with further detailed analyses of some of these cases within the book (for example, Brazil, and, more generally, Latin America).

The ranks of the nations under examination swell further thanks to the work of Yülek (2015), who under the category of industrial policy includes the cases of Ireland ('small open economy') and Israel ('The State and the Development of High Technology'), as well as the EU and Japan. Under the category of economic planning, on the other hand, he places the cases of Turkey, South Korea and South Africa.

Summing up, the strong and persistent 'structural change' must be regarded as the main road towards strengthening the competitiveness in manufacturing. It is essential to set up the right framework conditions for industry to develop the technologies and production capabilities needed to deliver this challenge. Overall, this is precisely the task of industrial policy as the broad economic literature mentioned at the beginning of this section shows.

The 'Jacquemin–Rodrik synthesis'

Few topics have aroused such extensive debate amongst economists of various schools and beliefs as industrial policy regularly does. However, it is equally true that few essays like that by Alexis Jacquemin (1987) have offered such a clear analysis of the various roles assigned to industrial policy (see in particular chapter 6). Professor Jacquemin wrote that depending on the stress attributed to the spontaneous settling of market forces, or on strategic behaviour, this will eventually lead to the choice of social model.

The contrasting position between the two paradigms (or points of view) that Jacquemin called – respectively – 'the efficiency of selection through market mechanisms' and 'the role of strategic behaviour (private or public) affecting these same mechanisms' are the *leitmotiv* of his well-known essay on *The New Industrial Organization: Market Forces and Strategic Behavior* – a contrast that could not fail to have an effect on economic policy choices and on industrial policy in particular.

So – he argued – 'for those who have full confidence in market mechanisms, the only real requirement is the existence of a healthy macroeconomic environment', whereas – he continues – 'there is a whole tide of research questioning whether the market alone can efficiently accomplish selections leading to new industrial organisations'. The author then developed the latter thought to arrive at the classic two-level argument that justifies an industrial policy:

i   'The long list of so-called market failures' (in this context R&D support in high-tech sectors is deliberately mentioned).[18]

ii   'A second level of argument in favour of a positive industrial policy goes beyond the consideration of failures inherent in certain markets. It concerns strategies that deliberately influence the transformation and the industrial reorganization of sectors, and nations.'

Alexis Jacquemin did not conceal his own preference. He also made use of numerous examples from those years, the 1980s (his overview takes into account the USA, Japan and, above all, Europe), and he levelled severe criticism of the methodological approach 'based on the idea that competitive processes ensure the survival of the fittest'.

Last, he dedicated himself to a study of the 'characteristics of an approach that allows for the existence of a strategic dimension in socio-economic behaviour'. Over the years several of his intuitions have shown great foresight, for instance the criticism of domestic policies in Member States that pursued the creation of 'National Champions'. On the other hand, the time squandered by our European companies compared to those in America and Japan – wrote Jacquemin (1987) – 'lead to the possibility of *a concerted European industrial policy that will help overcome industry strategies along national lines*, reduce barriers between national champions, and develop a large home European market for industrial applications'. It's precisely this insight that has reappeared in the EU a quarter of a century later; and this insight is even more valuable today because of the further extension(s) of the Single Market (i.e., the 1995 and 2004–2007 enlargements).

After Professor Jacquemin's work (in the 1980s) and more than a decade of silence on industrial policy (the 1990s) – when it fell victim both to its past mistakes and to the rise of a dominant ideology (the so-called 'Washington Consensus') – we quickly reach the 2000s. Halfway through the new decade a couple of seminal papers by Dani Rodrik (2004, 2008) shed light on what industrial policy really is at the start of the twenty-first century. To avoid misunderstandings, the adjective 'new' has been added to industrial policy, in order to distinguish it from the industrial policy of the past, which was focused on 'picking the winners' and, more generally, on excessive public intervention (above all by the nation-state) in the economy, mainly the state ownership of industrial and/or services enterprises and through 'state aids'.

Nowadays, the seminal works by Professor Rodrik that are usually referred to in the economic literature are those from 2004 and 2008, respectively entitled *Industrial Policy for the Twenty-First Century* and 'Normalizing Industrial Policy'. In both, the author illustrates 'his own' definition of industrial policy: 'I will use the term to denote policies that stimulate specific economic activities and promote structural change' (not only, he argues, in the manufacturing industry but also in all kinds of 'non-traditional activities' in agriculture or in services).

Like Jacquemin, Dani Rodrik starts from a conventional point of view for industrial policy, i.e. 'market failures' ('markets for credit, labor, products and knowledge', he adds) and the need to deal with them. Yet, like Jacquemin, there is more to Rodrik's thought: on 'policies for economic restructuring', he argues that in order to encourage diversification the task of industrial policy 'is as much about eliciting information from the private sector on significant externalities and their remedies as it is about implementing appropriate policies'. Thus,

> the right model for industrial policy is not that of an autonomous government applying Pigovian taxes or subsidies but of strategic collaboration between the private sector and the government with the aim of uncovering where the most significant obstacles to restructuring lie and what type of interventions are most likely to remove them ... It is innovation that enables restructuring and productivity growth.
>
> (Rodrik 2004)

What is fundamental is to get the policy *process* right, not to focus on the policy *outcomes*. As Rodrik (2004) puts it:

> We need to worry about how we design a setting in which private and public actors come together to solve problems in the productive sphere, each side learning about the opportunities and constraints faced by the other, and not about whether the right tool for industrial policy is, say, directed credit or R&D subsidies or whether it is the steel industry that ought to be promoted or the software industry.

Rodrik's vision of 'industrial policy as a discovery process – one where firms and the government learn about underlying costs and opportunities and engage in strategic coordination', is highly important for the success of the new EU industrial policy, which relies heavily on developing strong Research, Technology and Education policies. In his words, when industrial policy is viewed as an iterative and dialogic process, 'the traditional arguments against [it] lose much of their force ... For example, the typical riposte about governments' inability to pick winners becomes irrelevant.' Dani Rodrik has continued to promote the principles inspiring a modern industrial policy both by publishing other works (2008b, 2013), and – as we know from the Prologue – by taking an active part in *The Economist* debate of July 2010.

Bearing in mind both Alexis Jacquemin's and Dani Rodrik's insights, we have seen an industrial policy that 'overcomes industry strategies along national lines' thanks to combined efforts at the European level; and a policy that, thanks to a 'strategic cooperation' between the public and private sphere of the economy, is concerned above all with the provision of public goods for the productive sector. That is to say:

> Public labs and public R&D, health and infrastructural facilities, sanitary and phitosanitary standards, infrastructure, vocational and technical training can all be viewed as public goods required for enhancing technological capabilities. From this perspective, industrial policy is just good economic policy of the type that traditional, orthodox approaches prescribe.

We should call this policy 'The Jacquemin–Rodrik Synthesis'.

The worldwide 'manufacturing renaissance' and the European response

Gary Pisano, distinguished professor at Harvard Business School, one of the global meccas of Anglo-Saxon-style managerial culture, claims that:

> One of our key messages is to get students to appreciate that manufacturing involves a lot of knowledge work. There has almost been a whole generation of MBA students and managers who have been brought up on a false idea that manufacturing is kind of the brawn and not the brain, and that the country should focus on the brain.
>
> (Pisano 2011)

One could equally cite other works by Pisano (Pisano and Shih 2012), or other authors (Sirkin *et al.* 2012). It seems, therefore, that the winds are changing: can we reasonably hope for a profound change in attitude from the years when the 'pensée unique' ('Washington Consensus') was king? Perhaps we can. Alongside the intellectual debate within the United States, we point out the previously mentioned actions taken by President Obama, as well as his constant call for a needed 'revival' in manufacturing:

> Today, I'm calling for all of us to come together – private sector industry, universities, and the government – to spark a renaissance in American manufacturing and help our manufacturers develop the cutting-edge tools they need to compete with anyone in the world. With these key investments, we can ensure that [the US] ... remains a nation that 'invents it here and manufactures it here' and creates high-quality, good paying jobs for ... workers.
>
> (The White House 2011)

Now, if the winds of change are nigh, what will happen to *us*, in the sense of the European Union? The first lesson after decades of globalization is that no country is an island: neither in terms of the flow of goods, nor (more importantly) in terms of the flow of ideas. This is of even greater truth in the case of the EU. Data published regularly on a monthly basis by the European Central Bank (ECB 2014) shed light on the relative strength of European industry compared to that of America and Japan, as well as the relative strength of the EU as a world trade power. These data – referring as they do to what was formerly defined as the 'Triad' during the 1980s and 1990s – obviously do not tell the whole story, considering the growing influence of newly industrialized countries, developing nations and BRIC on the global economy. But we believe they *are* sufficient to make our point: the position of the EU from both perspectives examined here seems remarkable, even in comparison with its two traditional competitors.

With manufacturing and export numbers of this scale – along with others related to the European big players that we will inspect later – comes a concomitant

Table 1.6a Overview of major economic areas: structural indicators (value added by economic activity, % of total)[1]

	EU/euro area	*United States*	*Japan*
Agriculture, fishing and forestry	1.8/1.8	1.2	1.2
Industry (incl. construction)	25.0/25.2	20.0	26.8
Services	73.2/73.1	78.8	72.1

Note

1 China has recently been added: Agric. (10.1%), Ind. (45.3%), Serv. (44.6%).

Table 1.6b Overview of major economic areas: structural indicators (external, % of GDP)[1]

	EU/euro area	*United States*	*Japan*
Exports of goods and services	18.3/26.8	14.1	15.4
Imports of goods and services	17.5/24.8	17.5	17.1
Current account balance	0.3/1.2	−2.8	1.0

Source: ECB (2013).

Note

1 China has recently been added: Exp (26.3%), Imp. (23.5%), Current account balance (2.3%).

responsibility for the European ruling class in the fields of government, academia and business. It would indeed be paradoxical if, at the moment when the elite of the Anglo-Saxon culture rediscovered manufacturing, the EU was not putting all of its forces – intellectual and material – behind the evolution of its own manufacturing industry, *in primis* from the technological and knowledge-based perspectives.

After all, from the great Joseph Schumpeter (1911) on, we have learned that the quintessence of economic growth lies in 'creative destruction': the rise of new industries in place of the old ones. This lesson has been re-proposed in recent years – as we have already seen – by Rodrik (2004), and Stiglitz and Lin (2013) in their contributions on an industrial policy aimed at 'structural transformation', and at 'affecting the economic structure of the economy'. So what *is* the role of European manufacturing on the global scale? It is worth mentioning two analyses: Table 1.7 is drawn from research carried out by the McKinsey Global Institute (McKinsey 2012); Table 1.8, from a *Scenario* by Italy's Centro studi Confindustria (CsC 2013).

McKinsey (2012, 6) in its *Manufacturing the Future* first explains that manufacturing gross value added continues to grow globally: today, it

represents 16% of global GDP, and manufacturing value added grew from $5.7 trillion to $7.5 trillion (in 2000 prices) between 2000 and 2010. Both advanced and developing economies have experienced growth in manufacturing value

Table 1.7 Large developing economies are moving up in global manufacturing: top 15 manufacturers by share of global manufacturing value added

Rank	1980	1990	2000	2010
1	United States	United States	United States	United States
2	*Germany*	Japan	Japan	China
3	Japan	*Germany*	*Germany*	Japan
4	*UK*	*Italy*	China	*Germany*
5	*France*	*UK*	*UK*	*Italy*
6	*Italy*	*France*	*Italy*	Brazil
7	China	China	*France*	South Korea
8	Brazil	Brazil	South Korea	*France*
9	*Spain*	*Spain*	Canada	*UK*
10	Canada	Canada	Mexico	India
11	Mexico	South Korea[1]	*Spain*	Russia[2]
12	Australia	Mexico	Brazil	Mexico
13	*Netherlands*	Turkey	Taiwan	Indonesia[2]
14	Argentina	India	India	*Spain*
15	India	Taiwan	Turkey	Canada

Source: taken from McKinsey (2012).

Notes
Emphasis added for the EU member states.
1 South Korea ranked 25 in 1980.
2 In 2000, Indonesia ranked 20 and Russia ranked 21.

added.... Overall, in high-income economies, manufacturing value added grew by 2.7% a year from 2000 to 2007 ... In the same period, 26% of the total growth in value added in middle-income countries such as Brazil, China, and India was generated by manufacturing.

Second, McKinsey points out – publishing a detailed exhibit (see Table 1.8) – that 'large developing economies grew faster than established high-income economies. From 2000 to 2010, their share in global manufacturing value added almost doubled, from 21 to 39%' (p. 6).

While keeping in mind this and other fundamental trends that McKinsey's research points out ('the size of manufacturing sectors varies among economies, even those at the same stage of development', and 'manufacturing's share of GDP has fallen in all but the poorest economies', etc.), once again the global data present the image of a Europe that is certainly not headed off into the sunset. There were six European nations in the 'Top 15' in 1980 (Spain would not enter the EEC until 1986), and there are still five of them in 2010. The Netherlands has fallen out of the rankings, and, as one can see, the relative positions of the others (with the exception of Italy) have generally declined as a result of the effect on global manufacturing of the trends cited above. But we must mention how other EU nations that are not found in the global 'Top 15' still have robust manufacturing traditions. We are thinking of the Netherlands and of Sweden (subject of a detailed analysis in the McKinsey

Table 1.8 The new industrial world (% of global manufacturing output, in current US$)

	Average 1991–1992	Average 2001–2002	Average 2011–2012	Average annual growth rate, manufacturing output, % (2005 US$): 1990–2012
1 China	4.1	9.7	21.4	12.4
2 USA	21.8	24.7	15.4	2.4
3 Japan	19.4	13.4	9.6	−0.4
4 *Germany*	*9.2*	*6.9*	*6.1*	*1.7*
5 South Korea	2.4	3.1	4.1	7.7
6 India	1.2	1.9	3.3	7.5
7 *Italy*	*5.5*	*3.4*	*3.1*	*−0.7*
8 Brazil	2.1	1.7	2.9	2.2
9 *France*	*5.0*	*4.1*	*2.9*	*−0.1*
10 Russia	0.2	0.8	2.3	–
11 *UK*	*3.9*	*3.5*	*2.0*	*0.1*
12 Mexico	1.6	2.3	1.7	2.7
13 Canada	1.9	2.3	1.7	1.4
14 *Spain*	*2.4*	*2.2*	*1.6*	*−0.1*
15 Indonesia	0.8	0.9	1.6	5.7
16 Taiwan	1.5	1.6	1.5	5.1
17 *Netherlands*	*1.3*	*1.2*	*1.1*	*1.2*
18 Australia	1.0	0.8	1.0	1.0
19 Turkey	1.2	0.7	1.0	4.0
20 *Poland*	*0.3*	*0.6*	*0.9*	*7.0*
World				2.8
EU-15 + US + JAP	*73.3*	*64.9*	*45.5*	*1.0*
BRICs	7.6	14.1	29.9	8.0
EU-New	*1.1*	*1.6*	*2.4*	*4.6*

Source: taken from CsC (2013).

Notes
Countries ranked in order of total percentage of global manufacturing output, 2011–2012 average.
EU-New: Bulgaria, Poland, Czech Republic, Slovakia and Hungary.
EU nations in italics.

report ('Sweden outperformed its EU peers in manufacturing value added, helping it maintain a large manufacturing sector', p. 23)), not to mention the central–eastern countries of Europe that entered the EU during its period of enlargement.

We should continue our exercise – to shed light from a European perspective on world manufacturing – with a second step, going through the research undertaken by CsC-Confindustria (2013). The *Scenario* presented under the title 'Global industry has become multi-polar', describes the changes over the last 30 years, changes that have been marked by the rise of emerging economies. These – they write – 'have acquired an economic weight that is felt at the global level; the growth rate has been very high for China and India, for the economies of Eastern Europe (Poland in particular), Turkey, and Indonesia and Taiwan in Asia.' On the other side, the loss of share in advanced economies has a multifaceted character: in some cases (Japan, Italy, France) this has been caused by a change in the levels of production; in others (Germany, the Netherlands, the United States) by a lower rate of growth than those in emerging nations. South Korea occupies a unique position insofar as it is no longer an emerging nation, yet it still grows as if it were one.

(CsC 2013, 41)

Confindustria rightly describes a situation of 'nations on the rise', especially the set made up by BRICs and EU-New (see Table 1.6): their performance, in the space of two decades (from 1991–1992 to 2011–2012), has been truly spectacular, and they now account for one-third of global production (29.9 per cent + 2.4 per cent) from the 8.7 per cent (7.6 per cent + 1.1 per cent) at the beginning of this period. Nevertheless, the data for Europe in 2011–2012 are hardly irrelevant (CsC 2013, 43–44).

When – from our supranational perspective – we pick up the seven EU-15 countries belonging to the 'Top 20' (Germany, Italy, France, UK, Spain and the Netherlands), plus Poland and the EU-New, we arrive at the notable number of about 20 per cent. Taking into account the share of manufacturing production coming from all the other EU countries, it is possible to argue that almost a quarter of global production comes from Europe (the 27 old and new Member States). This portion is significantly higher than the ones of the US (15.4 per cent) and Japan (9.6 per cent). Moreover, viewed in its entirety as the 'European Union quota' – and not simply as the single portions of the Member States – this is even higher than any of the BRIC economies considered singularly, starting from the largest of them all (as can be seen from Table 1.6, China, the world's largest producer, is at 21.4 per cent).

Summing up, the lesson we can learn from both the McKinsey and Confindustria analyses is simple: the EU continues to have a primary role to play on the world's stage of manufacturing. Nonetheless, the supplemental responsibility that we have just spoken of demands a qualitative leap: in public discourse, in policy-making and in corporate strategies. Let me give a familiar example: Italy. The country's elites cannot limit themselves to crowing about Italian manufacturing achievements, even if these are significant: second place in the EU after Germany as a manufacturing power. The question becomes: what can Italy reasonably change or reform within its 'model of capitalism' so as to bring it as close as possible to the model of 'Rhine capitalism'? The same thing goes for all other Member States (in their own proportions), or at least for all others which believe that Germany truly represents a model to aspire to; a nation that, in the words of Horst Siebert (2005, 1), long-time economic adviser to Chancellor Kohl, has 'an open economy with a strong industrial base, producing about a third of its gross domestic product for export'.

And so let's return to the 'triangle of industrial policy' mentioned at the beginning of this chapter. There exists a field in which the process of European integration has led the EU, decade after decade, to speak with a 'single voice': trade policy (consider, for example, the role of the EU in the World Trade

Organization). Once again: there exists a field like competition policy where supranational jurisdiction is strong, and is an integral part of the *acquis communautaire* (consider the control of concentrations, the fines levied for abuses of dominant positions, the state aids control and so forth). But the third side of industrial policy – i.e. technological policy – is still primarily in the hands of single Member States. How far do we have to go before reaching the objective of an authentically European industrial policy, one where even this third side is genuinely Community oriented?

Since Article 130 of the Treaty of Maastricht (now Article 173), something has changed in the structure of the EU, and not by chance has a new series of Communications about industrial policy been approved by the European Commission since December 2002. We're speaking about an industrial policy that, more so now than in the past, is essentially a policy for promoting – according to the previously given definition – the 'structural change' of industry, therein bringing about an increase in 'knowledge investments', starting from R&D and human capital.

The fundamental question, at this point, is the following: is the idea of taking technological policy into the realm of supranational governance so very unthinkable, considering how the issues it involves are no less important than those of international trade and competition policy (the first two sides of the triangle), which have clearly gone past the confines of any single nation-state? Taking the case of R&D once again, we should keep in mind the positive externality that is inherent in this kind of investment.[19]

Connecting the third side of the triangle with a technological policy that is managed at the supranational level should be one of the cornerstones of the new European governance which has so long been spoken of, and where it seems that questions of a macroeconomic nature always predominate. Going back to Jacquemin, compared to the period when he worked in Brussels alongside President Delors, 'overcoming industrial strategies along national lines' is a step that has become even more necessary due to the dynamics of the global economy in the first decade of the twenty-first century. At that time, as already mentioned, the 'Triad' (EEC, USA, Japan) reigned, whereas now we are in the midst of the rise of the BRICs and, more generally, of those countries which the International Monetary Fund has called the 'Emerging and developing economies', which account for the majority of the additional growth of global GNP. All of this leads, as we know, to a different composition of global manufacturing production. Along with the data presented in Tables 1.6 and 1.7, the transformation is described by *The Economist* in its special report entitled 'A Third Industrial Revolution'. The London weekly writes in the section 'Back to making stuff':

> For over 100 years America was the world's leading manufacturer, but now it is neck-and-neck with China. In the decade to 2010 the number of manufacturing jobs in America fell by about a third. The rise of outsourcing and off-shoring and the growth of sophisticated supply chains has enabled companies the world over to use China, India and other low-wage countries as workshops.
>
> (*The Economist* 2012)

Much other data could be cited but it wouldn't change the substance of the story, which is that of the well-documented growing role of the BRIC nations and of all developing countries as the 'factories of the world'. It is however equally true that these countries also have become in recent years extraordinary new export markets for quality goods (from both the technological and design point of view), such as those produced in Europe (*Made in Italy* is a strong point among these), because of the sudden economic growth, spurred by industrialization, that these nations have experienced. Indeed, in global industry, is there not still room for a united Europe and, even more specifically, for its industry? The data on its economic 'structure' shown in Tables 1.2a and 1.2b, as well as in Tables 1.6 and 1.7, argue in favour of this enduring role, though with changing circumstances and players. There's more: a further positive reply comes to us when we look at global manufacturing from a particular perspective, that of the so-called 'European Champions'; those large enterprises which hold positions of leadership within the new genuinely globalized market.

A first assessment (definition and taxonomy) of the 'European Champions' has already been the topic of previous work (Mosconi 2009), while a new and updated analysis will be carried out in the next chapter. To be clear, we are talking about large multinational companies that have business operations in many European countries and, branching out expressly from its original European base, are often capable of carrying their growth strategies into the major extra-European markets (think of America and Asia). There are 'Champions' – those which we have named 'Type I' – that come about from joint initiatives of two or more governments: the success story of Airbus is the most famous example. But the prevailing typology of 'Champions' is another, that which we have named 'Type II', comprising large enterprises that erupted into the market thanks to cross-border mergers and acquisitions (M&As).

Economic history teaches that M&As, worldwide, tend to go in 'waves' that match relevant production, technology and financial transformations (Carlton and Perloff 2005). A couple of remarks: first, the wave that was developing with particular strength in the middle of the last decade and which had Europe as its main actor has partially dissipated in the wake of the subprime crisis of September 2008, but it has not passed in vain (there are many signs that indicate a certain upswing in M&As, even though we are still in the midst of a fragile macroeconomic situation). Second, the three extraordinary accomplishments of the EU in the past two decades – the internal market ('Objective '92'), the single currency (the euro and a system of fixed exchange rates) and the enlargement towards the East (which from an economic point of view should be understood as a further enlargement of the internal market) – have all positively influenced the success of the best European enterprises; a new European oligopoly has thus come about, and in this – by definition – the role of large firms is fundamental. At the same time, innovation has become the main determinant and driver of the ability to add value and to grow (Sapir *et al.* 2003; Aghion 2006; Brusoni and Malerba 2007).

It is certainly not news that large companies have for a long time been the cornerstone of the European economy (particularly in some Member States).

Many studies have highlighted their leadership position in certain industrial fields, though not without underlining the relative weakness of big European companies in some of the most promising new technologies (see the review in the next chapter).

This is where the most delicate question on policy lies: how to promote the structural change of European industry during the years which witnessed simultaneously – on the one hand – the internal market, the euro, the Eastern enlargement, and – on the other – new global challenges coming from the USA and the BRICs? One path, though admittedly not the only one,[20] lies in the 'European Champions' – those which have already proven themselves as well as those to come – benefitting from a new industrial policy that is able to manage, from a supranational position, the most relevant parts of R&D programmes, technological innovation and investment in human capital.

We would then be in the presence of an EU that speaks with a 'single voice' even in the field of technology policy, providing the latter with the same status that trade policy and antitrust already enjoy. This is the path that we propose in this setting, in particular because of the intrinsic strength of European manufacturing and its large enterprises. Can European technological capacity match this manufacturing strength? Or is there a gap that needs to be bridged? If so, by which methods and governance? We will attempt to answer these questions below.

The European innovation landscape and the triangle's third side

Paraphrasing the well-known 'Keynesian multiplier', nowadays we should define the new concept of a 'manufacturing multiplier'. Let's take the EU economy as a first example: according to the European Commission (2012), the current level of industry in Europe is around 16 per cent of GDP, but it 'still accounts for 4/5ths of Europe's export, and 80% of private sector R&D investment comes from manufacturing'.[21]

The same holds true at a worldwide level. McKinsey (2012) in the above-mentioned report shows that 'manufacturing contributes disproportionately to exports, innovation, and productivity growth', especially in the advanced world where 'it remains a vital source of innovation and competitiveness, making outsized contribution to research and development, exports, and productivity growth'. The figures speak for themselves: the manufacturing shares of exports and private sector R&D (respectively, 70 and 77 per cent) are much higher than the manufacturing shares of global GDP (16 per cent) and employment (14 per cent).[22]

If the main goal of the EU's renewed industrial strategy is to reverse the declining role of industry in Europe from 16 per cent of GDP 'to as much as 20% by 2020', there will be a strong incentive to strengthen R&D and innovation policies at the supranational level – since the 'multiplier' comes into play. The EU is lagging behind the US on the global innovation landscape, where Asia

Table 1.9 R&D big spenders: top seven countries and the EU, 2009

Country	R&D ($, billion)	Share of global R&D (%)	EU Member State
1 US	402	32	–
2 China	154	12	–
3 Japan	138	11	–
4 Germany	83	7	✓
5 France	48	4	✓
6 South Korea	44	4	–
7 UK	40	3	✓
Italy + Spain	25 + 20	–	✓
Sweden + Finland + Denmark	26	–	✓

Source: adapted from Veugelers (2013).

is rapidly rising. In comparison to the US, the European starting point is characterized not only by a lower level of R&D investment, a lower R&D intensity and a weaker specialization in high-tech sectors (European Commission 2011); the EU is also characterized by a fragmentation of R&D-related policies on national bases. Drawing a parallel with the previous section where the 'top manufacturers' have been ranked, here we show the big spenders on R&D.

Doing some simple calculations from the data shown in Table 1.9 (EU-8 = $242 billion), and adding all the other European countries demonstrates that 'the EU accounted for 23% of total global R&D in 2009, down from 27% in 1999', while 'the R&D performed in Asia represented only 24% of global R&D total in 1999. By 2009, Asia accounted for 32%, compared to 34% for North America' (Veugelers 2013).

Notwithstanding the competition coming from both the US and Asia, Europe still has a role to play as one of the world's most innovative economies. Despite the rise of Asia, the EU share of R&D (23 per cent) comes in second place just after the US (32 per cent), almost doubling both China (12 per cent) and Japan (11 per cent). In other words, is there not a European potential to be exploited? The reasons for a positive answer lies in the third side of the industrial policy triangle (i.e. technology policy), provided that this side should be shaped as the other two. Hence, the question becomes: why after a decade of Brussels-based new industrial policy thinking is the practice still far away from a fully integrated and supranational approach? The answer has many facets and, in part, is due to the fact that:

- The EU budget has remained essentially the same, with a substantial part (almost 40 per cent) of it still destined to agriculture (CAP), in spite of some changes made over the last decades.
- So far, this budget has not been thoroughly reformed, as the 'Sapir Report' (Sapir *et al.* 2003) commissioned by then President Prodi sought by creating a 'Fund for economic growth' amounting to 45 per cent of the total resources (i.e. about 1 per cent of the EU GDP).

- There is still a 'missing link in the new EU cohesion package' (Marzinotto 2012) – i.e. the use of EU Structural and Cohesion funds (2014–2020) 'to support long-term investment'. With the new European Semester process – so Bruegel's argument goes – 'consistency' should exist not only *across policy* areas but also *across national reform plans*: 'A European industrial policy strategy [Benedicta Marzinotto concludes] is what would contribute to enhanced coordination across countries.'
- The research and technology policy, while dealt with by some important EU programmes, is mainly carried out by the single Member States, each of them with its own research 'system' and its own policy for technological innovation (not to mention the further fragmentation of powers between central government and regions that occurs in many countries, Italy among them).
- The EU approved, in December 2012, a 'Unitary Patent package' composed of two regulations, and an Agreement on the Unified Patent Court, but it will be possible to apply for a Unitary Patent only after the entry into force of the above-mentioned Agreement on the Court (not before the beginning of 2015, and probably later, depending on when at least 13 contracting Member states will ratify the agreement).[23]
- The creation of large-scale European infrastructural networks (the *Trans-European Networks* of President Delors' White Paper (European Commission 1993)) has remained a dead letter for many years (decades).
- The Eurobonds, conceived by the Delors' White Paper itself to finance the *TENs* mentioned in the previous item, in spite of several types that have been devised since then, have not yet become part of the *acquis communautaire* (only some minor steps forward have been taken).[24]

Combining these seven reasons – which we will discuss more in depth in the next chapters – reveals the direct opposite of a transfer to the supranational level of policies and instruments (starting with R&D) that today are a substantial part of the new industrial policy. We shall look further at research and innovation, and what we can call the 'arithmetic of R&D' tells us these simple facts:

i   The gap between the US and the EU for R&D investments, which is measured at 1 per cent of GDP (the former invests almost 3 per cent, and the latter is skimming 2 per cent), is significant: to clarify the amount, it meant a difference of almost $70 billion in 1999, and more than $100 billion in 2009 (Veugelers 2013).

ii   In one of its most significant quantity targets, the 'Lisbon Agenda' (2000–2010) envisaged a 3 per cent R&D/GDP ratio for the EU by 2010, and the same target has been confirmed by 'Europe 2020' (2010–2020).

iii   The 'Research Framework Programme', which is the Community's most important tool in this field, was worth respectively €14.8 billion in its fifth edition (1998–2002), €19.2 billion in its sixth edition (2002–2006) and €55.8 billion in its seventh edition (2007–2013).

iv   Continuing with our simple arithmetic, we could ask: how many (multiyear) Research Framework Programmes would be needed – even if progressively increased in their budget(s) – to bridge the gap that historically divides the EU from the US, which has proved capable of holding on to its leadership in almost all high-tech production fields?

v   A tentative answer is showed in Table 1.10.

vi   From this to other questions that seek to give the issues a positive spin: in which other fields, if not those of science and technology, could the long awaited 'Centres of European Excellence' be built? Centres able to (re) attract hundreds of thousands of young researchers – those that *Time* magazine called 'Europe's Science Stars' (19 January 2004) – who have abandoned European countries to study and work in the United States? Why not combine, at least in key sectors, the resources (human and financial, both public and private) that each Member State dedicates to research and higher education undertaken at national levels and through national bodies and programmes?

With the creation of authentically European budgets in the field of the so-called (to quote the Commission) 'enabling technologies', would there not be a greater probability of inventing something that is really new, thus increasing the return on R&D spending? From this perspective, it does seem difficult to escape the need for an extensive revision of the Union's budget.

The European Commission is right to place R&D-intensive industries – and the most competitive sectors – on a different level because of the fundamental growth-enhancing effects they can have (Aghion *et al.* 2011). These are industries that often need radical innovations – downright changes of paradigm – considering that the EU is lagging behind the United States in terms of technological advancements, and in view of the new challenge coming from Asia and from the emerging countries in general – the famous BRICs among many others.

These industries require the implementation of a new industrial policy, like the one summarized by the 'Jacquemin–Rodrik Synthesis'.

Conclusions

At first glance, from 1990 through to the early 2000s – which at the beginning of this chapter I called a period of 'suspension' of the EU's industrial policy – there were certainly some extraordinary achievements in the Union: the 1992 programme for completion of the Single Market; the convergence towards Maastricht criteria and the birth of the euro; the historic enlargement towards the East.

Since the beginning of this century, on closer inspection, it has been possible to sense a change of attitude in a significant part of European elites: a change that has touched upon the economic role of the state. Hence, it is a short step to 'Industrial Policy in an Enlarged Europe' – as the first Commission's Communication (European Commission 2002) stated. The reason for this change is threefold: Europe's growth problem, which was already under way – as showed by the 'Sapir Report'

Table 1.10 Summing up R&D investments: global and EU vs US[1]

	R&D global investment ($bn)[2]	US share of global investment ($bn and %)[2]	EU share of global investment ($bn and %)[2]	EU–US total gap ($bn)	Framework programme:[3] total commitments ($bn)	Framework Programme:[3] annual commitments ($bn)	FP commitments/EU-US total gap year-over-year basis for the FP length
1999	641	244 (38%)	173 (27%)	70	17.1 (=€14.8)	4.3 (=€3.7)	4.3/70 → 6.1%
2009	1,276	402 (32%)	293 (23%)	109	73.7 (=€55.8)	10.4 (=€7.9)	10.4/109 → 9.6%

Source: author's elaboration based on Veugelers (2013, 2) and European Commission-DG Research.

Notes

1 R&D expenditures and FP commitments are nominal, expressed in $, PPP; see: http://stats.oecd.org/Index.aspx?datasetcode=SNA_TABLE4.
2 Veugelers (2013), www.bruegel.org.
3 European Commission-DG Research: for 1999, FP 5 (1998–2002); for 2009, FP 7 (2007–2013).

– when the European Commission approved the Communication in December 2002; the great economic crisis in Europe after the 2008 crash; and the pace of technological change in this twenty-first century. In fact, despite significant success at 'institutional' levels, the EU was not growing and introducing technological innovations in the measure that would have been needed. In some countries – beginning with the largest ones, which are those with the lowest growth rate – the idea began to emerge that attitudes of radical closure towards industrial policy were slowing down the structural transformations rather than fostering them. The European Commission, as we realized when we reviewed events, welcomed this stimulus, which was the context in which the new EU industrial policy was sketched.

Whereas at the height of the 1990s there was general consensus about the capability of market forces to find in themselves the most suitable answer to problems of growth, in the last decade a (growing) consensus has emerged for the need for renewed strategic interaction between the public and the private sphere of the economy, between the state and the market. To voice the issue in other terms, the last decade of the twentieth century was one of outdated industrial policy, whereas these decades of the new century have seen its re-launch, although under a decidedly different form.

Certainly, there may be a rediscovery of the economic role of the state on the condition, we might add, that trade liberalization is not considered an accident of history, the single market a useless device, competition policy and state aid regulations an annoying interference from 'Brussels bureaucrats' and so on. In a word: on the condition that the first two sides of the triangle will be saved.

Of course, both for the internal market (liberalization of public utilities as well as effective opening of other services) and for trade liberalization (barriers still existing in the Common Agricultural Policy), there is much to be done and barriers to demolish if a level playing field is really to be created. In general we can state that we cannot backtrack from what has been achieved: in other words, neither can we return to fragmentation of the single European market by building new barriers (or leaving in place those still in existence), nor can we return to protectionism, however it may be disguised. What is more: the Union cannot return to a competition policy that is more acquiescent towards firms and states.[25]

Here we open an important page regarding the relationship that Europe has historically developed between industrial policy and competition policy. In Giuliano Amato's (2005) words:

> The starting point is competition policy as European policy for building an integrated market, which is a legal and conceptual counter position to Industrial policy as a national policy for creating and defending national industry. There was a phase when the two policies cohabited, mainly due to the temporary Europeanization of the latter, then in the 1980s competition policy, an integration tool, clearly prevailed.

The Treaty of Maastricht arrived in 1992, amending the Treaty of Rome not only – as we well know – on the macroeconomic field (the Monetary Union), but also on the microeconomic front. At the time of the Treaty of Rome, industrial policy was considered the prerogative of a nation-state. With Maastricht, however, we arrived at the addition of the famous Article 130, expressly dedicated to 'Industry'. Of the interpretations that immediately emerged for this new article, Amato embraced what the European Commission had always upheld, that there was no contradiction between competition itself and the policies described in the new (at that time) Article 130. He argued:

> Basically, if the world has entered our common market, then we have to reposition and measure competitiveness in our businesses not within European boundaries, but within those of global economy. So, here the rules of competition become part of the whole, but they are not self-sufficient for development.
>
> (Amato 2005)

Summing up, at present the EU has its own ability to speak with 'one voice' in *trade policy*; besides that, *competition policy* is the only other area where the EU has exclusive competence (apart from the exchange rate of the euro).[26] In this chapter a common *technology policy* has been strongly suggested; a technology policy that, in turn, should be seen as an essential tool of the new European industrial policy.

In so doing, we understand that we are describing, above all, a change of attitude that is of no small significance, given how many biases still remain towards industrial policy (which until very recently was seen as damaging and *passé*). Those same biases, once again until very recently, even went against manufacturing itself, insofar as it was seen as an outdated economic activity that was no longer fashionable. We therefore recall our earlier quotation (see previous section) about the 'brain-brawn' binomial in manufacturing (Pisano 2011). The time is ripe for a complete re-evaluation of the role of manufacturing and industrial policy: they both matter. Europe, thanks to its traditions, has much to offer in this regard.

Notes

* The author would like to thank the international publishing house Springer for having granted permission to use, in the writing this chapter, sections from material that he had previously published under the title *The New Industrial Policy in Europe a Decade After (2002-2012)* in the volume edited by M. Yülek (2015), 'Economic Planning and Industrial Policy'.
1 'Les autores notent que la politique industrielle est la résultante d'un "triangle" formé par la politique de la concurrence, la politique commercial (échange extrérieures) et la politique technologique' (Cohen and Lorenzì 2000).
2 See: European Commission (1994, 1998).
3 The 28th Member State, Croatia, entered the EU on 1 July 2013.
4 See also: Visco (2004).
5 See: European Commission website http://ec.europa.eu/enterprise/policies/industrial-competitiveness/industrial-policy/index_en.htm.
6 Currently, the EU invests on average about 2 per cent of its GDP in R&D.
7 Sapir *et al.* (2003).
8 Padoa-Schioppa *et al.* (1987).

 9 One of the most important contributions of the 'Sapir Report' is its insistence on encouraging 'knowledge investments (education, research and development)' and the recognition of the gap between the EU and its main competitor, the US, with regard to resources invested in R&D, registered patents, the number of new successful companies, educational attainments of the population, etc.
10 The two following Communications did not change the approach: the 1994 Communication, 'An Industrial Competitiveness Policy for the European Union' (European Commission 1994), as well as the 1998 Communication, 'The Competitiveness of European Enterprises in the Face of Globalisation: How it can be Encouraged'.
11 Recent contributions on the probability/decision of internationalization are, for example, from a theoretical point of view: Conconi *et al.* (2013); from an empirical perspective: Bacchiocchi *et al.* (2012).
12 Prodi (2003), emphasis added.
13 In his Report ('A New Strategy for the Single Market') to the President of the European Commission, J. M. Barroso, the former Commissioner, Mario Monti (2010), in the same paragraph argues that:

> In Europe leaders are discussing the merits, and limits, of an active industrial policy. The return of interest for industrial policy goes parallel with a renewed attention to the importance of manufacturing for Europe's economy and a wide concern for the profound transformation of the European industrial base triggered by the crisis.

14 See the website: www.manufacturing.gov/welcome.html.
15 Nevertheless, on a separate occasion that same year, the German federal government (Federal Ministry of Economics and Technology 2010, 6) referred expressly to *industrial policy* as one of the 'priorities in Europe 2020'. The government, moreover, once again listed the 'megatrends' that are emerging (see Table 1.5) and from which Germany, thanks to its competitive industrial sector, can benefit: 'environmental and climate protection', 'future-proof mobility and energy solutions', 'state-of-the-art health technologies and everyday goods geared toward an ageing population'.
16 For an analysis of the UK case, we heartily recommend: Chang *et al.* (2013).
17 In the interest of thoroughness, and remaining with the most advanced nations in the world, we should also cite the case of France with its plan of €3.5 billion launched in September 2013. Writing from Paris, the *Financial Times* stated:

> In a high profile announcement at the Elysée Palace, President François Hollande laid out a 10-year industrial policy based on supporting no fewer than 34 sectors, spanning new technologies in areas ranging from renewable energy to robotics and medical biotech.
>
> (article by H. Carnegy, 12 September, www.ft.com)

18   Public authorities [the A. Jacquemin's argument goes] could then favour organizational forms that internalize the external effect of important technological choices and promote the emergence of poles of competition; through financial aids and specific public programs they would be required to support research and development in high-technology industries (microcomputers, aerospace, biotechnology) affected by important fixed and sunk costs.

19 Alexis Jacquemin (1987) was already talking about the need for this type of industrial policy at the end of the 1980s; more recently, many have returned to the topic, including Aghion *et al.* (2011).
20 Think only of the importance held by start-ups in the high-tech sectors, especially those that come out of academic settings. And there's no need to mention the importance of the SMEs, the backbone of all economies in the EU (see the overview at the end of Chapter 2: Boxes 2.1 and 2.2).
21 Then the Commission (2012) adds a footnote which deserves attention:

Industrial activities also have important spillover effects on production and employment in other sectors. For every 100 jobs created in industry, it is estimated that between 60 and 200 new jobs are created in the rest of the economy, depending on the industrial sector.

22 McKinsey (2012), like the European Commission, points out the changing boundaries between the different sectors (manufacturing vs services):

> Service inputs (everything from logistics to advertising) make up an increasing amount of manufacturing activity. In the United States, every dollar of manufacturing output requires 19 cents of services. And in some manufacturing industries, more than half of all employees work in service roles, such as R&D engineers and office-support staff.

23 By the end of 2014, only five Member States had done so. The 'Unitary Patent package' has been approved with the 'enhanced cooperation': Italy and Spain refused to participate because they disagreed on the decision to use only three official languages for the Unitary Patent (English, German and French). Despite this, Italy signed – but has not yet ratified – the agreement on the Unified Patent Court.

24 It is worth mentioning, among the most innovative and forward-looking proposals, the one called 'EuroUnionBond' put forward by Alberto Quadrio Curzio and Romano Prodi (2011, 2012), to which we will come back in Chapter 5.

25 There would be much to be said about this, even just thinking about European antitrust events in recent years: on one hand the severe decisions taken by the Commission regarding the General Electric-Honeywell merger (not approved) and the Microsoft case (convicted of abusing a dominant position); on the other hand, three Commission decisions against three concentration operations (Airtours/First Choice, Schneider/Legrand, Tetra Laval/Sidel), then overturned by the Court of First Instance. The stated aims of competition policy retain their complete validity, fully investigated by juridical doctrine and economic theory: the spreading of private economic power and protection of individual freedom and rights; protection of economic freedom of market competitors; assurance of consumer wellbeing through efficient allocation and production. On 1 May 2004 two new reforms became applicable, giving form and substance to new competition policy: (1) 'Antitrust': new Council Regulation No. 1/2003 for application of Articles 81 and 82 of the Treaty prohibiting restrictive practices and abuse of dominant positions, replacing a regulation dated 1962; (2) 'Merger control': new Council Regulation No. 139/2004 controlling concentrations of businesses, reforming the first regulation dated 1989. At that time, alongside these major legislative instruments, there was a further decision that is worth mentioning here. In fact, it is quite significant that the Commission's third Communication on new industrial policy (European Commission 2004a), issued on 20 April 2004, was flanked with another, connected Communication, by the title: 'A proactive competition policy for a competitive Europe' (European Commission 2004b). It underlines how 'the existence of efficient competition in the EU's internal market contributes in a decisive manner to the competitiveness of European industry since it promotes improvement of productivity and innovation'.

26 When describing Europe as 'Fragmented Power', André Sapir mentioned 'external monetary affairs', like trade and competition policies, as 'an exclusive competence of the Union', even if with 'two important qualifications'. More in general, in its Report, Bruegel's research team dealt with 'the fragmented character of the governance of Europe's external economic policy', coming to this conclusion:

> A common *external energy policy* and a *common migratory policy* are 'sine qua non' conditions for the EU to develop solid and healthy relationships with neighbours who possess vast energy and/or human resources that are vital to its security and well-being.

(Sapir 2007, 18)

References

Amato G. (2005) 'Politica Industriale e Politica della Concorrenza nell'Europa Unita', in F. Mosconi (ed.), *Le nuove politiche industriali nell'Europa allargata*, 2nd edn, Parma, Monte Università Parma Editore (95–108).

Aghion P. (2006) 'A Primer on Innovation and Growth', Bruegel Policy Brief, October (www.bruegel.org).

Aghion P., Boulanger J., Cohen E. (2011) 'Rethinking Industrial Policy', Bruegel Policy Brief, 16 June.

Aiginger K. (2012) 'A Systemic Industrial Policy to Pave a New Growth Path for Europe', WIFO Working Papers, No. 421, February.

Aiginger K. (2013) 'The "Greening" of Industrial Policy, Headwinds and a Possible Symbiosis', WWWforEurope, Policy Paper No. 3, May.

Bacchiocchi E., Florio, M. Giunta, A. (2012) 'Internationalisation and the Agglomeration Effect in the Global Value Chain: The Case of Italian Automotive Suppliers', *International Journal of Technological Learning, Innovation and Development*, 5, 3, 267–290.

Baldwin R., Wyplosz C. (2004) *The Economics of European Integration*, Maidenhead, McGraw Hill.

Bianchi P., Labory S. (eds) (2006a) *International Handbook on Industrial Policy*, Cheltenham, Edward Elgar.

Bianchi P., Labory S. (2006b) 'Introduction', in P. Bianchi and S. Labory (eds), *International Handbook on Industrial Policy*, Cheltenham, Edward Elgar (xv–xxii).

Brusoni S., Malerba F. (2007) *Perspectives on Innovation*, Cambridge, Cambridge University Press.

Budzincki O., Schmidt C. (2006) 'European Industrial Policy: Economic Foundations, Concepts and Consequences', 24 July (www.ssrn.com).

Carlton D. W., Perloff J. M. (2005) *Modern Industrial Organization*, 4th edn, Maidenhead, McGraw-Hill.

Cassi L., Corrocher N., Malerba F., Vonortas N. (2008) 'The Impact of EU Funded Research Networks on Knowledge Diffusion at the Regional Level', *Research Evaluation*, 4, 17.

Chang H.-G., Andreoni A., Kuan M. L. (2013) 'International Industrial Policy Experiences and the Lessons for the UK', in *The Future of Manufacturing*, UK Government Office of Science, BIS, London.

Cipolla C.M. (1967) *Clocks and Culture, 1300–1700*, London, Collins.

Cohen E., Lorenzì J.-H. (eds) (2000) 'Politiques Industrielles pour l'Europe', Paris, Conseil d'analyse économique, Rapport 26, La Documentation Française.

Conconi P., Sapir, A., Zanardi M. (2013) 'The Internationalization Process of Firms: From Exports to FDI', www.cepr.org/pubs/new-dps/dplist.asp?dpno=9332.

Council of the EU (2005) 'Presidency Conclusions of the European Council', Brussels, 23 March.

CsC (Centro Studi Confindustria) (2013) 'L'alto prezzo della crisi per l'Italia: Crescono i Paesi che costruiscono le condizioni per lo sviluppo manifatturiero', Scenari industriali, 4, Rome, June (www.confindustria.it).

De Bandt J. (1999) 'Practical Issues of Networking and Co-operation', in K. Cowling (ed.), *Industrial Policy in Europe: Theoretical Perspectives and Practical Proposals*, Routledge, London (152–163).

Dosi G., Llerena P., Sylos Labini M. (2005) 'Science–Technology–Industry Links and the "European Paradox": Some Notes on the Dynamics of Scientific and Technological Research in Europe', Pisa, S. Anna School of Advanced Studies, May (www.lem.sssup.it).

Economist, The (2010) 'Industrial Policy: This House Believes that Industrial Policy Always Fails', Economist Debates, July.

Economist, The (2012) 'Manufacturing and Innovation: A Third Industrial Revolution', Special Report, 21 April (www.economist.com).

European Central Bank (2013) *Statistics Pocket Book*, Frankfurt, July.

European Central Bank (2014) *Statistics Pocket Book*, Frankfurt, October (www.ecb. europa.eu).

European Commission (1990) 'Industrial Policy in an Open and Competitive Environment: Guidelines for a Community Approach' (COM (1990)556), Brussels, November.

European Commission (1993) 'Growth, Competitiveness, Employment: The Challenges and Ways Forward into the 21st Century' (COM (1993)700), Brussels, 5 December.

European Commission (1994) 'An Industrial Competitiveness Policy for the European Union' (COM (1994)319), Brussels, 14 September.

European Commission (1998) 'The Competitiveness of European Enterprises in the Face of Globalisation: How It can be Encouraged?' (COM (1998)718), Brussels, January.

European Commission (2001) 'The Economic Impact of Enlargement', Enlargement Papers, No. 4, June.

European Commission (2002) 'Industrial Policy in an Enlarged Europe' (COM (2002)714), Brussels, December.

European Commission (2003) 'Some Key Issues of Europe's Competitiveness: Towards an Integrated Approach' (COM(2003)704), Brussels, November.

European Commission (2004a) 'Fostering Structural Change: An Industrial Policy for an Enlarged Europe' (COM (2004)274), Brussels, April.

European Commission (2004b) 'Facing the Challenge: The Lisbon Strategy for Growth and Enlargement', Report of the High Level Group chaired by Wim Kok, Brussels, November.

European Commission (2004c) 'A Proactive Competition Policy for a Competitive Europe' (COM (2004)293), Brussels, April.

European Commission (2005a) 'Working Together for Growth and Jobs: A New Start for the Lisbon Strategy' (COM (2005)24), Brussels, February.

European Commission (2005b) 'Implementing the Community Lisbon Programme: A Policy Framework to Strengthen EU Manufacturing: Towards a More Integrated Approach for Industrial Policy' (COM (2005)464), Brussels, October.

European Commission (2006) 'Creating an Innovative Europe', Report of the Independent Expert Group on R&D and Innovation appointed following the Hampton Court Summit and chaired by Mr Esko Aho, Brussels, January.

European Commission (2007) European Commission DG Research, Third Status Report on European Technology Platforms at the Launch of FP7, Brussels.

European Commission (2010) 'Europe 2020: A Strategy for Smart, Sustainable and Inclusive Growth' (COM(2010)2020), Brussels, 3 March.

European Commission (2011) 'EU Industrial Structure Report: Trends and Performance', Directorate-General for Enterprise and Industry, Luxembourg, Publications Office of the European Union.

European Commission (2012) 'A Stronger European Industry for Growth and Economic Recovery: Industrial Policy Communication Update' (COM (2012)582), Brussels, 10 October.

European Commission (2014) 'For a European Industrial Renaissance' (COM (2014)14), Brussels, 22 January.

Federal Ministry of Economics and Technology (2010) 'In Focus: Germany as a Competitive Industrial Nation: Building on Strengths: Overcoming Weaknesses: Securing the Future', Berlin, General Economic Policy-Industrial Policy, October (www.bmwi.de).

Federal Ministry of Education and Research (2010) 'Ideas, Innovation, Prosperity. High-tech Strategy 2020 for Germany', Bonn, Innovation Policy Framework Division (www.bmbf.de).

Goldman Sachs (2003) 'Dreaming with BRICS: The Path to 2050', Global Economic Paper, No. 99, October (https://portal.gs.com).

Jacquemin A. (1987) *The New Industrial Organization: Market Forces and Strategic Behavior*, Cambridge, MA, MIT Press, 167–212.

Lin J., Chang H.-J. (2009) 'Should Industrial Policy in Developing Countries Conform to Comparative Advantage or Defy it? A Debate Between Justin Lin and Ha-Joon Chang', *Development Policy Review*, 27, 5, September, 483–502.

McKinsey (2012) *Manufacturing the Future: The Next Era of Global Growth and Innovation*, Seoul, San Francisco, London, McKinsey Global Institute and McKinsey Operations Practice, November.

Maicent E., Navarro L. (2006) 'A Policy for Industrial Champions: From Picking Winners to Fostering Excellence and the Growth of Firms', Industrial Policy and Economic Reforms Papers No. 2, Enterprise and Industry Directorate-General, European Commission, Brussels, April.

Marzinotto B. (2012) 'Industrial Policy: The Missing Link in the New EU Cohesion Package', Brussels, 26 April (www.bruegel.org).

Mazzucato M. (2014) *The Entrepreneurial State: Debunking Public vs. Private Sector Myths*, revd edn, London, Anthem Press.

Monti M. (2010) 'A New Strategy for the Single Market: At the Service of Europe's Economy and Society', Report to the President of the European Commission – J. M. Barroso, Brussels, 9 May (http://ec.europa.eu/bepa/pdf/monti_report_final_10_05_2010_en.pdf).

Mosconi F. (2005) (ed.), *Le nuove politiche industriali nell'Europa allargata*, 2nd edn, Parma, Monte Università Parma Editore.

Mosconi F. (2009) 'The Rise of "European Champions" in the Single Market: A First Assessment', in J. Kundera (ed.), *Economic Integration in the EU Enlarged: From Free Trade Towards Monetary Union*, University of Wroclaw, Cyfrowa Biblioteka Prawnicza, pp. 81–118.

Navarro L. (2003) 'Industrial Policy in the Economic Literature: Recent Theoretical Developments and Implications for EU Policy', Enterprise Papers No. 12, European Commission, Enterprise Directorate-General, Brussels.

OECD (2003) *The Source of Economic Growth in the OECD Countries*, Paris, OECD Publications.

OECD (2013) *Perspectives on Global Development 2013: Industrial Policies in a Changing World*, Paris, OECD Publications.

O'Mahony M., van Ark B. (eds) (2003) *EU Productivity and Competitiveness: An Industry Perspective: Can Europe Resume the Catching-up Process?* Luxembourg, Office for Official Publications of European Communities.

O'Sullivan E., Andreoni A., Lopez-Gomez G., Gregory M. (2013) 'What is New in the New Industrial Policy? A Manufacturing System Perspective', *Oxford Review of Economic Policy*, Special Issue on Industrial Policy.

Owen G. (2012) 'Industrial Policy in Europe since the Second World War: What has Been Learnt?' London, LSE, February (http://eprints.lse.ac.uk).

Padoa-Schioppa T., Emerson M., King M., Milleron J.-C., Paelinck J. Papademos L., Pastor A., Scharpf F. (1987) *Efficiency, Stability and Equity: A Strategy for the Evolution of the Economic System of the European Community*, Oxford, Oxford University Press.

Pelkmans J. (2006) 'European Industrial Policy', in P. Bianchi and S. Labory (eds), *International Handbook on Industrial Policy*, Cheltenham, Edward Elgar (45–78).

Pisani-Ferry J. (2005) 'Speeding up European Reform: A Master Plan for Lisbon Process', Munich Economic Summit, June, CESIFO Forum, What's Wrong With Lisbon? (www.cesifo-group.de).

Pisani-Ferry J., Sapir A. (2006) 'Last Exit to Lisbon', Bruegel Policy Brief, March.

Pisano G. (2011) 'Why Manufacturing Matters', *Harvard Business School Weekly Newsletter*, 28 March (http://hbswk.hbs.edu/item/6664.html).

Pisano G., Shih W. (2012) *Producing Prosperity: Why America Needs a Manufacturing Renaissance*, Cambridge, MA, Harvard Business Review Press.

Prodi R. (2003) 'Industrial Policy in an Enlarged Europe', Speech delivered at the Conference 'Industrial Policy in an Enlarged Europe' by the President of the European Commission, Brussels, 21 January, Speech/03/18.

Quadrio Curzio A., Prodi R. (2011) 'EuroUnionBond, Here is What Must be Done', 'Il Sole-24 Ore', 23 August (www.ilsole24ore.com).

Quadrio Curzio A., Prodi R. (2012) 'EuroUnionBond, Why are we Proposing Them Again?' 'Il Sole-24 Ore', 23 August (www.ilsole24ore.com).

Rodrik D. (2004) 'Industrial Policy for the Twenty-First Century', Harvard University, John F. Kennedy School of Government, Cambridge, MA, September (www.sss.ias.edu).

Rodrik D. (2008) 'Normalizing Industrial Policy', Commission on Growth and Development (International Bank for Reconstruction and Development/ World Bank), Working Paper No. 3 (www.sss.ias.edu).

Rodrik D. (2013) 'Green Industrial Policy', School of Social Science, Institute for Advanced Study, Princeton, NJ, September (www.sss.ias.edu).

Sapir A. (2003) 'The Economic Impact of Eastern Enlargement', Paper presented at the XXVII 'Convegno Nazionale di Economia e Politica Industriale', University of Parma, September, mimeo.

Sapir A. (2005) 'Globalization and the Reform of the European Social Model', Background document for the presentation in ECOFIN Informal Meeting, Manchester, 9 September.

Sapir A. (2007) (ed.) *Fragmented Power: Europe and the Global Economy*, Brussels, BruegelBooks, 31 August.

Sapir A., Aghion P., Bertola G., Hellwig M., Pisani-Ferry J., Rosati D., Viñals J., Wallace H. (eds) (2003) 'An Agenda for a Growing Europe: Making the EU Economic System Deliver', Report of an Independent High-Level Study Group established on the initiative of the President of the European Commission, Brussels, July 2003 (then published by Oxford University Press, 2004).

Schumpeter A. O. (1911/2008) *The Theory of Economic Development: An Inquiry into Profits, Capital, Credit, Interest and the Business Cycle*, trans. from German by Redvers Opie, New Brunswick, NJ, London, Transaction Publishers.

Siebert H. (2005) *The German Economy: Beyond the Social Market*, Princeton, NJ, Princeton University Press.

Sirkin H.L., Rose J., Zinser M. (2012) 'The US Manufacturing Renaissance: How Shifting Global Economics are Creating an American Come Back', University of Pennsylvania, Knowledge@Warton.

Stiglitz J. E., Yifu Lin L. (eds) (2013) *The Industrial Policy Revolution I: The Role of Government Beyond Ideology*, International Economic Association-IEA Conference Volume No. 151-I, New York, Palgrave Macmillan.

Stiglitz J. E., Yifu Lin L., Monga, C. (2013) 'Introduction: The Rejuvenation of Industrial Policy', in J. E. Stiglitz and L. Yifu Lin (eds), *The Industrial Policy Revolution I: The Role of Government Beyond Ideology*, International Economic Association-IEA Conference Volume No. 151-I, New York, Palgrave Macmillan (1–15).

Török A., Csuka G., Kovács B., Veres A. (2013) 'The "Resurrection" of Industrial Policy in the European Union and its Impact on Industrial Policy in the New Members Countries', WWWforEurope, Working Paper No. 26, July.

Veugelers R. (2103) 'The World Innovation Landscape: Asia Rising?' *Bruegel Policy Contribution*, Issue 2013/02, February.

Visco I. (2004) 'La crescita economica in Europa: ritardi e opportunità', *L'Industria*, XXXV, 2, 289–315.

White House, The (2001) *Economic Report of the President*, 'The Annual Report of the Council of Economic Advisers', Washington, DC, U.S. Government Printing Office.

White House, The (2011) 'Remarks by the President at Carnegie Mellon University's National Robotics Engineering Center', Pittsburgh, PA, 24 June (www.whitehouse.gov).

Yülek M. (ed.) (2015a) *Economic Planning and Industrial Policy in the Globalizing Economy: Concepts, Experience and Prospects*, Berlin, London, New York, Springer.

Yülek M. (2015b) 'Revisiting National Economic Planning and Industrial Policy: Concepts, Experiences and the Ecosystem', in M. Yülek (ed.) *Economic Planning and Industrial Policy in the Globalizing Economy: Concepts, Experience and Prospects*, Berlin, London, New York, Springer (3–27).

2   The new European oligopoly

The role of the 'European Champions'

Central to the Bain approach was the notion of barriers to entry as an explanation for the joint observation of high concentration and high profitability. As long as such barriers can be taken as exogenously given features of the underlying pattern of technology and tastes, then they can indeed serve as a candidate explanation for market structure. But once we pass beyond scale economies (to which Bain devoted much of his argument) to factors such as advertising intensity or R&D intensity, than we are dealing with entities that are themselves endogenously determined as part of an equilibrium system.

(Sutton 1998)

Introduction

Since its beginnings during the 1940s and 1950s at Harvard University, market structures and economic behaviour have been at the centre of all studies of Industrial Organization (IO). The process of European integration, which was going on concomitantly, offers an excellent case study for understanding growth strategies of enterprises in a market that is growing ever larger and more competitive. The following two sections are dedicated, first, to these two 'plots' and, second, to their interrelationship.

Out of this analysis of the Single Market, the crucial role of large enterprises will emerge, given their significant importance in a contemporary world of new economic powers in international markets and incessantly advancing technological innovation. The fourth section will thus offer a review of some of the most original studies that have been carried out on the Big European Players over the past few years.

In the same vein, the fifth section is devoted to our analysis of 'European Champions'. It starts by briefly describing the fundamental transformation of the economic landscape, and explains how this has changed – and will continue to change – the 'playing field' for European companies. It then provides a basic taxonomy of 'European Champions': first of all, we have the 'Champions' that we call 'Type I' and which have come about – at least at the initial stages – as a result of supranational cooperation and concerted public policy support for the development of technology in 'strategic sectors' involving firms from more than one EU country. In so doing, it looks at the undisputable success story of Airbus and asks whether there are other sectors where this approach could be replicated and how this could be reasonably done. We then note the emergence of another type of large European company: the 'Type II Champions'. These are companies that have taken form under the pressures of the Single Market and as a result of consecutive merger and acquisition (M&A) waves.

The final section concludes the chapter and gives a brief overview on the other side of the European industrial structure: small- and medium-sized enterprises (SMEs).

Two 'plots' from the 1950s...

Theory and practice have always shaped studies on Industrial Organization (IO); what has changed over the years within the discipline is the relative weight given to one or the other element. The proverbial 'swing of the pendulum' may be useful to illustrate the situation, albeit in summary form. Let's begin at the start of the 1950s at the fundamental moment when Joe Bain (1951, 1959) – building on the seminal papers of Edward Mason (1939, 1949) – published his pioneering work in which the celebrated Structure–Conduct–Performance (S–C–P) paradigm tied to the 'Harvard School' was formulated within the field of IO.[1]

This would be followed at the end of the 1960s by an initial, partial oscillation of the pendulum upon the success of the 'Chicago School', linked primarily to the name of George J. Stigler.[2] Nevertheless, cross-section analyses at the industry level were still at the centre of research agendas. Along the way, though, the traditional empirical structure became less and less satisfying as a method for explaining causal relationships, and the solution to these unsatisfying results lay in a new generation of theoretical clarification (1970s and first half of the 1980s). This is the era during which the pendulum swung as far as possible away from the position of S–C–P with the introduction of 'Game Theory': a fundamental theory, yes, for deepening our understanding of rational behaviour in small-number situations, but not always armed with a sufficient predictive capability. And the story doesn't end here, as the new dominant approach was about to be subjected to another oscillation.

The June 1987 volume of the *Journal of Industrial Economics* was published as a monograph with the following significant title: 'The Empirical Renaissance in Industrial Economics'. Towards the end of the 1980s, after two decades during which most studies focused on theoretical issues, there is thus a return of interest in empirical studies. As often happens when traditional practices return to favour, its new variation has somehow evolved in order to overcome the previous limitations recognized to be inherent in the original form.[3] In general, we can claim that a central role in the new IO was now played by the (different) interpretation of the evolution of market structures, no longer simply accepted as exogenous. The first two volumes of the *Handbook of Industrial Organization* (Schmalensee and Willig 1989), published precisely at this time, reflect this new form and learn from the theoretical and empirical advances made in the discipline. In the same vein – one that leads to a continually improved understanding of the analysis of the endogenous nature of market structures – we should mention the essays by Alexis Jacquemin (1987)[4] and John Sutton (1991).[5] Both manage to bridge the gap between the new generation of models linked to game theory and the more traditional empirical spirit; both are able to shed light on the strategic behaviours of economic agents. As a consequence, the pendulum, which had gone through wild and often unpredictable swings during the previous decades, has come to rest in a more centralized, more balanced position.

Rather than prolong (or go into greater depth about) this story, it would be better to now start out on a parallel journey. Let us thus return to the very beginning of the 1950s – the publication date of Bain's work – because it is exactly in this year, as a fortuitous coincidence, that the process of European integration had its formal beginnings. In fact, 1951 saw the introduction of the European Coal and Steel Community (ECSC): 'the first big federalist step', according to Baldwin and Wyplosz (2004, 10). Shortly thereafter, in 1957, the Treaty of Rome set the foundations for the creation of the European Economic Community (EEC):[6] this Treaty 'committed the Six to extraordinary deep economic integration' (Baldwin and Wyplosz 2004, 11). This commitment, in turn, has been brought to a more complete fruition between the second half of the 1980s and the first years of the 1990s – during the Jacques Delors presidency of the European Commission – thanks to the 'Single Market Programme' (SMP): it 'was set out in the celebrated Commission White Paper of June 1985 (*Cockfield Report*) and incorporated into the EU legal system by the 1986 Single European Act' (Baldwin and Wyplosz 2004, 20). These are also the years during which a second fundamental and brilliant goal of European integration – the first being the Single Market – began to take shape: the formation of a Monetary Union, which was brought into being by the Maastricht Treaty in 1992 ('Treaty on European Union').

There's more: the early 1990s, after the fall of the Berlin Wall, were without doubt the fundamental years for the launching of Eastern enlargement. This is the third successful goal we encounter on our brief excursus into European integration. Like the previous enlargements,[7] this one towards the Central and Eastern European Countries (CEECs)[8] should be primarily seen from an *economic perspective*, without neglecting its political and cultural significance. From this perspective, it means a further expansion of the Single Market: an expansion – as the SMP stated – of 'an area without internal frontiers in which the free movement of goods, persons, services and capital is ensured' – i.e. the size of the market has become bigger.[9] A Single Market in which 18 out of 28 Member States have, up to now, adopted a single currency, the euro.

The grave economic and financial crisis that has buffeted the EU with all its strength for six years now has naturally led to an underestimation of this potential. It behoves us then to focus our attention, for illustrative purposes, on the situation during the years immediately preceding September 2008.

Alberto Quadrio Curzio (2007), working with data related to Gross National Product (aggregate GNP, GNP per capita, its growth rate), exports and trade balance, foreign direct investment (FDI), trans-national corporations (TNCs) and even the Human Development Index (HDI), reaches some relevant conclusions about 'Europe and the United States under the test of globalization'. We cite two of these: the EU, in terms of GNP, 'is the greatest global economic power today'; and the EU 'in terms of trade is a more important and competitive power on the international scale than the United States'.

André Sapir (2007), in his introduction to *Fragmented Power*, draws a map of Europe and of the world, splitting apart the latter so as to reflect the traditional protagonists (USA, Japan, G7) and the newcomers (geographically close countries like Russia, emerging economies like China, India and Brazil, other developing nations). The image that develops around the mid-2000s – see Table 2.1 – shows how with just 7.6 per cent of global population, the EU-27 accounts for 20.4 per cent of global GNP. The corresponding figures for the United States are 4.6 and 20.1 per cent, while the BRICs have values of 43.2 and 26.6 per cent.

From these data, the first question that the united Europe must address, and which remains pressing today, is the perpetual gulf that separates the EU, in terms of per capita GNP, from the United States: if the EU-27 is given a value of 100, the USA has a value of 162.8. Consequently, this gap lifts the veil on the different dynamics of productivity growth, which since the middle of the 1990s has divided in stark fashion the two great economies that face each other from different sides of the Atlantic. But Sapir's data raise another relevant question, this time in relation to the emerging economies: during the period of 1998–2007, these enjoyed a growth rate in GNP that doubled or tripled (and in some cases, even more) the performance of the EU-27, which had a rate of 2.4 per cent (2.1 per cent in the euro area). Taken together, as we might have expected, we can say that there were both bright and dark spots in the process of European integration in the years just before the bankruptcy of Lehman Brothers.

We will return in the next chapter of this book to the events of the last five or six years, events which for many reasons have further debilitated some of the weaknesses of the European Union. At the same time, a long-term retrospective look of the period from the ECSC and the EEC (1950s) to the three success stories of the 1980s and 1990s (the Single Market, the euro and Eastern enlargement) offers confirmation of the value of the process of European integration.

...and two 'plots' that intertwine

Now, can we try to reasonably establish an early and partial connection between the two levels of analysis discussed above? We have summarized the two 50-year-old 'plots' (for a 'Focus on Italy', see Box 2.1 at the end of this chapter).

These are levels of analysis that are intrinsically different, but we believe that a connection can be made. At the very least, the historical moment seems auspicious. On one side, theory and practice seem to have found the right balance within studies of IO, in particular in the study of two rather important questions: (i) the determinants of market structures and the difference in the degree of

Table 2.1 Europe and the world

	Population (2005) (% of world)	GDP at PPP (2005) (% of world)	GDP per capita (2005) (EU-27 = 100)	GDP growth (1998–2007) (% per annum)
EU-27	**7.6**	**20.4**	**100.0**	**2.4**
(euro area)	(4.9)	(14.8)	(112.5)	(2.1)
Neighbours[1]	**10.9**	**8.5**	**29.1**	**4.2**
(Russia)	(2.3)	(2.6)	(42.1)	(5.4)
United States	**4.6**	**20.1**	**162.8**	**3.1**
Other advanced	**4.5**	**13.9**	**115.1**	**1.8**
(Japan)	(2.0)	(6.4)	(119.2)	(1.3)
Emerging economies[2]	**60.8**	**34.5**	**21.1**	**6.1**
(China)	(20.7)	(15.4)	(27.7)	(9.1)
(India)	(17.3)	(6.0)	(12.9)	(6.6)
(Brazil)	(2.9)	(2.6)	(33.4)	(2.4)
Other developing[3]	**11.6**	**2.6**	**8.3**	**4.3**
World	100.0	100.0	37.2	4.1
G7[4]	11.4	41.2	134.6	2.4
BRICs[5]	43.2	26.6	23.0	7.8

Source: Sapir (2007, 4).

Notes
1 Rest of Europe (including Russia and other CIS countries), Middle East and North Africa.
2 Developing Asia and Latin America.
3 Sub-Saharan Africa.
4 Canada, France, Germany, Italy, Japan, United Kingdom and United States.
5 Brazil, Russia, India and China.

concentration across different industries; (ii) the motivations and the effects of horizontal integration – through M&As, joint ventures, etc. – and the consequent trade-offs between market power and efficiency.[10]

On the other side, the process of European integration needs to rediscover the *élan* of past decades both as a means for overcoming the crisis and for completing its model of economic governance, first of all among the nations in the euro area, but without forgetting the more general outline for structural economic and social reforms for the entire EU (previously the 'Lisbon Strategy', then 'Europe 2020' as we will see in Chapter 4). Nevertheless, the principle of 'One Market, One Currency' contributed to the construction of a level playing field, within which enterprises could formulate their growth strategies on a genuinely continental, or pan-European, basis: it is from this perspective that we will devote our attention, in the next two sections, to the big European players, speaking in particular of 'European Champions'.

This new playing field obviously does not mean that differences have disappeared. Again, it does not make all countries and companies the same, especially in terms of growth opportunities. On the contrary, when the Monetary Union celebrated its (first) ten-year anniversary in May 2008, the differences within the euro area were significant. Jean Pisani-Ferry *et al.* (2008), in their report on this first decade, analysed – among other things – the divergence in the relationship between 'real exchange rates and export performance in the euro area'.[11] Germany's performance has been literally astonishing, and notable have been the differences between the North and the South of Europe (which have been intensifying, as is sadly known, in the years since the big crash of 2008).

Summing up, the EU (euro area) Member States are not all equal. A relevant part of the explanation of this diversity can be found in *macroeconomic* management (a topic which falls outside the scope of this work). But a not-insignificant part of this same explanation – as we will shortly see – is found in *microeconomic* features; i.e. the countries' industrial structure and the firms' behaviour: 'S–C–P' still matters, even if redefined from Harvard's first paradigm of the 1940s and 1950s. Returning to the question raised above, the purpose is to offer empirical evidence to our positive response about the intertwining of the two 'plots', which we can reduce to a single storyline: the new European oligopoly.

Our emphasis will fall on large enterprises, often on multinationals, as will become clear in the pages that follow. No one wishes to undervalue or deny the role played by SMEs in the economies of almost all the EU Member States, be they old (Western countries) or new (Eastern countries).[12]

Nevertheless, we believe that our emphasis on large enterprises is justified on two accounts – in this context – from a methodological point of view.

The first has to do with the 'pro-competitive effect' à la Baldwin–Wyplosz, mentioned above and in Chapter 1. This effect, they argue

> put pressure on profits, and the market's response is 'merger mania'. That is, the pro-competitive effect squeezes the least efficient firms, prompting an industrial restructuring where Europe's weaker firms merge or get

bought up. In the end, Europe is left with a more efficient industrial structure, with fewer, bigger, more efficient firms competing more effectively
with each other.

The history of European integration teaches that an important wave of M&A in
the manufacturing sector was felt, not accidentally, during the years of the Single
Market Programme (1985–1992). And even though there would still be a fairly
high level of M&A activity in the years immediately following, another peak
would be achieved towards the end of the 1990s: the years of the euro and the
New Economy. In 2001, the collapse of stock market values worldwide in the
wake of the failure of many of the new dot.com companies inevitably slowed
M&As. But once the initial panic had passed and normal rhythms were re-
established, a 'new frontier' began to open up in the EU via Eastern enlargement
(2004). At the same time, the Monetary Union was paying off one dividend after
another. As we will show in the section on 'European Champions', it is in these
years that M&A activity picks up speed again in the EU, led both by large manufacturing enterprises and by services (banks, insurers and public utilities). We
will also see how the crash of 2008 has slowed but not nullified this activity,
which has even returned to the fore over the last two years (2012–2013).

But there is, as we stated before, a second methodological justification, one
that is related to what the European Commission has called the 'Top R&D
investing companies' (Joint Research Centre and European Commission 2013).
In fact, *The 2012 EU Industrial R&D Investment Scoreboard* (*The Scoreboard*)
'includes the 1500 companies investing the largest sums in R&D in the world
while maintaining an EU focus by complementing this coverage including the
top 1000 R&D investing companies based in the EU'.[13] *The Scoreboard*'s key
messages tell us that 'performance of the world's top R&D investors regained
pre-crisis level in 2011', and the 'EU based companies increased R&D investments by 8.9%, above world average'. As far as companies and industries are
concerned, the report points out that

> Toyota Motor leads the R&D ranking in 2011, with Volkswagen climbing
> to third place from sixth last year. Companies in the ICT sector continue to
> show the largest R&D increases in the top ranks. As in 2010, R&D growth
> figures of the EU Scoreboard sample are to a large extent driven by the auto-
> mobiles sector, with BMW (21.6%) and Renault (19.4%) leading the
> increases.

And finally:

> Companies showing high performance over the last decade (at least doub-
> ling sales) operate in the ICT and health related sectors,[14] all of high R&D
> intensity. The US is strengthening its relative specialisation in these high
> R&D intensive sectors that account for the largest amount of R&D and the
> largest numbers of high performers. No significant shift of structure towards

these high R&D intensive sectors is observed in the EU-based *Scoreboard* companies over the last decade.

(pp. 5–12)

A new industrial policy, one with the goal of strengthening the third side (technology policy), is exactly what we advocated in Chapter 1. The role of enterprises that are capable of growing within the Single Market and of increasing their investments in R&D, technology and highly skilled human capital is of vital importance.

It follows that now more than ever something profoundly important is taking place in the (enlarged) European Single Market, especially in manufacturing given its role for economic growth. This affirmation begs the question: *what* is changing within European industry? Reformulated into the terms of our present topic: which Europe will we discover from the perspective of big industrial players? This is the issue to which we will now turn.

The big players in Europe: a summary

Introduction

Many studies in recent years have focused on the large European enterprises that have successfully exploited the potential of the Single Market, and that in many cases have then been able to move out from this European base on to the global stage, where they match their strengths with American and Asian competitors (and more generally, with emerging nations). In this section we will review some of the most authoritative and original works on the subject, while in the next section we will present our own investigation into the 'European Champions', and propose a possible taxonomy of them ('Type I' and 'Type II').

'Farewell National Champions': the 'trend towards Europeanisation of Europe's largest companies'

The first study in our series, *Farewell National Champions*, is the one published seven years ago by Bruegel (Véron 2006), the Brussels-based think-tank. The author investigated Europe's 100 largest listed companies vis-à-vis the American counterparts, asking himself: where exactly is 'home' for a modern corporation? His survey showed that

> the share of European sales in their total revenue is almost identical, on average, to the share of US revenue for the US Top 100, at 65%. The share of their national (or, for smaller countries, regional) base is on a rapidly declining trend and stands at 36.9% of global revenue in 2005 against 50.2% in 1997.

It follows that for Europe's 100 largest firms 'their home market is increasingly Europe as a whole rather than any particular country within it'.

Véron (2006) called all of this 'the trend towards Europeanisation' of Europe's largest companies, stressing the 'policy challenge'. In fact, this trend, he argued,

> undermines the effectiveness of policies aimed at national economic performance through the support of 'national champions' – when this support takes place at group rather than plant level. Moreover, it lowers the obstacles to the mobility of corporate headquarters within European borders. This could set the stage for more regulatory competition in the future in areas which include securities law, taxation and corporate governance. European policymakers need to adapt this new landscape.

It is not irrelevant to note that during the same years of the publication of Véron's data which demonstrated the 'Europeanisation' of large European enterprises, more than one government intervened to block cross-border mergers, giving birth to a phenomenon called 'economic patriotism'. France assumed the position of the leading protectionist Member State, but it was not alone in Europe in pursuing the double standard of a closed-door policy towards inward investments and a simultaneous enthusiasm and support for outward-bound investments;[15] nor did the US remain untouched by this phenomenon.[16] With hindsight, we can state that this 'phenomenon' was no more than just a collection of individual cases at one moment in time (the mid 2000s), and that these did not interrupt in any significant way the basic tendencies behind enterprise growth in the European Single Market.

We see evidence of this both in the summary of this section and in the following analysis of 'European Champions'. As *The Economist* rightly noticed at the time: 'Europe's nationalisms cannot reverse or perhaps even much affect the market-opening action of their companies. But they may increase its costs' (2 March 2006).

The Bruegel reports on the 'internationalisation of European firms'

There are three Bruegel reports published on the 'internationalization of European firms'. The first one – 'The Happy Few' (Ottaviano and Mayer 2007) – focused on 'the characteristics of European firms involved in international activities through exports or foreign direct investment ("internationalised firms", IFs)'. This first analysis of firm-level evidence revealed that: (i) 'IFs are superstars'; (ii) 'IFs belong to an exclusive club'; (iii) 'The pattern of aggregate exports, imports and foreign direct investment (FDI) is driven by the changes in two "margins". The "intensive margin" refers to average exports, imports, FDI per firm. The "extensive margin" refers to the number of firms actually involved in those international activities'; (iv) 'The "extensive margin" is much more important'. In short, Ottaviano and Mayer pointed out

> the international performance of European countries is essentially driven by a handful of high-performance firms. Moreover, the opening up of trade and

FDI triggers a selection process whereby the most productive firms substitute the least productive ones within sectors. This is good for productivity, GDP and wages.

The second Bruegel report – *Of Markets, Products and Prices: The Effect of the Euro on European Firms* (Fontagné *et al.* 2009) – was published two years later and, first, confirmed 'the consensus that emerges from a growing body of literature: contrary to expectations trade flows have not increased meaningfully since the introduction of the euro'.[17] However, as Bruegel's Director argued in his Foreword (Pisani-Ferry 2009), 'trade effect cannot be measured by trade volumes alone ... As important, if not more so, is *who* is trading and at *what prices*'. The authors answered both issues: (i) on the 'who issue', they find that 'the increase in the number of exporting firms has remained small. For the typical euro-area SME, life has not changed with the single currency and the market remains primarily national'; (ii) 'Fortunately there is better news about the *what price issue*. Here the euro has resulted in less volatile and lower prices, especially within the euro area, and this is a clear plus for consumers.'

It was just in 2009 that Bruegel, together with its partners,[18] launched the EFIGE (European Firms in a Global Economy) project, in order to conduct a multi-country company survey on firm internationalization and performance relying on new and internationally consistent data.[19] In so doing, a report with the title *The Global Operations of European Firms* (Barba Navaretti *et al.* 2011) was then published: the third report of our series.

Among the main messages of this report – a six-point list of 'Facts' – we should draw our attention on the following: (i) 'In all countries, firms involved in international markets are, in general, *larger, more productive, more skill intensive and more innovative*'; (ii) 'The international performance of European firms is primarily explained by firm-specific characteristics' – i.e. '*it is firms that are at the heart of competitiveness*'; (iii) '*Companies that internationalise successfully their sales or their production have similar features in all European countries*. Size, productivity, the skill intensity of the workforce and the ability to innovate are positively related to firms' export performance in all countries'; (iv) '*Internationalisation patterns of countries differ mainly because nations differ in their internal industrial structures* – i.e. in the distribution of their firms' characteristics, such as *size and sectoral distribution*, and *innovative capacity and productivity*'; (v) 'The fact that firm characteristics are of central importance raises new challenges for policy. Should policy making aim to foster those firm-specific drivers of internationalisation? ... The importance of firms' characteristics [Bruegel's answer goes] *supports the view that policies focused on improving the general business environment, on reforming institutional, regulatory, infrastructural or other factors that hinder long term investments, innovation capabilities and firms' growth, are likely to be more effective in strengthening international competitiveness than targeted intervention, such as measures for export promotion.*'

'Who are the Champions?'

In its survey of 'European Business' (10 February 2007), *The Economist*, quoting an analysis by McKinsey, argued that 'Europe has 29% of the world's leading 2,000 or so companies, broadly in line with its 30% share of world GDP. It punches its weight in most global industries except IT, where America is leagues ahead' (see Figure 2.1).

In the same survey, referring to *Fortune*'s rankings of world companies, the British weekly wrote again:

> Europe has for many years played a large part in global business. A table compiled by *Fortune* (2006) magazine shows that half the world's 30 leading companies by revenue are European. But in two key sectors Europe trails badly: high-tech (which mostly means IT) and life sciences.

Mediobanca's 'multinationals'

The last study here summarized is *Multinationals: Financial Aggregates (387 companies)*, annually undertaken by R&S–Mediobanca (2013);[20] in Table 2.2, we present the essential data for the 2013 edition, the latest available (the eighteenth edition).

'Our survey [R&S points out] covers the leading industrial, telecommunications companies and utilities in the world, all considered at group level. The survey covers a total of almost 64,000 companies including consolidated subsidiaries' (R&S 2013, xvii).

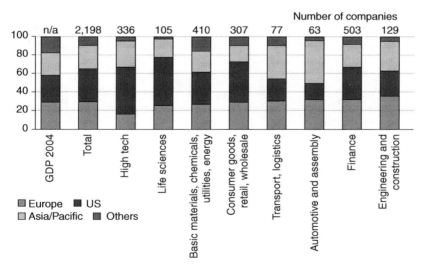

Figure 2.1 'Punching its weight. Number of companies in Global 2000 by region and sector, %' (source: McKinsey (quoted in The Economist, 10 February 2007)).

Table 2.2 Big players: 'multinationals in 2011'

	No. of companies	Net sales in € billion	Total assets[1] in € billion	No. of employees in '000
Europe	156	3,915	3,921	9,912
North America	68	2,875	2,403	6,466
Japan	38	1,482	1,646	3,923
Total, triad regions	*262*	*8,272*	*7,970*	*20,301*
Asia-Russia	50	1,801	1,911	5,788
Rest of the world	23	485	760	1,325
Total, industrials	*335*	*10,558*	*10,641*	*27,414*
Telecoms	29	973	1,317	3,013
Utilities	23	675	1,327	1,201
Total	*387*	*12,206*	*13,285*	*31,628*

Source: Mediobanca (2013).

Note
1 Excluding intangibles.

In Appendix II.1, starting from the results of this 2013 survey focusing on the ten-year period 2002–2011, we will publish an ad hoc elaboration made by R&S–Mediobanca, which focuses on the manufacturing of the Triad, for an overall number of 233 enterprises (in fact, the 'total industrials' includes also the energy enterprises).

On the whole, by taking a look at the highlights published in Table 2.2, the status of Europe is already confirmed when we analyse the world's big players in the manufacturing industry. Quoting Mediobanca researchers: 'Globally, the majority of industrial activities as measured by total net sales are located in Europe (37.1%), followed by North America (27.2%).'

Obviously – as we learned from the previous surveys summarized in this paragraph – the overall data conceal both geographical (among the EU countries) and sectoral differences. With regard to the first aspect, the survey states

> the companies analysed here do not all show the same degree of domestic presence. Measured by total net sales as a percentage of GDP in their respective home countries, the U.K. has the highest concentration of multinationals in Europe, followed by Switzerland-Liechtenstein; Italy and Spain have the lowest, the latter two featuring prevalently small and medium-sized enterprises.

As for the second aspect, the R&S survey continues,

> it is worth noting the low presence of electronics in Europe, where this sector accounts for only 10.4% of aggregate net sales, the lowest percentage in the world; at the opposite end of the spectrum there is North America (33.8%) followed by the Asian–Russian area (29.2%). Europe leads North

America and Japan especially in the chemical-pharmaceutical sector, with 48.2%, in the food and drinks industry, with 44%, and in mechanical engineering, with 40.2%. Japan leads North America in the automotive sector, with 31%, but is below the European share (37.5%).

Europe has an industrial specialization that we are getting familiar with and that we will investigate further both in the next section, which focuses on the *Fortune* 'Global 500', and in the next chapter, which is dedicated to a reflection on 'capitalism models', among which the 'Rhine Model', which stands out for its strong industrial base.

Having completed this summary, it is time to deal with the issue at hand: the 'European Champions' in the making.

The age of the 'European Champions'

Introduction

'The European Union will be able to exploit the chances offered by the single market – and this is my firm conviction – only if we decide to create European Champions in areas … such as electrical energy, postal services, etc.' (Merkel 2006). These are the views expressed by the German Chancellor, Mrs Merkel, on 9 May 2006 during the 'European Forum' of the WDR, which could be backed up by other positions she took in that period. In fact, Mrs Merkel had already referred to 'European Champions' on at least two other formal occasions, such as at the press conference that concluded the European Council in Brussels (23–24 March 2006) and a speech she gave on 2 May, when the first stone was laid for the 'N3 – Arnstadt Engine Servicing Centre', in which she specifically mentioned the joint venture between Lufthansa and Rolls-Royce as an example of 'European Cooperation'.

These statements – the benefits that the Single Market and companies capable of growing on a continental basis can bring to our prosperity, and, in a more general sense, the need to develop a 'European way of thinking' about competitiveness – taken together have contributed to bringing to the forefront the issue that now goes by the name of 'European Champions'. Naturally, emphasis needs to be placed on the adjective, since the noun might bring to mind – as if by magic – the 'National Champions' of the past: and no one today can reasonably think that this instrument, typical of the industrial policies of European countries during post-Second World War years, is still apt for competing in the new international context. So it is not simply a question of vocabulary.

Now, the question that comes to mind is: in what do the two model-types of 'Champions' – the 'National' of the 1960s and 1970s (and beyond) and the 'European' of the 2000s – differ? Like all developing issues, this one is the subject of lively discussion and at the present time offers no unambiguous definitions that one can ascribe. By simply googling the expression 'European Industrial Champions' and patiently looking at the very first pages that come up on the search engine, one realizes that discussion is still wide open. On the other hand, it is true that with the passing of time important empirical evidence is being gathered (see the previous section) that could allow us to make a first attempt at understanding the defining characteristics of 'European Champions' or, at least, 'big European players'.

This section – as already mentioned – tries to provide an inaugural definition of 'European Champions', explaining how they differ from the former 'National Champions'. It starts by briefly describing the fundamental transformation of the economic landscape that has been underway for more than a decade now, and explains how this has changed the 'level playing field' for European companies. It focuses on the competition brought about by globalization and by the rise of the new industrialized countries, on the ICT revolution, and on the challenges and opportunities brought about by the Eastern enlargement of the EU.

The transformation of the world's economic landscape at a glance

The economic context facing European firms today is significantly different from that prevailing during much of the second half of the twentieth century. Three developments have brought about this remarkable change: globalization and the rise of the 'new' emerging economies; the ICT revolution; and, at home, the consolidation of the Single Market, the birth of the euro and the enlargement to the East.

Without going into a discussion on the many definitions of the term 'globalization', we shall employ it here to refer to two major trends that have had an enormous impact on the world economic system in the last two decades or so. On the one hand, there has been not only an increasing free flow of circulation of the factors of production (goods, services, labour and capital) but also an increasing speed and ease of relocation of technologies and production processes (think of the 'great unbundling' originally described by Richard Baldwin (2006)). On the other hand – and very much influenced by the above – there has been the rise of new world economic giants: China, first and foremost, but more in general all the well-known 'BRICs economies' (Goldman Sachs 2003), followed by the 'Next 11 (N-11)' (Goldman Sachs 2007a).[21] The whole group of emerging markets and developing economies[22] has been regarded by the Western industrialized countries – at the same time – as a source of cheap labour, a platform for their business operations (via FDI), an important market for their products and services (via exports) and a strong competitor in the technological race. Table 2.3 describes the competition between the two major groups of countries: something like the (old) West vs the (new) East.

A great facilitator of these globalizing trends has been another major development: the revolution in information and communication technologies (ICT). This is considered to have been one of the driving forces of America's 'New economy' during the second half of the 1990s (for an excellent review see Council of Economic Advisers (The White House 2001)), and a driving force behind the gap in productivity growth levels between Europe and the US.

Table 2.3 G7 vs BRICs in perspective (US$ billions)

| | 'BRIC' economies | | | | G6[1] | | | | | | BRIC[2] | G6[3] |
	Brazil	China	India	Russia	France	Germany	Italy	Japan	UK	USA		
2000	762	1,078	469	391	1,311	1,875	1,078	4,176	1,437	9,825	2,700	19,702
2050	6,074	44,453	27,083	5,870	3,148	3,603	2,061	6,673	3,782	35,165	84,201	54,433

Source: adapted from Goldman Sachs (2003), *Global Economic Paper No 99*, 1 October.

Notes
1 Goldman Sachs analysts removed Canada from the present G7 configuration due to its negligible weight in terms of total GDP.
2 It is the sum of Brazil, China, India and Russia as reported in the left hand column of the table.
3 It is the sum of G6 in its present configuration, as reported in the right hand column of the table (from France to USA); according to these projections of the GDP, only USA and Japan will continue to be part, from now until 2050, of this (hypothetical) club of the major industrialized countries in the world.

Furthermore it is felt that the use of ICT in other industrial or service sectors has been crucial in determining their respective productivity performances (European Commission 2001; O'Mahony and van Ark 2003).

Finally, developments in Europe during the last 20 years have also had a tremendous impact on the level playing field for European companies. The completion of the Single Market has progressively been consolidated through the gradual privatization of state-owned companies, on the one hand, and the increasing – even if patchy – liberalization of markets in various sectors, on the other. The impact on competition within the Single Market has been impressive, with the M&A waves in the energy, manufacturing and financial sectors being prominent examples (see next sub-section). In addition, the economic importance of 'Eastern enlargement' cannot be underestimated: it has offered Western European (i.e. EU-15) companies access to new markets and cheaper resources, while at the same time raising competitive pressures significantly, especially in the border regions; the Eastern countries have gained in both employment opportunities and technological know-how. In short, enlargement has brought about new opportunities for a pan-European reorganization of companies, on the condition that goods, services, capital and labour are allowed to freely circulate within the Single Market (European Commission 2001; Sapir 2005).

To sum up, the combined impact of these three developments on European industry are enormous and multifaceted. The EU companies now face increased competition from many fronts – not only, as it was in the 1980s, from the US and Japan (the old 'Triad'), but also from the 'BRICs' (and from Asian countries in general). National governments have become increasingly unable to protect and support the once 'favoured' firms or industries. At the same time, innovation (Sapir *et al.* 2003; Aghion 2006; Brusoni and Malerba 2007) has become the main determinant and driver of the ability to add value and to grow.

The effects of the 2008 economic crisis posed a stumbling block to many of these processes; the significant slowing of economic growth experienced by the Central-Eastern countries of Europe is one of many such indicators. The 'new frontier' that was being opened by their entry into the EU is a frontier that has, in truth, remained as such, as the most recent data on economic growth display (European Commission 2014a).[23]

Yet this is a crisis that has – as we argued in Chapter 1 – given birth to a new awareness throughout the Western world of the central role played by manufacturing in achieving lasting, real economic growth.

In the meantime, technological progress and globalization have not slowed down one whit; rather, they have continued on their path – so much so that it has become the norm to speak of a 'new industrial revolution' – and will continue to do so for the foreseeable future. As often happens in history, what is destined to change is the relative strength of the main actors (in this case, nations). An important OECD study (2012) 'Looking to 2060: A Global Vision of Long-Term Growth', gives us the opportunity to glimpse the changes predicted for the next 50 years.

As Table 2.4 clearly shows, 'there will be major changes in the composition of global GDP', which is

> expected to grow at around 3% per year over the next 50 years, but wide variations are forecast between countries and regions. Fast-growing emerging countries will be the principal driver of the long-term outlook. Growth rates of emerging countries will eventually slow, converging towards those projected for the OECD area ... In parallel, the relative size of economies will change radically over the next 50 years. The combined GDP of China and India will soon surpass that of G7 economies and will exceed that of the entire current OECD membership by 2060.
>
> (OECD 2012, 1)

In the face of such data, there is a strong temptation to borrow Francis Fukuyama's (1992) celebrated prophecy and apply it not to the 'universalization of Western liberal democracy as the final form of human government', but to the unstoppable rise of Asian (and more generally, Eastern) economies.

Are we thus on the eve – or the cliff – of another 'End of History'?

But this would appear be, once again, a false prophecy, or at the very least a hasty one, as Fukuyama's was eventually deemed to be in light of historical events.[24] But let's get back to us. Manufacturing in Europe, as we saw in the preceding chapter in the rankings of McKinsey and Confindustria (both sources use data from IHS Global Insight), is hardly a lost cause. The decline of the EU in relative terms compared to the emerging economies of the planet – a decline shown both in the data from Goldman Sachs on the BRIC and from the OECD on 2060 – should not lead us to underestimate the solidity of the European oligopoly or the muscles that it is still able to flex.

As a final conclusion, we can say that the Big European Players are real, and that they play a fundamental role on the global stage. It is to the analysis of this role that we now turn in the final section of this chapter: however, we will start

Table 2.4 Changes in the composition of global GDP[1] – percentage of global GDP in 2005 PPPs

	2011	*2030*	*2060*
United States	23	18	16
Japan	7	4	3
Euro area	17	12	9
Other OECD	18	15	14
Other non-OECD	11	12	12
China	17	28	28
India	7	11	18

Source: OECD (2012, 8).

Note
1 Global GDP is taken as sum of GDP for 34 OECD and 8 non-OECD G20 countries.

with perhaps the most famous 'European Champion' of them all (the EADS Company, builder of Airbus), which we will call 'Type I', before looking at 'Type II' Champions, those which were formed (and are still being formed) in the Single Market, especially through M&A transactions.[25]

'Type I' 'European Champions': is the Airbus case a model?

Bringing together all the various insights and policy advice that have been put out by the Commission in various documents on industrial or research and technology policy over the past decade (2002–2012, see Chapter 1), we can see which sectors/industries/technologies have gained most prominence in the last few years: ICT, energy, defence, space, biotechnology and pharmaceuticals.

It is evident that the core businesses of firms in these sectors are all very high-tech and R&D intensive. In order for European companies to develop a leading edge in such sectors, two factors are absolutely crucial: first, they must have access to a high level of financial resources in order to conduct R&D at the required level; second, they must be able to hire excellent researchers, engineers and managers – human capital – who have the right skills and knowledge to come up with new and innovative production, organizational and management outputs. As a result, developing strong European Research, Technology, and Education policies, overcoming the segmentation of policies of individual national governments, is key to any 'champions-related policies for innovation and growth of economies'.

Of course, this is not an argument for returning to the old-fashioned policy where politicians and economists were inclined to 'pick winners', i.e. companies or sectors to be promoted and supported with public money. Indeed, today three policies – diametrically opposed to the old approach – must play a fundamental role. First, the strict enforcement of competition policy, not only in terms of mergers control but also with regard to state aid, should foster the development of excellent European companies able to take on global markets. Second, the completion of the Single Market, in particular in the services sector, is crucial for the future development and competitiveness of European industry in general, and not only of European Champions. Finally, well-designed welfare and labour market reforms should be completed in order to accommodate industrial restructuring.

Rejecting the old 'picking the winners' philosophy, the argument for strengthening the European Research, Technology and Education policies has a different basis, i.e. the theoretical and empirical insights gained recently with regard to sectors at or approaching the 'technological frontier', heavily dependent on high R&D spending and subject to externalities as well as to scale and scope effects. However, the vital question at this point is: are the numerous policy tools and approaches adopted by the Commission over the last few years directed at the same goal, that is, towards the creation of new European Champions (which we label 'Type I' or 'Airbus-model Champions': big European firms that have stemmed from multilateral governmental cooperation and public funding in very sensitive sectors)? An equally important question is whether they *should* aim to achieve this goal. Answering these questions is not at all easy, as the liveliness with which the issue is being debated throughout Europe shows. Any attempt to do so, however, must look not only at the (hopefully) pan-European research and technology policy, as we have done so far, but also at the evolution of market concentration.

The economic literature suggests that in some cases and sectors too low a concentration level cannot bring about either equilibrium or optimal solutions and, despite an increase in the size of the market, the degree of concentration may remain far from zero (Sutton 1998, 2007). There are four key factors that shape concentration by 'bounding it from below', away from the zero value that the idealistic competitive setting requires: the need for R&D spending, economies of scope, a critical size for being innovative and financial requirements.

Markets where R&D effectiveness is important will see a higher level of concentration, because a fragmentized market may lead to dispersive and unprofitably duplicated research spending. In such a situation, the returns for a high-spending new entrant will be large, making it profitable for one (new) firm to outspend the research outlays of the incumbents. Clearly, then, the case in which only small low-spending firms subsist would not be a stable configuration of the market (see, in particular, Sutton 1998).

The sectors identified by the Commission as needing a joint European presence – biotechnology, ICT, energy and aerospace – can be seen to a certain extent as the kind of sectors this literature is talking about. These sectors require a strong European presence for at least two different but related reasons. First, the high level of R&D outlay required in order to be competitive in the global market is difficult to attain at the national level. Second, the high R&D spending requirement induces the market structure to change, by bringing about a higher level of concentration, which makes it worthwhile for Europe to address this process.

The argument applies for the 'Airbus case', whose successful experience can be regarded as the emblematic pathway to follow in other sectors for the emergence of new European Champions. This, however, can be regarded only as a general principle, because we have to bear in mind what Paul Seabright (2005) found in his assessment of the 'Airbus experience': that it has been 'a rather special case whose applicability to other project and sectors is fairly limited' due to the technological characteristics of the aerospace sector, i.e. with 'high fixed costs of production, variable costs of production that fall significantly with scale, [and] products [that] are somewhat less differentiated than in other comparably high-technology sectors such as motor vehicles and precision instruments'.

Thus, although the recent proliferation of policies at the EU level has been of the right kind, there is a danger that their results will in practice be limited for the reasons identified by Seabright above. In other words, the success of Airbus cannot be replicated with ease on all of the 31 ETPs, six JTIs, ten FP7 programmes etc., because not all these sectors have the characteristics of the aerospace programme that have facilitated the accomplishment of Airbus.

Therefore, there is a danger that vital funds and other resources allocated at the EU level are being distributed too thinly for them to have a significant effect on the competitiveness of European industry and on the development of 'Type I' European Champions. Thus, it is necessary to refocus the EU Technology Policy with this insight in mind, and also to concentrate efforts on those sectors where a genuinely tight 'strategic cooperation between the private and the public sectors' (Rodrik 2004) is likely to emerge.

Having explained in detail the policy context surrounding Europe's firms, what is natural to do at this point is to examine how the wider process of EU integration itself is bringing about a transformation of the European market structure and the creation of a new type of 'European Champions' – a type driven and supported by market forces alone.

'Type II' European Champions: something new afoot?

In order to elucidate what we mean by 'Type II' Champions, let's take a look at an authoritative empirical study on the subject – *Fortune* 'Global 500: The World's Largest Corporations' – presented here alongside some of our own observations (further information is to be found in Appendix II.2).

In general terms, the relative strength of European industry in the global scenario has already been displayed from a macroeconomic point of view by the publication of data on the importance of industrial activity and on export performances (see Tables 1.6a and 1.6b, Chapter 1). From a microeconomic perspective it is possible to find another way of looking at this strength: that is, the performance of European *big players*. In addition to the review presented in the previous section, reference must be made to the most distinguished source on this score: the annual rankings by *Fortune*. Table 2.5 presents the essential data of this classification.

At first glance, the position held by Europe's industrial giants, when looked at through international eyes, comes out clearly from these data, and it confirms – from a microeconomic perspective – the empirical data that had already been seen at the macroeconomic level (value added by economic activity and exports). What can a closer analysis of these rankings reveal?

Let's begin with the first ranking from *Fortune* (2014). When presenting the 'Local Angle' (i.e. 'Global 500' ranked within countries), the American magazine writes in its summary: 'There are now 95 China-based companies on the 'Global 500', up from 89 last year. Four U.S. corporations fell off the list, leaving a total of 128.'

Fortune *'Global 500': a glance at their geographical distribution*

The summary above does not make mention of the position of the EU, which, on the one hand has witnessed the departure of nine companies over the last three years covered by 'Global 500' (from 137 to 128), but which has at the same time shown itself to be neck and neck with the USA (128 vs 128). In addition – as

Table 2.5 Big players: *Fortune* 'Global 500' (2013): the world's 500 largest corporations ranked within countries

Countries/macro-areas[1]	2011	2012	2013
Austria	1	1	1
Belgium	4	3	2
(Britain/Netherlands)[2]	(1)	(1)	(1)
Denmark	1	1	1
Finland	1	1	1
France	32	31	31
Germany	32	29	28
Great Britain	26	26	27
Ireland	2	2	2
Italy	9	8	9
Luxembourg	2	2	1
Poland	1	1	1
Netherlands	12	11	12
Spain	8	8	8
Sweden	4	3	3
Hungary	1	1	–
Total EU	*137*	*129*	*128*
Brazil	8	8	7
Russia	7	7	8
India	8	8	8
China	73	89	95
Total BRICs	*96*	*112*	*118*
United States	132	132	128
Canada	11	9	10
Mexico	3	3	3
Total North America	*146*	*144*	*141*
South Korea	13	14	17
Japan	68	62	57
Singapore	2	2	2
Thailand	1	1	1
Taiwan	6	6	5
Malaysia	1	1	1
Indonesia	–	1	2
Total South-East Asia	*91*	*87*	*85*

Source: adapted from *Fortune* (2012, 2013, 2014), 'The Global 500'.

Notes
1 In order to complete the full list, in Europe we must also consider (2012, 2013 and 2014 respectively): 15, 14 and 13 for Switzerland; 1, 1 and 1 for Norway; for Turkey, 1, 1 and 1. In the Middle East: 1, 1 and 1 for Saudi Arabia; 1, 1 and 1 for the United Arab Emirates. In Latin America, 1, 1 and 1 both for Colombia and Venezuela, plus 1 in 2014 for Chile. Finally, 9, 8 and 8 for Australia, bringing the total to 500.
2 Unilever.

shown in Table 2.5 – the EU presence in this ranking was superior to that of the US in 2011 (137 vs 132) while in 2012 it fell slightly behind (129 vs 132). Taking this battle to the continental level (Europe vs North America), the situation is almost perfectly balanced (143 vs 141).[26] And when looking at the third member of the (old) Triad – Japan, reduced to 57 companies in 2013 – we see that the EU has more than doubled that number in the 'Global 500'.

What, then, can we say about the comparison between the EU and the BRIC nations, where the Chinese presence is of particular importance? Looked at in terms of total numbers, the EU still has a larger portion of big players in 2013 (128 vs 118), though the lead has narrowed compared to the previous years (137 vs 96 and 129 vs 112), and not insignificantly (from 41 corporations to ten).

Widening the field to include other 'emerging nations' (using the IMF definition and/or members of the G20, the N-11, etc.), we notice how the *Fortune* rankings give an ever clearer picture of the rapid changes taking place on the global economic stage. To the 118 BRIC corporations from Table 2.5, we must add all of the other Asian (30, Japan excluded) and Latin American (three) companies, which brings the total to 151. This number is greater than the European total (128 for the EU and 143 for Europe as a whole). In any event, the sum of corporations in the category we have called 'emerging' requires grouping together nations that are geographically distant and very different culturally/ politically, and which are linked by trade agreements (in most cases, and in small sub-groups). The history of the EU is different, starting from the largest Single Market in the world, which by common consent represents the force behind European integration. Will it continue to be so in the foreseeable future?

In an attempt to answer this question, the initial data on the geographical distribution of the 'Global 500: The World's Largest Corporations' must now be confronted with some fundamental structural economic indicators. Then, in the last part of this section, we will move towards an ad hoc census of the cross-border M&As that have taken place in the European Single Market over the last decade. In fact, M&A activity that seeks to reinforce European enterprises (the Champions) is, in and of itself, a symptom of the market's health, a health that is further stimulated by the fact that 18 of the 28 Member States share the same currency.

Table 2.6 places these two sets of data side by side for the major global economic powers, using for GDP the 'global vision' of the OECD (see Table 2.4). The 383 corporations divided here into five macro-areas represent almost 77 per cent of the 'Global 500' both in terms of their total number and in terms of their total revenue.

The euro area accounts for 17 per cent of global GDP (the far-right column), a percentage that becomes significantly higher when its portion of the 'Global 500' is calculated: 19 per cent (number of corporations) and 21.2 per cent (total revenue). The same – or rather, a more than proportional incidence of the 'Global 500' itself compared to GDP – can be said for the other two historically great industrial powers, the USA and Japan, and starting from 2013 for China as well (in the previous years it had three similar values, all around 17 per cent).[27]

Table 2.6 Why Europe has a role to play

	Fortune 'Global 500' 2013[1]		Revenues ($ millions)	% of total world revenues	'Global GDP' 2011[2]	
	Number of corporations (and % of total no.)				% of Global GDP (in 2005 PPPs)	
World	*500 (100%)*		*31,058,432.4*	*100.0*	*100.0[3]*	
1 Euro area	95 (19)		6,701,954.4	21.6	17	
2 US	128 (25.6)		8,558,906.4	27.5	23	
3 Japan	57 (11.4)		3,085,732.9	9.9	7	
4 China	95 (19)		5,839,179.7	18.8	17	
5 India	8 (1.6)		367,025.9	1.2	7	

Source: author's elaboration.

Notes
1 *Fortune* (2014).
2 OECD (2012, 8): 'Global GDP is taken as sum of GDP for 34 OECD and 8 non-OECD countries'.
3 For 2011: other OECD 18%, other non-OECD 11%.

The data published in Table 2.6 give us the opportunity to carry out a further analysis of the relative strength of the largest corporations of various global economic powers. The average revenue of the 95 corporations in the eurozone ($69,279.09 million) is the highest in the world, followed by that of the 128 US corporations ($66,866.45 million), the 95 Chinese ($61,465.05 million), the 57 Japanese ($54,138.71 million) and the eight Indian ($45,878.13 million). This average revenue of the eurozone is amply larger than the average of the entire 'Global 500' ($62,116.86 million, European corporations included).

But prosperity is not guaranteed. As we know, the OECD's vision of the world at 2060 shows that the GDP of the euro area is destined to decline significantly, already by 2030. It is of the greatest import to be fully aware of this trend; underestimating it would be a serious mistake. But it would be an equally serious mistake to underestimate the productive base that Europe (and the euro area in particular) still represents for the world today. Strengthening this base would provide an important contribution to the European growth problem, perhaps the most pressing issue in Europe for years. And as we saw in Chapter 1, an adequate 'new' industrial policy (one that links all three sides of the 'triangle') would contribute to this strengthening.

But this strengthening can never be truly virile without the involvement of industrial enterprises, starting with the largest of them. What do the more than 100 corporations in the EU from the 'Global 500' produce? Is manufacturing still the prevailing core business among them? We must take a look at their industrial specializations before moving our analysis forward into M&As.

No one is surprised any longer that the top positions in the 'Global 500' are occupied by oil and gas and energy companies (in 2013, six of the top seven, with the exception of Wal-Mart at number one). The highest spots – the top 30, let's say – are also well represented by telecommunications (and utilities in general) and finance (banks). But it is in these first 30 positions that manufacturing demonstrates its long-lasting importance in each of the great world economic zones. We find: Volkswagen (eighth), Toyota Motor (ninth), Samsung Electronics (13th), Apple (15th), Phillips 66 (19th), Daimler (20th), General Motors (21st), Exor Group (24th),[28] Ford Motor (26th), and General Electric (27th). Some of these corporations are even on the rise compared to 2011, such as the first two carmakers and Apple (up from 55th two years ago). When we look at the top 50, other colossal names – paragons of global manufacturing quality – come up: Honda Motor (45th), and Hewlett-Packard (50th). And widening further the field to the top 100, our list grows to include: Siemens (58rd), Nissan Motor (61th), BMW (68th), International Business Machines (71st), Nestlé (72th), Basf (75th), Hitachi (78th), Boeing (90th), Procter & Gamble (92th) and Hyundi (100th) – while Airbus Group comes in at the 103rd slot (up from 114th).

We could go on, but we believe that the first 100 positions are sufficient to reveal both the relative strengths of nations and their main specializations: automotive and chemical in Germany, automotive and consumer electronics in Japan (and South-East Asia), automotive, IT and consumer goods in the USA.

At this point, though, our study necessitates an *infra-European* comparison of EU Member States to shed light on the various paths towards business growth. And a comparison among the Big Five of the EU should be adequate for our task. Table 2.7 focuses on the manufacturing enterprises that appear in the 'Global 500' for each of these five nations. What becomes immediately clear is the reality of the 'varieties of capitalism' that stretch across Europe, with Germany (the 'Rhine Model') defending and upgrading its robust industrial base, and Great Britain (the 'Anglo-Saxon Model') choosing the route of finance (this theme will be picked up again in the next chapter).

In truth, Italy too has preserved its solid industrial base, and it remains the second largest manufacturing economy in Europe (after Germany) and one of the largest in the world. It is, however, an industry that is concentrated in the Centre-North regions of the country and which comprises primarily SMEs and industrial districts rather than large corporations (which in Italy tend to operate in the finance, energy and utilities sectors). Put another way, the 'Global 500' – by its very nature – underestimates the importance of Italy in European manufacturing, while the opposite is true in the case of France, whose manufacturing forces (in and of themselves not particularly significant) are concentrated in large corporations: let's call it a *sui generis* case (or capitalism). Spain, more similar to Italy, has very few corporations in the 'Global 500' and in the same sectors (energy, Tlc and banking), once protected from competition and still today subject to heavy government regulation. But Spain's backbone of SMEs and industrial districts is decidedly more fragile than Italy's, making it difficult to postulate a 'Mediterranean Model' from this perspective.

To round out the data in Table 2.7, Appendix II.2 gives a more complete extract of the 'Global 500 Ranked Within Countries', which details the significant role played by the EU's big five on the world's manufacturing scene primarily thanks to excellent performance of Germany.[29]

If the EU-based corporations in the 'Global 500' are already, by definition, 'Champions', there are many other medium and large enterprises in the Single Market that are pursuing growth strategies (primarily through external growth via M&As, joint-ventures, etc.) that are destined to become tomorrow's Champions. Perhaps, in reality, they have already become so: it is now time to turn our attention to the new tendencies afoot in Europe.

Cross-border mergers and acquisitions (M&As) and the reshaping of the European market structure

The focus of this subsection will be on (large) European firms' recent behaviour, and especially on the growth strategies they are adopting in light of the increasing completion of the level playing field – the European Single Market. In many of the sectors we mentioned so far in our discussion, a strong M&A wave has swept through in the last decade, with many deals being of a cross-border nature and leading to the emergence of what we will label 'Type II' European

Table 2.7 A tale of two capitalisms

	Total corp(s) from *Global 500*	Of which: manufacturing corp(s)[1]	Manufacturing revenues – $ millions (and % of total revenues of each country)	Top five in country's manufacturing ranking (country's total ranking/'Global 500' rank)
Britain	27	5	141,602.9 (8.9%)	Glaxo Smith Kline (14/265), BAE Systems (22/455), AstraZeneca (23/468), Rolls-Royce Holdings (26/489), British American Tobacco (27/499)
France	31	10	264,586.1 (12.7%)	Peugeot (9/119), Saint Gobain (14/180), Renault (17/190), Sanofi (19/238), Chistian Dior (21/289)
Germany	28	11	723,467.0 (35.1%)	Volkswagen (1/8), Daimler (3/20), Siemens (5/58), BMW Group (6/68), Basf (7/75)
Italy	9	1	150,996.9 (20.7%)	Exor Group (2/24)[2]
Spain	8	–	–	–

Source: author's elaboration based on *Fortune* 'Global 500' (2014).

Notes
1 Energy and construction not included.
2 The revenues of Exor Group combined automotive (Fiat and Fiat Industrial, now FCA) with many other service activities.

Champions. Moreover, as long as the Single Market continues to release its potential through deepening (think of the adoption of the euro) and widening (think of Eastern enlargement) measures, we can expect this new type of European Champion to consolidate even further as a result of future M&A activity.

These strategies make a crucial contribution to the emergence of those 'global champions' which Barry Eichengreen (2007) – in his review of the role of the institutions that contributed most to European integration from the Treaty of Rome onwards – called 'firms with the scale and scope needed to compete internationally'.

To sum up, what are the most important facts that appear from the ten-year wave of M&As occurring in Europe? Several well-known databases are monitoring worldwide M&A activity in general terms,[30] and the European Commission itself continuously monitors deals in the context of its institutional duties.[31] Our analysis takes a necessarily narrow view, as Table 2.8 shows: since Eastern enlargement (2004) M&A activity has been split into two periods, using the 2008 crash as the breaking point (as in the case with the *Fortune* ranking, additional information will be presented in Appendix II.3).

What can we learn from the European cross-border deals that have taken place in the periods under scrutiny? The lesson, at least, is fivefold:

i   The entire spectrum of economic activities and industrial sectors has been involved in the M&A wave: everything from mining to commercial services.

ii   The financial system (banks, insurance companies and stock exchanges) was the catalyst for many operations – for better or for worse, we might add. During our first period (2004–2008), operations of a certain 'industrial' nature were predominant, seeking to extend the presence of banks in the nations of Eastern enlargement; while in the second period (after September 2008), enormous public resources had to be invested in bailout operations of European financial markets (banks above all).

iii The macro-sector of oil and gas and public utilities – at an equal level to the financial system – was the setting for many operations, taking advantage of the processes of privatization and liberalization of markets which were launched by all EU governments during the 1990s.

iv   The image that comes forth out of manufacturing – European and global – is that of an economic activity that has by no means fallen from grace. All industries – from steel to fashion to defence to space, and so on[32] – concluded numerous operations both before and after the breaking point of September 2008. These are sectors characterized both by different levels of technology and by diverse levels of contamination by the services sector (for example, throughout ICT, the immaterial/intangible component is predominant).

v   The size of the main actors and the frequency of operations in the first period show Europe's leading position in M&A activity in the middle years of the 2000s.[33] The crisis that followed the bankruptcy of Lehman Brothers, and in particular the chaos that it created in financial markets worldwide, brought an inevitable shrinking of operations in 2009, 2010 and 2011; however, there has been a healthy rebound of operations over the past three years.

As we have already said, our 'sample' of M&As makes no claim of being exhaustive (in part because this would take us well beyond our means and our ends). A complete tally of the thousands of operations that take place every year can be found in the official sources mentioned above. Our objective, we should recall, was more focused: study the European Single Market both from the perspective of market structure and from the perspective of enterprise behaviour. This analysis has revealed the role of the big players, whom we have renamed 'European Champions'.

Overall, the underlying strategy of Europe's biggest firms is to concentrate on their core business, therefore using M&As to carry out a strategy of 'horizontal integration'. There seems to be a widespread consensus that a takeover is more likely to pay off when companies are in the same or similar industries, because they tend to offer greater opportunities for exploiting economies of scale and scope (the famous argument for 'synergies').

Notwithstanding the centrality of a European-oriented M&A wave – and the trend towards 'the Europeanization' of European companies – two other perspectives deserve attention. First of all, *transatlantic* alliances and deals are not rare: examples include the takeover of Lucent Tech. by Alcatel, the joint venture between STMicroelectronics and Intel and, more recently (April 2014), the Nokia takeover completed by Microsoft; in the financial system, the NYSE's agreed bid for Euronext (the Paris-based stock exchange operates bourses in Paris, Amsterdam, Brussels and Lisbon), creating the first transatlantic stock market (at the exact moment when Deutsche Börse was withdrawing its proposed merger with Euronext for a pan-European solution). Second, step by step, BRIC-based companies are entering the European stage – the successful bids of Indian-based Mittal Steel (for the French Arcelor) and Tata Steel (for Corus, an Anglo-Dutch competitor) spring immediately to mind. And both perspectives are destined to become more and more forceful. It is enough to consider on the one hand, the recent signing of the *Transatlantic Trade and Investment Partnership* by the EU and the US, and, on the other, the rising role played on the global economic stage by all emerging nations, with China and India in the lead.

If, here at the end of our analysis of the current M&A wave, we turn briefly to politics, we have to raise the issue of economic nationalism (or patriotism) and the concomitant policy of protectionism. The assumption behind the behaviours of many European national governments is that the nationality of ownership matters. The 'Type II' European Champions, since they are the final outcome of market-opening activities by firms (beginning from the biggest ones), appear to be more coherent with the EU Treaties than any attempt at protecting 'National Champions'.

Table 2.8 A sample of the main 'European' cross-border M&As, 2004–2014

Industry/sector	2004–2008	2009–2014 (October)

Finance (banks, insurance, stock markets)	Santander – Abbey National
	UniCredit[1] – HVB
	BNP Paribas – BNL
	ABN Amro —Antonveneta[3]
	Crédit Agricole – Emporiki Bank
	Royal Bank of Scotland/Santander/Fortis – ABN Amro[4]
	Assicurazioni Generali – PPF Group (Czech Republic), and Assic.
	    Generali – Banca del Gottardo
	UniCredit – Ukrsotsbank (Ukraine), and AFT Bank (Kazakhstan)
	Intesa SanPaolo – BOF Leasing (Slovakia)
	Crédit Agricole – Cariparma
	Euronext – NYSE (*transatlantic*)
	LSE – Borsa di Milano
	Deutsche Börse – ISE, International Securities Exchange
	    (*transatlantic*)
	US Nasdaq Stock Market – OMX (*transatlantic*)[5]
		2008–2009: Commerzbank – Dresdner Bank[2]
		2010: Banco Financiero y de Ahorros SA –
		    FROB Fondo de Reestructuración Ordenada
		2011: Caixa d'Estalvis de Catalunya – FROB
		    Fondo de Reestructuración Ordenada
		2012: Ageas – Ageas SA/NV
		2013: CVC Capital Partner – Cerved Group SpA

ICT and media	Telefonica – 02
	Alcatel – Lucent (*transatlantic*)
	Nokia – Siemens (*network divisions*)
	Mondadori – EMAP France
	Thomson Corp. – Reuters
	News Corporation – Dow Jones (*WSJ*)
	Telefonica[6] – Telecom Italia
	RCS Media Group – Recoletos
	Mediaset – Endemol
		2011: Wind Telecom SpA (Weather Investments
		    SpA) – VimpelCom Ltd
		2011: Société Française du Radiotéléphone SA –
		    Vivendi SA
		2011: Autonomy Corp Plc – Hewlett-Packard
		    Vision BV (*transatlantic*)
		2012: Deutsche Telekom – MetroPCS
		    (*transatlantic*)
		2013: Dentsu Inc. (*From Japan*) – Aegis Group
		    Plc

continued

Table 2.8 Continued

Industry/sector	2004–2008	2009–2014 (October)
Manufacturing/I (pharma and biotech, food)	UCB – Schwarz-Pharma Nycomed – Altana Bayer – Schering Merck – Serono Schering-Plough – Organon BioSciences (transatlantic) Astra-Zeneca – MedImmune (transatlantic) Novartis – Alcon (from Nestlé)[7] Pernod Ricard – Vin&Spirit	2013: Siemens AG – Invesys Rail Ltd (UK) 2013: Microsoft – Nokia (transatlantic) 2013: Vodafone Vierte Verwaltungs AG – Kabel Deutschland Holding AG 2013: Google – FlexyCore (transatlantic) 2014: Portugal Telecom SGPS SA – Oi Sa (from Brazil) 2014: Publicis Group SA – Omicorp Group (transatlantic) 2011: Genzyme Corp – Sanofi-Aventis SA (transatlantic) 2011: Nycomed International Management GmbH – Takeda Pharmaceutical Co Ltd (transatlantic) 2011: Alcon Inc. – Novartis AG (transatlantic) 2012: Alliance Boots GmbH – Walgreen Co (transatlantic) 2012: Actavis-Watson Pharmaceuticals Inc. 2012: Nestlé SA – Pfizer Nutrition (transatlantic) 2012: Heineken – Asia Pacific Breweries Ltd (from EU to Asia) 2013: Bayer – Conceptus (transatlantic) 2013: AstraZeneca Plc – Pearl Therapeutics 2014: Novartis – GlaxoSmithKline[8] 2014: Actavis – Forest Laboratories 2014: Medtronic Inc. – Convivien Plc (transatlantic) 2014: AbbVie – Shire (transatlantic)

Category		
Oil and gas, utilities[9]	Iberdola – Scottish Power Suez – Electrabel AEM & EDF – Italenergia Enel – Endesa Suez & La Caixa – Agbar ENI – Burren Energy, and ENI – Distrigas[10]	2011: GDF Suez Energy Europe & International – International Power Plc 2011: Petrohawk Energy Corp – BHP Billiton Plc (*transatlantic*) 2012: Electrabel SA – International Power Plc 2013: Energetický a Prumyslový Holding 'EPH' – Slovak Gas Holding 2013: Fincantieri (Cantieri Navali Italiani) – STX OVS AS 2014: LetterOne Group – RWE Dea AG 2014: Altice Nubericable – SFR Vivendi
Manufacturing/II (luxury goods and fashion)	PPR – Puma Luxottica – Oakley (*transatlantic*)	2011: LVMH[11] – Bulgari 2011: PPR[12] – Brioni 2011: E-Land – Mandarina Duck 2012: E-Land – Belfe, Lario 1898, Coccinelle 2013: LVMH SA – Loro Piana 2013: Guccio Gucci SpA (Kering Group, previously PPR) – Richard Ginori 2013: PAI Partners SAS – Marcolin
Manufacturing/III (automotive)	Porsche – Volkswagen (VW), and previously VW – Scania (-> Man + Scania in the commercial-vehicles division) Tata Motors – Land Rover and Jaguar (UK-based firms owned by Ford and bought by a BRIC's corporation) Fiat's three joint ventures with Severstal (Russia), Tata Motors (India), Chery Auto (China)	2009: Fiat – Chrysler[13] (*transatlantic*) 2012: Audi – Ducati[14] 2012: Volkswagen AG – Porsche AG[15]

continued

Table 2.8 Continued

Industry/sector	2004–2008	2009–2014 (October)
Manufacturing/IV (space and defence, mechanics, electrical equipment, etc.)	Finmeccanica – SELEX Sensors and Airborne Systems, and Finmeccanica – DRS Technologies (*transatlantic*) Brembo – Hayes Lemmerz (*transatlantic*)	2012: Cooper Industries Plc – Eaton Corp (*transatlantic*) 2013 (April): Siemens – Invensys Rail 2013: General Electric Co – Avio SpA (*transatlantic*) 2013: ASML Holding NV – Cymer Inc. (*transatlantic*) 2013: Ltd – Ceram Tec GmbH 2014: General Electric – Alstom – Energy Division (*transatlantic*)
Manufacturing/V (steel)	Mittal (*from BRICs*) – Arcelor Tata Steel (*from BRICs*) – Corus Tenaris – Hydril (*transatlantic*)	2013: Fives – OTO Mills (subsidiary of the Marcegaglia Group) 2013: Chicago Bridge & Iron Company – The Shaw Group Inc.
Construction and infrastructure	–	2013: Concessions SaS – ANA Aeroportos de Portugal SA 2014: Holcim – Lafarge
Mining	Bhp Billinton – Rio Tinto[16]	–
Commercial services (retailing and travel firms, property management, etc.)	TUI – First Choice Thomas Cook – My Travel Autogrill (with Altadis) – Aldeasa (2005) Autogrill – Alpha Group Plc (2007), and Autogrill – World Duty Free Europe (2008), and full control of Aldeasa (2008) Air France/KLM – Alitalia[17]	2008: Lufthansa – Swiss International Airlines 2009: Lufthansa – Austrian Airlines, and 2012: Lufthansa – BMI (British Midland International) 2010: British Airways – Iberia 2012: Terra Firma Capital Partners – Annington Homes Ltd

Source: author's elaborations based on corporate reports and media releases (updated October 2014).

Notes

1 Additionally, in May 2007, UniCredit acquired Capitalia in Italy's domestic market.

2 Previously (2002–2008) Dresdner Bank was a subsidiary of the insurance corporation Allianz.

3 During 2007 Banco Santander acquired Banca Antonveneta through its participation in a three-way break-up bid for ABN Amro. Subsequently, Banca Monte dei Paschi di Siena buys Antonveneta from Santander.

4 Before: Barclays Bank's unsuccessful offer for ABN Amro.

5 Agreement between Nasdaq and Bourse Dubai to buy OMX, where Dubai receives Nasdaq's stake in the London Stock Exchange plus a 19.9% stake in the US exchange operator.

6 Together with some of Italy's biggest financial companies (Assicurazioni Generali, Intesa Sanpaolo, Mediobanca).

7 A total of 25% of Alcon (contact lens and eye drop), an American firm owned by Nestlé, which has an option to sell its remaining 52% between 2010 and 2011.

8 Acquisitions of Glaxo Cancer Drugs.

9 Domestic M&A (i.e. 'National Champions'): Gaz de France (GDF) + Suez.

10 After exclusive talks between Suez and Eni to sell Distrigas stake.

11 LVMH (Moet Hennessy Louis Vuitton SA), owned by Mr Bernard Arnault, bought in 2010 a stake in Hermes International.

12 The group owned by Mr François Pinault (previously Pinault-Printemps-Redoute) includes other brands such as, for example, Gucci and Yves Saint Laurent.

13 They signed in June 2009 a strategic alliance brokered by the US government, one day after the Supreme Court cleared the path for the deal. Fiat will initially take a 20% stake in the company; its share can go up to 35%.

14 In 1998 the German carmaker bought Lamborghini.

15 A takeover of one by the other has been on the cards since October 2008 when Porsche failed to buy up Volkswagen, racking up more than €10 billion in debts but falling short of the 75% of shares targeted. The German car company responded by purchasing 49.9% of Porsche. On July 2012, VW bought up the remaining 50.1% of Porsche.

16 Ongoing. On 1 February Chinalco (China) in a team up with Alcoa (USA) to buy a strategic 9% stake in Rio Tinto. On 5 February, BHP Billton increased its offer for Rio Tinto which was rejected by Rio. BHP is expected to respond with an increased price offer for Rio.

17 Air France had then withdrawn its offer to buy Alitalia.

SMEs, makers and the new industrial revolution: a short account

The great transnational firms – the 'European Champions' that we spoke so much about in this chapter – have both the necessary size and know-how of their American counterparts to conduct their own R&D activities in their own laboratories and patent their own inventions. They also have the capacity and the resources to compete independently or in partnership with universities, research centres and other firms, in the important Community level funding *calls* for research and innovation (previously the seven Framework Programmes, now the Horizon 2020).

Not to mention the strategic role that European Champions play in supporting numerous supply chains. To give just a single truly transnational example, take the case of a great Swedish multinational – 'The world's leading food processing and packaging solutions company' – which has its headquarters for Southern Europe in a traditionally industrial city in the region of Emilia-Romagna. More than 800 people work in this office, half of them in R&D, design and planning. Up to this point, nothing special: that's how it is when you are looking at large firms that work in medium-high or high-tech sectors. Where do the productive district and the supply chain come in? Exactly at the point where the machines that have been envisioned and designed by the multinational are not built on site, but are placed into the hands of a family owned, highly specialized mechanical engineering firm. This firm is located in the same geographic zone that produces fully operational machinery for the multinational, passing work along down the line to its own subcontractors.

In so doing, information flows easily and rapidly between the multinational and the specialized suppliers, technological spillovers guarantee constant spread of knowledge and innovations, and everyone involved – entrepreneurs, executives and workers – thus becomes gradually more specialized in their fields, developing and perfecting necessary skills.

And so all three of the Marshallian 'sources of industrial localization' have a concrete impact on this territory. These are, according to Paul Krugman's (1991) re-reading of the original: 'labor market pooling', 'intermediate inputs' and 'technological spillovers'.[34]

These reasons (the virtuous circle that flows between large multinationals and small businesses working in districts/clusters) as well as others (such as the significant weight of SMEs in the EU), lead us to conclude this chapter, which at the beginning was focused on the 'European Champions', with a closer look at precisely those SMEs. Box 2.1 examines the issue from a European perspective; Box 2.2 goes into further depth on the important case study of Italy.

We should start by making one minor premise with respect to the 'new industrial revolution'; the third such revolution according to most historical-economic analyses, following the first – the mechanization of the textile industry – and the second – starting from the mass production of automobiles.

The thesis that Chris Anderson (2012) first expressed in his book *Makers* is constantly finding more supporters, and has been used in innumerable practical applications around the world. His thesis is that the '3D printer' – which the author considers the contemporary equivalent of the power loom – will open countless new opportunities for the 'smallest businesses and for digital craftsmen', because it presents the possibility of 'printing objects the way you would print a piece of paper, creating a private factory'.

If we also keep in mind that today, right alongside 3D printers, we find nanotechnologies, new materials and ever-more intelligent robots and software, it follows that not a few SMEs will truly be able to benefit from this 'new industrial revolution'.

This same argument shaped the core of Peter Marsh's (2012) book, the subtitle of which – *Consumers, Globalisation and the End of Mass Production* – explains one of the author's strongest theses: 'the greater focus on tailor-made goods aimed at specific individuals and industry users'. Despite the (slightly) different breakdown of the great changes wrought by manufacturing since its beginnings (Marsh postulates that we are currently in the fifth great leap), the finish line is the same. The international success of many niche products is made possible today by great technological advances, including computers, semiconductors, lasers, the Internet and nanotechnology, to name just a few that made their appearance during the final decades of the twentieth century; on the Internet of Things and the new Industrial Revolution, see also Roland Berger (2014) and Goldman Sachs (2014).

Box 2.1 A focus on SMEs/I

The 'cylinder' from Hamburg to Florence and the leading role of Germany as an 'industrial nation'

'The cylinder that goes from Hamburg to Florence' has been defined by Romano Prodi (2009) as the heart of the European manufacturing system. He pointed out – referring in particular to Italy – that

> once there was the well-known 'blue banana' in Europe; now there is a cylinder that goes from Northern Europe (primarily Germany), and reaches central Italy: the result is that up to Florence we have a productive system similar to the German one.

In general terms, many official documents of the European Union (primarily, the European Commission in Brussels) showed increased attention towards small- and medium-sized (SMEs) enterprises, the 'backbone' of the European manufacturing system. Two important elements are worth mentioning: (i) the adoption of the *'Small Business Act' for Europe* (SBA) by the European Commission in June 2008; (ii) the activation, again in 2008, of the *SME Performance Review* (http://ec.europa.eu/enterprise/policies/sme/facts-figures-analysis/performance-review/index_en.htm).

What is an SME as defined in EU law (EU recommendation 2003/61)?

There are two main factors determining whether a company is an SME: (i) the number of employees, and (ii) either turnover or balance sheet total.

Table A

Company category	Employees	(either) Turnover	(or) Balance sheet total
Medium-sized	<250	≤€50 m	≤€43 m
Small	<50	≤€10 m	≤€10 m
Micro	<10	≤€2 m	≤€2 m

The 'European SBA' applies to independent enterprises of fewer than 250 employees (which is 99 per cent of the total), and has three main purposes:

First, to establish

> a set of 10 principles to guide the conception and implementation of policies both at EU and Member State level. These principles ... are essential to bring value added at the EU level, create a level playing field for SMEs and improve the legal and administrative environment throughout the EU.

Second, 'a set of new legislative proposals which are guided by the "Think Small First" principle'. Third, 'a set of new policy measures which implement these 10 principles according to the needs of SMEs both at Community and at Member State level'.

If this is the regulatory framework that most accurately defines the development of European SMEs, what is their numerical consistency, also in view of a comparative analysis? To answer this question we can use the data published in the *SME Performance Review*, which, in turn, consists of two main sections: *Annual Report on European SMEs* and *SBA Fact Sheets*.

From the last edition of this *Report* we learn that

> across the EU28 last year, some 21.6 million SMEs in the non-financial business sector employed 88.8 million people and generated €3,666 trillion in value added. Expressed another way, 99 out if every 100 businesses are SMEs, as are 2 in every 3 employees and 58 cents in every euro of value added.

> (European Commission 2014c, 6)

Given this overall picture, we would now like to draw attention to the figures published in the various *SBA Fact Sheet(s)*, which we have simply reorganized in Table 2.9 that follows by size (SMEs), rather than by single Member States (as they appear in the European Commission's website); the comparison is limited to the largest four economies of the EU, plus Spain. A more detailed table showing the four categories of enterprises will be published in the Appendix II.4.

Table 2.9 shows, for example, that Italy has the highest number of enterprises (3.7 million, about twice the number of any other country); at the same time, the breakdown by size (see Appendix II.4) shows how Italy – compared to its main European partner/competitor – presents a clear predominance of 'micro enterprises'. This is evident when considering all the three parameters used: 94.4 per

Table 2.9 SMEs in the EU's biggest economies: basic figures

	Number of enterprises			Number of employees			Value added		
	Number	Share	EU-27 Share	Number	Share	EU-27 Share	€bn	Share	EU-27 Share
Italy	3,694,288	99.9%	99.8%	12,028,799	80.0%	66.5%	422	68.0%	57.6%
France	2,483,844	99.8%	–	9,108,188	62.6%	–	501	58.5%	–
Germany	2,147,569	99.5%	–	16,348,724	62.2%	–	745	53.8%	–
Spain	2,239,814	99.9%	–	8,129,205	74.9%	–	284	64.8%	–
UK	1,666,725	99.6%	–	9,387,822	52.4%	–	473	49.8%	–

Source: adapted from European Commission (2013).

cent are microenterprises (against only 81.7 per cent in Germany); they employ 46.1 per cent of workers (18.5 per cent in Germany) and generate 29.8 per cent of the value (15.1 per cent in Germany). Correspondingly, Italy is under-represented, still in comparison with Germany as well as the other biggest countries, in the category of large enterprises.

As we already know from the 'structural indicators' showed in Chapter 1 (ECB 2014), today the EU – in comparison with the two other major (advanced) economic areas in the world – still presents an industrial basis (24.7 per cent of the value added for industry including construction) that makes it more similar to Japan (23.8 per cent) than the United States (18.7 per cent).

A broader image is provided by OECD data (2014) – found in Appendix II.5 – which indicate Europe (both the EU-28 and the eurozone) at 22 per cent of value added from industry (including energy but excluding construction, which alone accounts for another roughly 6 per cent); Japan is at 20.5 per cent, with 5.6 per cent in construction. Aside from the BRICs, we should also cite the results obtained by Norway (where industry reaches the exceedingly high 36.6 per cent), by Switzerland and Turkey (both above 20 per cent), not to mention many other emerging nations such as Indonesia (40.4 per cent), Korea (33.8 per cent), Mexico (29.6 per cent), South Africa (29.3 per cent), Chile (27.7 per cent).

Continuing with the EU, its economic structure could be broken down at the single Member States level and focused on manufacturing. The data (see Figure 2.2, and a more comprehensive survey in the Appendix II.6) suggest that the European manufacturing basis has shown a good degree of resilience, at least in large countries, Germany and (Northern) Italy, that form the two ends of the 'cylinder' envisaged by Romano Prodi (2009).

Germany in particular has been the object of the greatest attention in recent years due to its extraordinary economic performance, especially in exports. Both in the economic literature and in the process of policy-making, it represents an excellent test for trying to understand how the attitude towards industry has changed

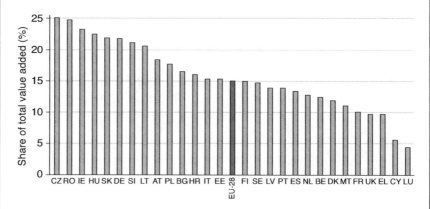

Figure 2.2 Manufacturing's share of total value added in the EU and in Member States (source: European Commission 2014).

Note
Columns represent 2013 shares in all cases except Bulgaria, Romania (2012 shares); current prices.

over the last ten years. An official document from the German federal government (Federal Ministry of Economics and Technology 2010) sheds some light on this change, starting from the description – which had become quite vogue in the international media at the beginning of the century – of Germany as 'the sick man of Europe'. The government writes: 'Many experts advocated adopting the Anglo-Saxon model. One of the remedies prescribed, in particular, was a stronger focus on the services sector.'

The Federal Ministry continued its analysis by highlighting the transition – in a few short years – from the earlier 'laggard' version of Germany to: (i) 'one of the best locations for doing business'; and (ii) a nation observed by others 'with a mixture of suspicion and admiration'. What had happened in the meantime? The answer comes from the selfsame document:

> Germany's competitiveness stems from several successful reforms and a relatively high level of specialisation in industrial manufacturing. Compared to other countries, Germany's manufacturing sector is a key factor of its macroeconomic performance. According to data compiled by the OECD in 2008, industry accounted for 23.1% of the gross value added in Germany. This figure was considerably lower in France (11.9%), the United Kingdom (12.3%) and the US (13.3%).
>
> (Federal Ministry of Economics and Technology 2010, 6)

The 'Introduction (Germany's International Competitiveness)' to this report then concludes:

> While Germany's neighbours are ambivalent about the country's export success, it is increasingly recognised that a strong and broadly diversified industrial base remains crucial for a successful European future.... Not surprisingly therefore, industrial policy is a priority in 'Europe 2020', the new European growth strategy for the coming decade.
>
> (Federal Ministry of Economics and Technology 2010, 6)

The subject of Europe 2020 will be expounded in Chapter 4; for now, we shall pick up the thread of Europe's 'cylinder' once again. This cylinder should not be interpreted in strictly geometrical terms, but as a metaphor that can visually transfer the key developments underway. Therefore a cylinder that could be extended from the top northwards to include some manufacturing regions of Denmark and Netherlands, and, through the Baltic Sea, Sweden and Finland. Again, it could be extended from the bottom (Italy) southwards, beyond Emilia-Romagna and Florence, along the Adriatic coast.

Finally, there are other areas (countries and/or regions) that should be mentioned for their industrial performance at the EU level. These contribute to the expansion the cylinder eastwards; i.e. towards many countries of the historical Enlargement of 2004 (and 2007): Czech Republic, Hungary, Romania, Slovenia and Slovak Republic, with manufacturing share of total value added not only higher than the EU-27 average (15.2 per cent), but also close to the German level of 25 per cent.

Confirmation of the industrial strength of more than one of the *newcomers* from Central-Eastern Europe can be found from the *OECD Factbook* that we cited earlier: Czech Republic, Hungary, Slovak Republic and Slovenia have all demon-strated a value added of more than 25 per cent from their manufacturing vigour (see again Appendix II.5).

The technological level in Eastern countries, of course, is not yet comparable to that of Western EU-15 Member States. However, we are in the presence of coun-tries that have long been the destination of numerous de-localizations of Western enterprises and are the destination of a remarkable flow of FDI.

Summing up, in all these cases we are in the presence of countries (or regions) that generate between one-quarter and one-fifth of their value added *directly* (i.e. in a strict sense) in the manufacturing sector of the economy, to which the value added in construction must be added (about 5–6 per cent everywhere) in order to calculate the GDP share of 'industry' as a whole. Moreover, the assessment of the real contribution offered by industry to a country's (or one of its regions') eco-nomic growth should include the value added *indirectly* generated – the one in the service sector (today equal to at least 70 per cent in all the formerly known 'indus-trialized' economies) that depends on manufacturing activities. Let us think of pro-duction support services, such as R&D, education, design, marketing, advertising, banking, finance, transport and logistics, and so on.

Studies of this nature have begun to be carried out, and they can be quite sur-prising, as in the case of Catalonia, for example, one of the main European manu-facturing regions (Tomàs and Munoz 2009). The methodology uses input–output tables with over 150 entries: in Catalonia the weight of the industry according to traditional calculations is 22 per cent of the GDP, whereas with the addition of ser-vices associated with production (what the study defines as 'the new industry') it reaches 63 per cent of the GDP.

A study quoted by the European Commission (2014b, 1) in its last Communi-cation on industrial policy casts light on the economic importance of industrial activities towards other economic factors, such as employment: 'Nearly one in four private sector jobs is in industry, often highly skilled, while each additional job in manufacturing creates 0.5–2 jobs in other sectors' (Rueda-Cantuche *et al.* 2013).

In the previous chapter, we evoked the idea of a 'manufacturing multiplier', suggested as a paraphrase of the more famous 'Keynsian multiplier.' In this light, we should listen one more time to the document of the German federal government – amply cited above – which reminds us that 'almost 90% of commercial R&D expenditure' comes from German industry's 'capacity for innovation'.

Box 2.2 A focus on SMEs/II

The Italian case

One final brief note about Italy. In a chapter dominated by European issues, Italy cannot be the main object of investigation per se, even though 'Italian' issues can be found in many places. For example, the extent to which enterprises in Italy are actively participating in the reshaping of the European oligopoly. In the space available here, we can only partially sketch the two parallel histories – those delin-eated at the beginning of this chapter – as they relate to an Italian perspective. Even a short excursus within the classical studies of Industrial Organization (IO) would reveal the 'long and illustrious tradition' that Italy enjoys in this field: this was the judgement once passed by Alexis Jacquemin, expressly citing works by Paolo Sylos Labini, Siro Lombardini, Franco Momigliano and Romano Prodi.

The late professor of IO from Louvain-la-Neuve was given this opportunity in the 'Preface to the Italian Edition' (Jacquemin 1991) of the innovative textbook by Jean Tirole (1988). The books mentioned are the following: S. Lombardini, *Concorrenza, monopolio e sviluppo economico* (1976); F. Momigliano, *Economia industriale e teoria dell'impresa* (1975); R. Prodi, *La diffusione dell'innovazione nell'industria italiana* (1971); P. Sylos-Labini, *Oligopolio e progresso tecnico* (1975).

Similarly, the history of Italy's role in the process of European integration (from the ECSC to the Monetary Union via the Treaty of Rome and the Single European Act), would be sufficient proof of the visionary political decisions made throughout the decades from the 1950s on, as would the positive impact of those decisions on Italy's economic performance (both at the macro- and microeconomic level).

The 'Italian Story' takes on its full importance right at the nexus of our two plots, the result of the structural impasses that still impede the country's economic growth. As already stated, a specific investigation of this is beyond the scope of this Box. There is just enough space to mention a few theses that, as a sample of the growing literature on the subject, outline future research agendas. The Rodolfo De Benedetti Foundation (Barba Navaretti *et al.* 2007) highlighted the restructuring processes undertaken in the Italian economy in the age of euro (e.g. the rebound in exports since 2006): processes that 'can be seen in particular at the organizational level of companies, more so than in terms of changes within the specialized sectors'. The Research Department of Mediobanca (R&S–Mediobanca 2008) in its studies on so-called 'Fourth Capitalism', has in its turn raised questions about the most important conclusions drawn by Barba Navaretti *et al*.

The arguments are published in *Riflessioni su 'Come sta cambiando l'Italia'*, the volume by the De Benedetti Foundation where the essay by Barba Navaretti *et al.* is published, and are available online at the Research Department of Mediobanca's website (www.mbres.it) in the section dedicated to 'Quarto Capitalismo': www.mbres.it/ita/mb_pubblicazioni/quarto_capitalismo.htm#.

R&S–Mediobanca underlines the special role played by 'geographical place' in ensuring success in global markets: enterprises are formed and expand in those places where the local society has accumulated the necessary skills and capabilities. The same Research Department, along with its colleagues from Unioncamere, has since periodically published their research on roughly 4,000 'medium-sized industrial enterprises' (Mediobanca-Unioncamere 2013) that specialize in 'Made in Italy' products and focus on niche markets of highly innovative content. In this regard, the difference between these two theses is less stark than would immediately appear, seeing as how both underline the role of the most efficient and dynamic enterprises.

Admitting that the insufficient growth rate in productivity remains the primary unresolved issue for the Italian economy (CsC (Centro studi Confindustria) 2006, 2008), a not-insignificant number of positive elements must be mentioned here in conclusion.

During the years of the euro, positive, in some cases excellent results have not been achieved by coincidence. They are the natural result of a series of strategic actions taken by Italian companies, or at least by a significant section of these companies. In fact, as already observed, the 'Euro Age' has encouraged profound restructuring at the *microeconomic* level of the single enterprise and/or territorial system where more dynamic companies emerge and expand.

Two investigations by the Istituto di Studi e Analisi Economica (ISAE 2008, 2009) provided detailed studies, respectively, of 'Comportamenti d'impresa' ('Firm behaviours'), and 'Ciclo, impresa, lavoro' ('Cycle, firm, employment'). In both cases the main conclusions of the analysis point in the same direction of an ever more visible upgrading in the quality of Italian industrial products, particularly products intended for exports. Citing the 2008 Report:

> The improvement in Italy's performance in foreign markets reflects the path of causality that goes from productivity to exports.... This suggests that in the 2000s, a skimming process of Italy's exports began to the benefit of those with an already high productivity. In addition to this, the analysis shows that the inclination to sell abroad has increased with the increase in company size. At the same time, Italian operators working on behalf of third parties have been penalised.... Another interesting phenomenon is that the fewer the foreign sales, the greater the number of sold products: in other words, the most 'polarised' companies were those able to increase their focus on international markets.... Moreover, the effect associated with the entry of new operators (commonly known as extensive margin) was higher than the increase in exports by companies already present in the single currency (intensive margin).

A point raised by these analyses leads directly to the question of firm size. In fact, ISAE, in describing the new strategic behaviour of many companies, has drawn our attention to the fact that positive behaviour, such as the inclination to sell abroad, increases in tandem with the size of the company. On the other hand, operators working on behalf of third parties are penalized, where it is reasonable to assume that a large number of micro enterprises are concentrated.

We stressed the fact at the beginning of this Box that something significant has changed within Italian industry during the years of the euro.

Other evidence of this can be found in the publications of the Bank of Italy, starting with the well-known 'Considerazioni finali' of the Governor (www.bancaditalia. it). In May 2008, for example, Mario Draghi stated:

> As we noted here one year ago, some elements within the production system have begun to restructure; the adoption of the Euro and its consequential disciplinary effect have played a role in this. Our studies indicate that this structural change cuts through all industries. Both in traditional and advanced producers, alongside those companies that have closed their doors or are facing serious difficulties, we find others that have been able to make a qualitative leap in their competitive capacity. The mortality rate of enterprises has gone up; but those that survive have increased their profitability and their internationalization. The medium-sized category is expanding.
>
> (Banca d'Italia 2008, 9–10)

The following year, the 'Considerazioni finali' (Banca d'Italia 2009) showed a subdivision of companies (operating in industry and services) into three categories.

The first two can be attributed to companies with at least 20 employees, many of which are already undergoing a process of restructuring. The difference between them is that there are 'financially sound companies' on one hand (first category) and those that in order to grow 'became indebted' on the other hand, and now face 'decline of cash flows, freeze on bank loans, and difficulty in accessing the capital market' (second category).

As the Governor continues, 'small companies of less than 20 employees are suffering from the crisis', which represents the third category:

> There are almost 500.000 in total in manufacturing only, with less than two million employees. The very survival of those operating as sub-contractors of major companies, by which they are subjected to order cuts and payment delays, is at risk.
>
> (Banca d'Italia 2009, 10)

In the same vein, the Servizio Studi of the Bank of Italy (Bugamelli *et al.* 2009) investigated 'The Euro and Firm Restructuring'. Starting from the realization that between 1998 and 2005 the productive specialization of the manufacturing industry did not change significantly either in Italy or in the eurozone, the authors demonstrate that profound restructuring has taken place within single sectors. Restricting the analysis to the Italian case (interviews with entrepreneurs and use of the INVIND database: companies of more than 50 employees) the role of single enterprises and their strategic behaviour emerges. In their words (Bugamelli *et al.* 2009):

> Since the adoption of the euro, companies have shifted their focus on production to upstream and downstream activities such as R&S, design, marketing and distribution.... The shift is more drastic in traditional and low technology activities.... And there is a distinct decrease in the number of workers (or 'blue collars'), in line with the theory that companies are shifting away from production. The lower the technological content of the sector, the more significant the decrease. Interestingly, in the pre-Euro Age it was the opposite: low-technology companies used the devaluation of the currency to recover price competitiveness and intensify their dependence on low-skilled work force. We have not found evidence that employment flows (or job flows) have increased after the introduction of the euro; restructuring seems to have led to a reallocation of the work force more within the companies rather than among them.

The structure of Italy's industry as it emerges from the figures displayed in Table II.4a (see Appendix II.4) has a second feature that goes hand in hand with the high number of micro enterprises – i.e. the modest presence of large companies.

Why has this factor increasingly become a problem? The economic and social role of SMEs is certainly not under discussion: in many Italian territories, both the diffuse presence of SMEs and their organization in highly specialized territorial networks have contributed to generate and distribute wealth as well as increase social cohesion. In Italy the historical and contemporary role of industrial districts (IDs) has been of constant import. Giacomo Becattini, a distinguished scholar, often makes reference to a 'capitalism with a human face':

> ID processes exemplify the presence and action of competitive forces that Marshall would have called 'chivalrous', and that are not dominated only by opportunism, shirking or pure cut-throat rivalry, but rather are infused also with rules that reward fair, open, and trustworthy behaviours and punish – often tacitly and informally, albeit effectively – cheating or breaching.
>
> (Becattini *et al.* 2009, xxxiii)

All in all, IDs have found their place in the national and international division of labour. This is true in particular for Italy:

> Since their 'statistical discovery' (in 1987) [as Fabio Sforzi (2009, 341) points out in his chapter in Becattini *et al.*'s *Handbook*] IDs were considered 'more' (in addition to large firms) and 'different' (for their assumed uniqueness) in the Italian economy compared to other industrialised countries. Then, with the crisis of large firms, IDs appeared to most as a 'new best way' to industrialisation.

When SMEs, and in particular microenterprises, constitute the bulk of an industry structure, the critical point – today more than ever in Italy as well as everywhere in the EU – lies in the dynamics of productivity.

From the interesting analysis conducted in the *2009 Annual Report* of the *SME Performance Review*, we understand that SMEs directly contribute to 67 per cent of employment in the EU, while their contribution to the value added to the cost of factors is lower (58 per cent) than that suggested by employment. On the contrary, large EU enterprises employ 33 per cent of staff, and contribute to the value added to an extent of 42 per cent. As a result, European SMEs have a lower than average work productivity.

The differences in labour productivity by firm size, as the authors write (Audretsch *et al.*, 2009), 'are only partially explained by the differences in sector structure' because a lower than average labour productivity 'is an intrinsic characteristic of the typical SME'. The conclusion is that:

> a typical SME is either too small to exploit the economies of scale or it is less capital-intensive. Another explanation could be the use of less qualified work force in SMEs, taking into account that the cost per work unit is lower.

As previously mentioned, if we focus our attention on Italian enterprises the question of productivity in SMEs, which also has a European flavour, emerges in all its importance. Italy is known to have suffered for over ten years from a *gap* in growth of productivity compared to other large EU countries. This dynamic, in turn, is at the origin of the low economic growth of the country on a European scale (Daveri and Jona-Lasinio 2005).

Yet the positive results achieved by many regional economies in foreign markets (or the surplus in trade balance) signal that the strength of Italian enterprise is rooted in the territory. It is worth remembering that these companies fall within the 99.9 per cent of SMEs with fewer than 250 employees, and that operate primarily, to use the expression of the Fondazione Edison (Fortis 2009), in the '4 As'; i.e. 'the four majors' of 'Made in Italy': '*Abbigliamento* (apparel and fashion), *Arredo casa* (furniture and interior decoration), *Automazione* (automation and mechanical engineering), *Alimentari* (food and beverages)'.

How do we reconcile these differences? In other words: is there something missing from the standard analyses on (low) growth in productivity and (positive) performance in international trade? Are we in the presence of a new 'Italian paradox'?

To answer these questions we must study the link between innovation and productivity, considering therefore a wider range of innovative activities compared to the expenditure in (codified) R&S only. SMEs implement innovation(s) in a non-conventional way by creating tacit knowledge: 'There is no shortage of topics, old or new, for any IO research programme that wishes to examine the "metamorphosis" of the Italian productive system as seen from a wider European perspective.'

In a paper presented at the 11th European Network on Industrial Policy (EUNIP) 2008 International Conference (Mosconi 2008), I used this word *metamorphosis* (defined as 'a major change in the appearance or character of someone or something', www.merriam-webster.com) for the first time to refer to the transformations taking place in the so-called 'Emilian Model'. This is an economic model that has for decades now been an object of interest in the international literature (not only the celebrated article 'The Emilian Model: Productive Decentralisation and Social Integration' by Sebastiano Brusco (1982), but also the works of Piore and Sabel (1984) and Porter (1990), which refer to this model on more than one occasion).

The region of Emilia-Romagna has had, since the 1960s, an economy with a markedly robust manufacturing base, a high capacity for export and a significant degree of social cohesion, so much so as to resemble even the most important German *Länder*. A particularly relevant feature of this economy resided – and still resides – in the role played by spatial aggregations of firms in the territory: Marshallian districts and/or clusters. Confronted by the changes ushered in by the European economy (the birth of the euro, Eastern englargement) and the global economy (the rise of the BRICs, among others), the model obviously could not sit on its laurels. Hence the 'metamorphosis' that we have tried to study and elucidate through a research programme that I coordinate at the University of Parma (Mosconi 2011, 2012): a metamorphosis that has been, by and large, positive when we consider the success of a new elite of medium-sized enterprises that have become niche players on a global scale, and the role this economy plays in both FDI inflows and outflows.

Obviously, all regions of Italy deserve deeper investigation into their own relative transformations, starting with those that fall within the 'cylinder' that we spoke of in the previous Box. In fact, recent years have seen a significant rise in empirical studies conducted in Italy in the academic and non-academic worlds.

In addition to the Research Departments cited earlier in this Box, we can mention the following (which is not, we readily admit, a complete list):

i   the two quarterly scientific journals for industrial/applied economists, collected in the Società Italiana di Economia e Politica Industriale (SIEPI): *l'Industria – rivista di economia e politica industriale* (published by Il Mulino, Bologna), and *Economia e Politica Industriale – Journal of Industrial and Business Economics* (published by Franco Angeli, Milan);

ii   the Research Departments of the two largest Italian banks, which are also among the biggest in the eurozone: Intesa SanPaolo (ISP, which publishes quarterly the *Monitor dei distretti*) and UniCredit;

iii the two important think-tanks based in Bologna – Nomisma and Prometeia (the latter, for example, publishes the *Analisi dei settori produttivi* in collaboration with ISP) – which came into being many decades ago from an initiative by a group of respected University of Bologna economists working at the then Istituto di Scienze Economiche under the intellectual guidance of the late professor Beniamino Andreatta;

iv other think-tanks, of more recent stamp, specializing in the study of industrial districts, such as the Osservatorio Nazionale Distretti Italiani and Fondazione Nord-Est, as well as the most important Italian daily business newspaper, *Il Sole 24 Ore* (for example, 'Il viaggio nei Distretti' undertaken by journalists of *Il Sole* in 2012 and edited by P. Bricco, M. Maugeri and G. Oddo).

The journal *l'Industria*, in particular, in publications of very recent stamp, has investigated many of the themes presented in this Box. Among others, we mention the following: (i) 'The Structural Transformation of the Italian Industrial System', edited by C. Pozzi (2012), with an introductory article by A. Arrighetti and F. Traù (2012) – 'Far from the Madding Crowd: Competence Development and New Evolutionary Paths of Italian Industrial Firms' – and commentary by S. de Nardis, F. Guelpa, D. Iacobucci, and F. Schivardi; (ii) the essay written by a group of ISTAT researchers (Causo *et al.* 2014), 'The Internationalisation of the Italian Manufacturing Firms During the Crisis: Winners and Losers in the Global Market', which makes use of the 'new ISTAT databases … to pinpoint both the firms' potential and obstacles'; (iii) in the same issue, 'The Forum: Which Industrial Policies for the Future of Italy?', coordinated by the journal's editor in chief, Enzo Pontarollo (2014). Also worthy of mention is the very recent work by Di Vico and Viesti (2014) on this same topic.

Notes

1 For a recent contribution on Joe Bain's seminal work and 'the origins of industrial economics', see: Bianchi (2013).
2 The two influential articles, 'The Economies of Scale' in 1958, and 'A Theory of Oligopoly' in 1964 were, amongst others, republished by Stigler himself in *The Organization of Industry* (1968).
3 In our case, three new trends tried to overcome the limits of case studies and cross-section analyses. The 'empirical renaissance' referred to by the journal consists of: (i) the use of new sources of data or datasets, collected in new methods with respect to the past; (ii) the growing use of the advances made in economic theory and in econometric methods; (iii) the movement away from industries and towards enterprises as the object of investigation (Bresnahan and Schmalensee 1987, 371–378). It is worth remembering, as the editors themselves noted, how little these new essays resemble those from the 1960s and 1970s, even if they come out of the same tradition of cross-section studies.
4 In the previous chapter, the 'industrial policy' implications of Jacquemin's thinking (1987, ch. 6) have already been scrutinized.
5 It is of great relevance that in Sutton's second book, dedicated to the evolution of market structures, his example of 'endogenous sunk costs' are R&D investments in the high-tech industries (Sutton 1998), whereas in his first book these costs were represented by advertising in the food and drink industry (Sutton 1991).
6 The other Treaty signed in Rome on 25 March 1957 created the European Atomic Energy Community (Euratom). These three institutions – the ECSC, the EEC and Euratom – were merged into the 'European Communities' (EC) in 1965.

7 First enlargement (1973): UK, Ireland and Denmark – while Norway refused EEC membership in a referendum; second enlargement (1981): Greece; third enlargement (1986): Spain and Portugal; fourth enlargement (1995): Austria, Finland and Sweden.

8 Cyprus, the Czech Republic, Estonia, Hungary, Latvia, Lithuania, Malta, Poland, Slovakia and Slovenia entered the EU on 1 May 2004, with Romania and Bulgaria in 2007.

9 After the 'historic milestone' of 2004 (and 2007), it was Croatia's turn, entering on 1 July 2013.

10 It is the third and latest volume of the *Handbook of Industrial Organization*, edited by Armstrong and Porter (2007), that presents the state of the discipline; particular mention must be made of the chapters by J. Sutton (2007) on 'market structure', which takes as its reference point the essay by Schmalensee and Willig (1989, chapter 16) in the first volume of the *Handbook*, and by M. Whinston (2007) on 'horizontal mergers', which updates the chapter by A. Jacquemin and M. E. Slade (1989, chapter 7).

11 See, in particular, the chapter written by Pisani-Ferry *et al.* (2008, 73–74):

> It was noted that enduring divergences in prices developments could be observed within the euro area, which possibly resulted in real exchange rate misalignments. In their words, the so-called competitiveness channel was too slow and too weak to prevent boom-and-bust cycles fuelled by excessively low real interest rates. As the boom ended, Spain and Ireland, the two champions of the euro's first decade, plunged into deep and probably long recession.

On the same subject, see also: Pisani-Ferry and Posen (2009).

12 According to the 'Commission recommendation 2003/361/EC' (European Commission 2003) – valid since 1 January 2005 – concerning the definition of 'micro, small and medium-sized enterprises (SMEs)', the 'category is made up of enterprises which employ fewer than 250 persons and which have an annual turnover not exceeding EUR 50 million, and/or annual balance sheet total non exceeding EUR 43 million' (article 2). Within the SME category: *microenterprise*, fewer than ten persons and annual turnover and/or annual balance sheet total does not exceed €2 million; *small enterprises*, fewer than 50 persons and annual turnover and/or annual balance sheet total does not exceed €10 million. As a matter of fact, 'microenterprises' (with a maximum of ten persons), according to data from the *SME Performance Review* – which is analysed in Box 2.1 – account throughout the EU for more than 90 per cent of the total number of firms, roughly 30 per cent of total employment and 21 per cent of the value added.

13 More in detail, *The Scoreboard* (pp. 13–14):

> concentrates on the analysis of the world's top 1500 companies that invested more than approximately €35 million in R&D in 2011. The sample comprises companies based in the EU (405), the US (503), Japan (296) and other countries (296) including Switzerland, Taiwan, South Korea, China, India, Norway, Australia, and a further 20 countries. A sample consisting of the top 1000 R&D investing companies based in the EU is analysed separately in chapter 6; these all have R&D investment exceeding €3.8 million.

14 In this report, 'health related sectors' mean 'pharma, biotech and medical equipment'.

15 During 2005 and 2006 – following an accurate reconstruction (Sabatier 2006) – the French government foiled the acquisition of the Danone Group, maker of yogurt and mineral water, by the American giant Pepsico, and pushed for the recent merger between water utility company Suez and the national gas company GdF to prevent Suez becoming prey to the Italian energy concern Enel. In addition, the government chaired by Dominique de Villepin introduced legislation designed to block hostile takeovers of French companies in 11 'strategic sectors'. Meanwhile, Spain blocked 'a German company taking over one of its own energy producers' (respectively, E.ON

and Endesa); Poland thwarted 'the purchase of several of its banks by Italians', while Italy did the same for some time, 'as evidenced by the long-running battle in 2005 to fight off the takeover of Antonveneta bank by the Dutch giant ABN Amro'; and Germany 'staunchly defends its "Volkswagen law", protecting its auto industry from foreign predators'. The blocked takeover of Italy's Autostrade by the Spanish group Abertis could also be added to the list.

16 In the same years – P. Sabatier (2006) added – 'Outside the EU one need only look at the spat over the acquisition of six US port operations of P&O by Dubai Port World or remember the furore over the Chinese oil firm CNOOC attempting to buy Unocal'; a subsequent takeover was made by Chevron (US).

17 Trade flows – Fontagné *et al.* (2009) wrote – 'may have grown by a couple of percentage points at most'.

18 The Centre for Economic Policy Research (CEPR) and other partners from seven countries (www.efige.org).

19 The newly collected *EU-EFIGE/Bruegel-UniCredit survey* of 15,000 manufacturing companies in seven EU countries: Austria, France, Germany, Hungary, Italy, Spain and the UK.

20 R&S–Mediobanca's definition of its study is given in the following:

> *Objective*: a study of the aggregate accounts of the largest multinationals in the world. *Object*: companies with sales over 3 billion Euros, equal to at least 1% of the total sales in its respective area or nation. *Sectors*: manufacturing and energy industry, telecommunications and utilities; businesses not involving manufacturing are not included: construction, finance, etc. *Geographic Area*: global, divided into three macro-areas: Triad (Europe-North America-Japan), Asia-Russia, and the Rest of the World.

21 Looking 'Beyond the BRICs' – to quote the title of Goldman Sachs' paper (2007) – a set of 11 countries emerged; the 'Next 11' (N-11) include: Bangladesh, Egypt, Indonesia, Iran, Korea, Mexico, Nigeria, Pakistan, Philippines, Turkey and Vietnam.

22 'Emerging Market and Developing economies', instead, is the expression proposed by the International Monetary Fund in its 'World Economic Outlook(s)' (see, for example, the latest one (IMF 2014, 2)), where it is possible to see their aggregate growth projections (5.0 for 2015) and to find subsets of countries such as: 'Commonwealth of Independent States', with Russia among them (projected rate of growth for 2015: 1.6 per cent); 'Emerging and Developing Asia' (e.g. China, India and ASEAN-5: Indonesia, Malaysia, Philippines, Thailand, Vietnam), growing at 6.6 per cent; 'Emerging and Developing Europe' (2.9 per cent); 'Latin America and the Caribbean' (e.g. Brazil and Mexico), growing at 2.2 per cent; 'Middle East, North Africa, Afghanistan, and Pakistan' (3.9 per cent); Sub-Saharian Africa (e.g. South Africa), growing at 5.8 per cent. A further sign of how the world's economic geography is changing can be found in 'The Group of Twenty (G20)' composition. 'The G20 was formally established in Sept. 1999 when finance ministers and central bank governors of seven major industrial countries met in Washington' – the web page shows (www.g20.org) – while starting from November 2008 'it brings together finance ministers and central bank governors from 19 countries … plus the European Union'. Together with the G7 countries and the four BRICs, there are: Argentina, Australia, Indonesia, Republic of Korea, Mexico, Saudi Arabia, South Africa and Turkey. Again from the web page: 'G20 members represent almost: 90% of global GDP; 80% of international global-trade; 2/3 of the world's population lives in G20 member countries; 84% of all fossil fuel emissions are produced by G20 countries.'

23 The 'main economic indicators' published in the '2014 Autumn Economic Forecast' (European Commission 2014a) also shed light on medium range tendencies. In 2000–2004 and 2005–2009, GDP grew, in the majority of these countries, between 3 and 7 per cent (real gross domestic product, five-year average). This was followed by

a four-year period (2010, 2011, 2012 and 2013) of ups and downs for both the old EU-15 and the newcomers from the East. The forecasts for 2014, 2015 and 2016 give positive GDP growth both for the countries belonging to the euro area (Estonia, Latvia, Lithuania, Slovenia and Slovakia) and the other EU Member States (Bulgaria, Czech Republic, Croatia, Hungary, Poland and Romania), with the best performance coming once again from the Baltics (with growth rates around 3–3.5 per cent), and respectable growth (GDP growth above 2 per cent and towards 3 per cent) in many others.

24 Among the events that followed the hypothetical 'End of History', we recall the 'clash of civilisations' – as postulated by Samuel P. Huntington (1996) – that the world has been experiencing since the fall of the Berlin Wall, as well as the not-exactly liberal democratic nature of the two principle 'emerging countries', China and Russia.

25 For a first assessment, see: Mosconi (2009).

26 Considering, in 2014 (with 2013 data), Europe as a whole we must add to the big EU players: 13 for Switzerland, one for Norway and one for Turkey; whereas, considering the North American continent (or NAFTA) we must add to the big US players: ten from Canada and three from Mexico.

27 India presents a very different case as an economy experiencing great growth but with very few big Indian players based in-country. It is, more than anything, a nation where many Western groups have established significant portions of their operations in a process of delocalization, especially in the IT sector. Nevertheless, in the world of international finance, India has at least two very famous groups: the group led by business tycoon Ratan Tata shows up twice in the rankings (Tata Motors and Tata Steel), while the other tycoon of Indian capitalism (Lakshmi Mittal, 'the steel tycoon') shows up under the heading of Luxembourg, site of the legal headquarters of the colossal ArcelorMittal, created in 2006 through the merger of Arcelor and the Mittal Steel Company.

28 Exor S.p.A. is the Italian holding company – controlled by the Agnelli family – with a controlling stake in automaker FIAT and FIAT Industrial (CNH and Iveco). During the year 2014, FCA (Fiat Chrysler Automobiles) was formed by merging FIAT and Chrysler.

29 Many other Member States of the EU should deserve attention for their performances in the 'Global 500': for example, Benelux (the Netherlands in particular); as an aside, *Fortune* lists the headquarters of the multinational Unilever (140th position) simultaneously in Britain/Netherlands – a singular case in the entire ranking. We should find other examples in the Scandinavian countries (Finland with Nokia, Sweden with Volvo and Ericsson). The CEEC nations that entered with the enlargement of 2004 are – as one might expect – poorly represented: Hungary and Poland have only a single corporation apiece, and operating in the same sector (oil and gas). Last, outside the EU but firmly within Europe, we must make note of Switzerland, site not only of world-famous financial giants, but also of important industrial corporations such as Nestlé, Novartis, Roche Group and ABB.

30 On global M&As, to give an example, Dealogic is the most cited source in *The Economist*'s articles and surveys referring to this topic.

31 In light of the Council Regulation (EC) No. 139/2004 (Council of the European Union 2004), the European Commission, explaining 'which mergers get reviewed by the EU', points out that

> in principle [it] examines only larger mergers with a *European dimension*, meaning that the merging forms reach certain *turnover thresholds*. About 300 mergers are typically notified to the Commission each year. Smaller mergers which do not have an EU dimension may fall instead under the remit of Member States' competition authorities.

Then, the Commission explains:

> There are two alternative ways to reach turnover thresholds for EU dimension. The first alternative requires: (i) a combined worldwide turnover of all the merging firms over €5,000 million, and (ii) an EU-wide turnover for each of at least two of the firms over €250 million. The second alternative requires: (i) a worldwide turnover of all the merging firms over €2,500 million, and (ii) a combined turnover of all the merging firms over €100 million in each of at least three Member States, (iii) a turnover of over €25 million for each of at least two of the firms in each of the three Member States included under ii, and (iv) EU-wide turnover of each at least two firms of more than €100 million. In both alternatives, an EU dimension is not met if each of the firms archives more than two third of its EU-wide turnover within one and the same Member State.
>
> (see: http://ec.europa.eu/competition/mergers/procedures_en.html)

32 Pharmaceuticals and biotech are also industry sectors where many deals are occurring: here, high R&D intensity and the growing necessity to outspend for this sort of investment seems to be the main engine.
33 From a European point of view, the M&As waves are also reflected in the number of 'notified cases' being filed every year by the European Commission-DG Competition. The 'notifications' were 402 in 2007 up from 168 in 1997, a decade earlier, while the following years showed many ups and downs (from 348 in 2008 to 259 in 2009, and from the latter to 274 in 2010 and 309 in 2011; and finally, from over 300 to 283 in 2012 and 277 in 2013). For the full list from 1990 till today, see the following statistics: http://ec.europa.eu/competition/mergers/overview_en.html.
34 Today, the experiences of industrial 'Districts' and/or 'Clusters' go well beyond the traditional boundaries of Western industrialized countries; for an analysis of 'Industrial Clusters' as policy tools to boost industrialization in the world's largest emerging economy (China), see: Frattini and Prodi (2013).

References

Aghion P. (2006) 'A Primer on Innovation and Growth', Bruegel Policy Brief, October, www.bruegel.org.

Anderson C. (2012) *Makers: The New Industrial Revolution*, New York, Random House.

Armstrong M., Porter R. H. (eds) (2007) *Handbook of Industrial Organization*, vol. 3, Amsterdam, North-Holland/Elsevier.

Arrighetti A., Traù F. (2012) ' "Far from the Madding Crowd": Sviluppo delle competenze e nuovi percorsi evolutivi delle imprese italiane', *L'industria*, 1, January/March, 7–59.

Audretsch D., van der Horst R., Kwaak T., Thurik R. (2009) 'First Section of the Annual Report on EU Small and Medium-sized-sized Enterprises', EIM Business & Policy Research, Zoetermeer, 12 January.

Bain J. (1951) 'Relation of Profit Rate to Industry Concentration: American Manufacturing, 1936–1940', *Quarterly Journal of Economics*, 65, 293–324.

Bain J. (1959) *Industrial Organization*, New York, John Wiley & Sons.

Baldwin R. (2006) 'Globalisation: The Great Unbundling(s)', 'Globalisation Challenges for Europe and Finland', Finland's EU Presidency Programme, September.

Baldwin R., Wyplosz C. (2004) *The Economics of European Integration*, Maidenhead, McGraw-Hill.

Baldwin R., Barba Navaretti G., Boeri T. (eds) (2007) *Come sta cambiando l'Italia*, Bologna, Il Mulino.

Banca d'Italia (2008) 'Considerazioni finali del Governatore', Assemblea Ordinaria dei Partecipanti, Rome, 31 May (www.bancaditalia.it).

Banca d'Italia (2009) 'Considerazioni finali del Governatore sul 2008', Assemblea Ordinaria dei Partecipanti, Rome, 29 May.

Barba Navaretti G., Bugamelli M., Faini R., Schivardi F., Tucci A. (2007) 'Le imprese e la specializzazione produttiva dell'Italia. Dal macrodeclino alla microcrescita?' in R. Baldwin, G. Barba Navareti, T. Boeri (eds), *Come sta cambiando l'Italia*, Bologna, Il Mulino (37–115).

Barba Navaretti G., Bugamelli M., Schivardi F., Altomonte C., Horgos D., Maggioni D. (2011), 'The Global Operations of European Firms: The Second EFIGE Policy Report', *Bruegel Blueprint*, XII.

Becattini G., Bellandi M., De Propris L. (eds) (2009) *A Handbook of Industrial Districts*, Cheltenham, Elgar.

Bianchi P. (2013) 'Bain and the Origins of Industrial Economics', *European Review of Industrial Economics and Policy*, 7, December (www.revel.unice.fr/eriep/).

Bresnahan T., Schmalensee R. (1987) 'The Empirical Renaissance in Industrial Economics: An Overview', *Journal of Industrial Economics*, XX, XV, 4, 371–378.

Brusco S. (1982) 'The Emilian Model: Productive Decentralisation and Social Integration', *Cambridge Journal of Economics*, 6, 167–184.

Brusoni S., Malerba F. (2007) *Perspectives on Innovation*, Cambridge, Cambridge University Press.

Bugamelli M., Schivardi F., Zizza R. (2009) 'The Euro and Firm Restructuring', Bank of Italy, 'Temi discussione', n. 716, Rome, June; the work has been published in: Alesina A., Giavazzi F. (eds) (2009) *Europe and the Euro*, Chicago, University of Chicago Press.

Causo S., Costa S., Luchetti F., Monducci R., Rossetti S. (2014) 'L'internazionalizzazione delle imprese manifatturiere italiane durante la crisi: vincitori e vinti nel mercato globale', *L'industria*, 1, January/March, 3–27.

Council of the European Union (2004) Council Regulation (EC) No. 139/2004 of 20 January on the Control of Concentrations between Undertakings (the EC Merger Regulation) (www.eur-lex.europa.eu).

CsC (Centro studi Confindustria) (2006) 'Produttività e attrattività del Paese: i nodi da sciogliere', *Quaderni di ricerca*, December.

CsC (Centro studi Confindustria) (2008) 'Cambiare per crescere: la performance del Paese nel contesto internazionale', *Rapporti monografici del CsC*, April.

Daveri F., Jona-Lasinio C. (2005) 'Italy's Decline: Getting the Facts Right', *Giornale degli Economisti*, 64, 4, 365–410.

Di Vico D., Viesti G. (2014) Cacciavite, *Robot e Tablet. Come far ripartire le imprese*, Bologna, Il Mulino.

Economist, The (2007) 'Who are the Champions? A Special Report on European Business', 10 February (www.economist.com).

Eichengreen B. (2007) *Back to Rome?* 26 March (www.telos-eu.com).

European Central Bank (2014) 'Statistics Pocket Book', Frankfurt, September (www.ecb.europa.eu).

European Commission (2001) 'The Economic Impact of Enlargement', *Enlargement Papers*, 4, June.

European Commission (2002) 'Industrial Policy in an Enlarged Europe' (COM (2002)714), Brussels, December.

European Commission (2003) 'Commission Recommendation of 6 May Concerning the

Definition of Micro, Small and Medium-sized Enterprises' (2003/361/EC), *Official Journal of the European Union.*

European Commission (2008) ' "Think Small First": A "Small Business Act" for Europe', Communication from the Commission (COM (2008)394), Brussels, 25 June.

European Commission (2013) 'SBA Fact Sheet for France, Germany, Italy, Spain, and the UK', Brussels, Directorate-General for Enterprises and Industry.

European Commission (2014a) '2014 Autumn European Economic Forecast: Slow Recovery with Very Low Inflation', Brussels, 4 November.

European Commission (2014b) 'For a European Industrial Renaissance' Communication from the Commission (COM(2014)14), Brussels, 22 January.

European Commission (2014c) 'Annual Report on European SMEs 2013/2014: A Partial and Fragile Recovery', Brussels, SME Performance Review, July.

European Commission (2014d) 'European Competitiveness Report 2014: Helping Firms Grow', Directorate-General for Enterprises and Industry, Commission Staff Working Document, SWD(2014)277, Luxembourg, Publication Office of the European Union.

Federal Ministry of Economics and Technology (2010) 'In Focus: Germany as a Competitive Industrial Nation: Building on Strengths – Overcoming Weaknesses – Securing the Future', 'General Economic Policy, Industrial Policy', Berlin, October.

Fontagné L., Mayer T., Ottaviano G. (2009) 'Of Markets, Products and Prices. The Effects of the Euro on European firms', EFIGE Report, *Bruegel Blueprint*, VIII.

Fortis M. (2009) *La crisi mondiale e l'Italia*, Bologna, Il Mulino.

Fortune (2012) 'The Global 500: The World's Largest Corporations', July.

Fortune (2013) 'The Global 500: The World's Largest Corporations', 22 July.

Fortune (2014) 'The Global 500: The World's Largest Corporations', 21 July.

Frattini F., Prodi G. (2013) 'Industrial Clusters in China: Policy Tools for Further and more Balanced Development', *European Review of Industrial Economics and Policy*, 5, January (www.revel.unice.fr/eriep/).

Fukuyama F. (1992) *The End of History and the Last Man*, New York, The Free Press.

Goldman Sachs (2003) 'Dreaming with BRICS: The Path to 2050', Global Economic Paper, no. 99, October (https://portal.gs.com).

Goldman Sachs (2007a) 'The N-11: More than an Acronym', Global Economic Paper No 153, March.

Goldman Sachs (2007b) 'Beyond the BRICs: A Look at the "Next 11"', April (www.goldmansachs.com).

Goldman Sachs (2014) 'The Internet of Things: Making Sense of the Next Mega-Trend', *Equity Research*, 3 September (www.goldmansachs.com).

Huntington S. P. (1996) *The Clash of Civilizations and the Remaking of World Order*, New York, Simon & Schuster.

IMF (2014) 'World Economic Outlook (WEO): Legacies, Clouds, Uncertainties', October (www.imf.org).

ISAE – Istituto di Studi e Analisi Economica (2008) 'Rapporto Isae: Previsioni per l'economia italiana – Comportamenti di impresa', March (see 'Introduzione a sintesi', pp. v–xx, and Chapters 1, 2 and 3, pp. 163–225).

ISAE – Istituto di Studi e Analisi Economica (2009) 'Rapporto Isae: Previsioni per l'economia italiana – Ciclo, imprese, lavoro', February (see 'Introduzione e sintesi', pp. v–xxii, and Chapter 1, pp. 175–189).

Jacquemin A. (1987) *The New Industrial Organization. Market Forces and Strategic Behavior*, Cambridge, MA, MIT Press, 167–212.

Jacquemin A. (1991) 'Prefazione all'edizione italiana', in J. Tirole, *Teoria dell'organizzazione industriale*, Milano, Hoepli (XXI–XIV).

Jacquemin A., Slade M. E. (1989) 'Cartels, Collusion, and Horizontal Merger', in R. Schmalensee, R. Willig (eds), *Handbook of Industrial Organization*, vol. 1, Amsterdam, Elsevier-North Holland (415–473).

Joint Research Centre and European Commission (Directorate-General for Research and Innovation) (2013) *EU R&D Scoreboard: The 2012 EU Industrial R&D Investment Scoreboard*, Luxembourg: Publications Office of the European Union.

Krugman P. (1991) *Geography and Trade*, Cambridge, MA, MIT Press.

Lombardini S. (1976) *Concorrenza, monopolio e sviluppo economico*, Milano, Franco Angeli.

Marsh P. (2012) *The New Industrial Revolution: Consumers, Globalization and the End of Mass Production*, New Haven, CT, London, Yale University Press.

Mason E. S. (1939) 'Price and Production Policies of Large-Scale Enterprise', *American Economic Review*, suppl. 29, 61–74.

Mason E. S. (1949) 'The Current State of the Monopoly Problem in the United States', *Harvard Law Review*, 62, 1265–1285.

Mediobanca – Unioncamere (2013) 'Le medie imprese industriali italiane', Milano-Roma (www.mbres.it/ita/mb_pubblicazioni/imprese.htm).

Merkel A. (2006) 'Rede von Bundeskanzlerin Dr. Angela Merkel auf dem WDR Europa-Forum am 9. Mai 2006 in Berlin' (www.bundesregierung.de).

Momigliano F. (1975) *Economia industriale e teoria dell'impresa*, Bologna, Il Mulino (2nd edn 1983).

Mosconi F. (2008) 'The Metamorphosis of the 'Emilian Model': A First Assessment', Paper presented at the 11th EUNIP International Conference, University of Deusto. San Sebastian, Spain, 10–12 September

Mosconi, F. (2009) 'The Rise of 'European Champions' in the Single Market: A First Assessment', in J. Kundera (ed.), *Economic Integration in the EU Enlarged: From Free Trade towards Monetary Union*, University of Wroclaw, Cyfrowa Biblioteka Prawnicza (81–118).

Mosconi F. (2011) 'La metamorfosi del "Modello Emiliano": un'introduzione', *L'industria*, 4, October/December, 573–576.

Mosconi F. (2012) (ed.) *La metamorfosi del 'Modello emiliano': L'Emilia-Romagna e i distretti industriali che cambiano*, Bologna, Il Mulino.

O'Mahony M., van Ark B. (eds) (2003) *EU Productivity and Competitiveness: An Industry Perspective: Can Europe Resume the Catching-up Process?* Luxembourg, Office for Official Publications of European Communities.

OECD (2012) 'Looking to 2060: A Global Vision of Long-term Growth', OECD Economics Department Policy Note, 15, November.

OECD (2014) *OECD Factbook 2014*: *Economic, Environmental and Social Statistics*, Paris, OECD, 6 May (www.oecd-ilibrary-org).

Ottaviano G., Mayer T. (2007) 'The Happy Few: The Internationalisation of European Firms: New Facts based on Firm-level Evidence', *Bruegel Blueprint*, 3, November.

Piore M. J., Sabel C. F. (1984) *The Second Industrial Divide: Possibilities for Prosperity*, New York, Basic Books.

Pisani-Ferry J. (2009) 'Foreword', in 'Of Markets, Products and Prices', EFIGE Report, *Bruegel Blueprint*, VIII, viii–ix.

Pisani-Ferry J., Posen A. (eds) (2009) *The Euro at Ten: The Next Global Currency?* Brussels, Bruegel Books.

Pisani-Ferry J., Aghion P., Belka M., Von Hagen J., Heikensten L., Sapir A. (2008) 'Coming of Age: Report on the Euro Area', *Bruegel Blueprint*, 4, January.

Pontarollo E. (ed.) (2011) 'Forum: Quali politiche industriali per il futuro dell'Italia?' *L'industria*, 1, January/March, 125–154.

Porter M. E. (1990) *The Competitive Advantage of Nations*, London, Macmillan.

Pozzi C. (2012) 'Introduzione: la trasformazione strutturale del sistema industriale italiano', *L'industria*, 1, January/March, 3–5.

Prodi R. (1971) *La diffusione dell'innovazione nell'industria italiana*, Bologna, Il Mulino.

Prodi R. (2009) 'Industria pilastro del paese', newspaper article by F. Locatelli, in *Il Sole 24 Ore*, 10 September, p. 2.

Quadrio Curzio A. (2007) 'Europa e Stati Uniti alla prova della globalizzazione', *il Mulino*, LVI, 431, 3, 387–397.

R&S (Ricerche e Studi)–Mediobanca (2008) 'Riflessioni su "Come sta cambiando l'Italia (a cura di R. Baldwin, G. Barba Navaretti e T. Boeri)"', 15 February (www.mbres.it).

R&S (Ricerche e Studi)–Mediobanca (2013) 'Multinationals: Financial Aggregates', Milan (www.mbres.it).

Rodrik D. (2004) 'Industrial Policy for the Twenty-First Century', Harvard University, John F. Kennedy School of Government, Cambridge, MA, September (www.sss.ias.edu).

Roland Berger Strategy Consultants (2014) 'Industry 4.0: The New Industrial Revolution: How Europe will Succeed', *Think Act*, March (www.rolandberger.com).

Rueda-Cantuche J. M., Sousa N., Andreoni V., Arto I. (2013) 'The Single Market as an Engine for Employment through External Trade', *JCMS: Journal of Common Market Studies*, 51, 5, 931–947.

Sabatier P. (2006) 'Europe Faces Globalization: Part I', *Yale Global Online*, 16 May (www.yaleglobal.yale.edu).

Sapir A., Aghion P., Bertola G., Hellwig M., Pisani-Ferry J., Rosati D., Viñals J., Wallace H. (eds) (2003) 'An Agenda for a Growing Europe: Making the EU Economic System Deliver', Report of an Independent High-Level Study Group established on the initiative of the President of the European Commission, Brussels, July 2003 (then published by Oxford University Press, 2004).

Sapir A. (2005) 'Globalization and the Reform of the European Social Model', Background document for the presentation in ECOFIN Informal Meeting in Manchester, 9 September.

Sapir A. (ed.) (2007) *Fragmented Power: Europe and the Global Economy*, Brussels, Bruegel Book.

Schmalensee R., Willig R. (eds) (1989) *Handbook of Industrial Organization*, vol. 1–2, Amsterdam, North-Holland/Elsevier.

Seabright P. (2005) 'National and European Champions: Burden or Blessing?', CESIfo Forum, 2 (www.cesifo-group.de).

Sforzi F. (2009) 'The Empirical Evidence of Industrial Districts in Italy', in G. Becattini, M. Bellandi, L. De Propris (eds), *A Handbook of Industrial Districts*, Cheltenham, Elgar (327–342).

Stigler G. (1968) *The Organization of Industry*, Homewood, IL, Richard D. Irvin.

Sutton J. (1991) *Sunk Costs and Market Structure: Price Competition, Advertising, and the Evolution of Concentration*, Cambridge, MA, MIT Press, 167–212.

Sutton J. (1998) *Technology and Market Structure: Theory and History*, Cambridge, MA, MIT Press.

Sutton J. (2007) 'Market Structure: Theory and Evidence', in M. Armstrong, R. H. Porter (eds), *Handbook of Industrial Organization*, vol. 3, Amsterdam, North-Holland/Elsevier (2301–2368).

Sylos-Labini P. (1975) *Oligopolio e progresso tecnico*, Torino, Einaudi.

Tirole J. (1988) *The Theory of Industrial Organization*, Cambridge, MA, MIT Press.

Tomàs E. B., Munoz C. V. (2009) 'La nova indùstria: el sector central de l'economia catalana', Papers d'economia industrial no. 26, Generalitat de Catalunya – Observatori de prospectiva industrial, Barcelona, Febrer.

Véron N. (2006) 'Farewell National Champions', *Bruegel Policy Brief*, 4, June.

Whinston M. D. (2007) 'Antitrust Policy Toward Horizontal Mergers', in M. Armstrong, R. H. Porter (eds) *Handbook of Industrial Organization*, vol. 3, Amsterdam, North-Holland/Elsevier (2369–2440).

White House, The (2001) 'Economic Report of the President', Annual Report of the Council of Economic Advisers, U.S. Government Printing Office, Washington, DC.

3 Industrial policy and 'models of capitalism'

> When we think of the morality of markets, we think first of Wall Street banks and their reckless misdeeds, of hedge funds and bail-outs and regulatory reform. But the moral and political challenge we face today is more pervasive and more mundane – to rethink the role and reach of markets in our social practices, human relationships, and everyday life.... Altruism, generosity, solidarity, and civic spirit are not like commodities that are depleted with use. They are more like muscles that develop and grow stronger with exercise. One of the defects of a market-driven society is that it lets these virtues languish. To renew our public life we need to exercise them more strenuously.
>
> (Sandel 2012)

Introduction

What can we mean by a 'model of capitalism' in a world without the Berlin Wall, a world that has revealed the coexistence in the Western industrialized countries of at least two forms of socio-economic organization: the 'neo-American model' and the 'Rhine model', to borrow the famous distinction made by Michel Albert (1991a)? What can it mean in the Western world that was moulded between the falls of the Berlin Wall and Lehman Brothers, a period during which the *market* was given the all-powerful function of regulating economic activity and the distribution of wealth, relegating the state to the background?

The devaluation of industrial policy, from the 1990s on, was the progeny of this cultural and intellectual climate. As we have tried to describe in Chapters 1 and 2 though, things have been changing in recent years both in terms of the introduction of new ideas (for example, that which we have called the 'Jacquemin–Rodrik Synthesis'), and in terms of concrete policy decisions (like the programmes for boosting manufacturing put into place both by the USA and the EU). Moreover, the difficult 'European' response to the 2008 economic crisis – described in the final chapter – has brought us towards a more general reconsideration of the respective economic roles of the state and the market. This reconsideration of the state's economic role appears to be particularly significant when looking at the macroeconomic topic *par excellence*: the effects of austerity measures (or fiscal discipline) on growth in various EU nations. This change of attitude should also encompass a microeconomic perspective, taking into account the European policies on competitiveness. It is within this context that a 'new' European industrial policy has been developing, step by step.

After having described the goals (the structural change *à la* Schumpeter) and the substance (knowledge-based investments) of the new industrial policy, we have now reached the moment in this third chapter to place it within the larger picture described above. Our reference points are thus the 'models of capitalism'.

The chapter is organized as follows: in the next section we will illustrate our own overview of the 'models of capitalism', trying to highlight for each model the economic institutions it relies on. Focusing our attention in particular on the EU (the US for better or for worse represents a homogeneous capitalism), in the third section we will proceed posing this question: is there any convergence among the great models that have emerged after the fall of the Berlin Wall, or are the diverging elements still prevailing? While the distinction among the models has often been centred on the financial system (bank vs stock exchange) and/or the welfare systems, it is in the industrial specialization that we find another difference. In the fourth and fifth sections we will try to shed light on the different specializations in a medium-to-long-term view (from the 1980s up to now). The final section draws the conclusions with a reflection on the possibility – in this age in which manufacturing is rediscovered – to converge towards a real 'European' model of capitalism, in which the new industrial policy aimed at increasing 'knowledge investments' will play the role it deserves. It may be a possibility now, after years in which finance and *short-termism* dominated the economic scene.

Capitalism vs capitalism

The literature on the *models* ever since the publication of Albert's book has spread out in all directions. In truth, works of extraordinary importance for understanding the differences that already existed in the Western world (the structures of the economy, corporate governance, etc.) had already been published before the fall of the Wall, even though during this period the debate over economic policy was primarily focused on the distinctions between free-market economies and planned economies. From this perspective, the years of 1989–1990 represent a genuine watershed moment.

Let us therefore return to the question posed in the first sentence of this chapter: what can we mean by a 'model of capitalism'? To our mind, this definition signifies the entire spectrum of institutions that shaped the economic life in our liberal democracies: institutions which on one side support and protect citizens, and which on the other are in place so as to guarantee the proper and efficient functioning of markets. Figure 3.1 offers a schematic view.

The two categories of economic institutions are characterized, as one might imagine, by numerous interrelationships, and when they are well designed, they complement each other. What's more, they share – as can be seen – a common origin.

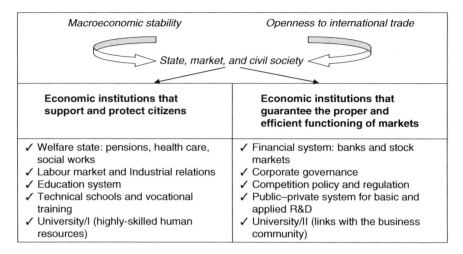

Figure 3.1 A 'model of capitalism': a schematic view.

In fact, all these economic institutions come from the configuration that the state–market–civil society relationship assumes in each given capitalistic system. Experience tells us that it is not an immutable relationship that is established once for all time, nor is it identical across national boundaries; on the contrary it appears to be historically determined and geographically differentiated. Political and economic doctrines evolve; our democracies alternate between governments of different ideological stamps; there are accidents of history, and so forth and so on. All of these contribute to the malleable borders between state, market and society within our 'models of capitalism'.

It is with capitalism that we have experienced 'the great transformation', to quote the title of the seminal work by one of the great thinkers of the twentieth century, Karl Polanyi (1944): the transformation through which social relations came to be defined by economic relations. A look at events from a historical perspective – so goes Polanyi's argument – shows that previous economic systems were *embedded* in the social system, and, thus, relationships of reciprocity, redistribution or for the public good were much more frequent than marketplace relationships. In this original text on the institutional aspects of social organization and on the social backdrop against which economic classes and relationships develop, Polanyi makes clear his diffidence towards one of the basic assumptions of classical and neoclassical political economy: that the 'market society' is a 'natural' evolution of human existence. The 'self-regulating market', which according to Polanyi's analysis is the most important of the four institutions of the nineteenth century (the other three being the balance-of-power system, the gold standard and the liberal state), is 'the fount and the matrix of the system': 'Our thesis [he continues] is that the idea of a self-adjusting market implied a stark utopia.'

Since the years of *The Great Transformation*, almost nothing has changed as profoundly as the relationship between the state, the market and civil society. These changes, associated in particular with the United States, have also consistently (and perhaps in some cases with greater force) affected our Europe. Looking at it from the perspective of production, we have passed from the days of the formation of so-called 'flag carriers' operating under the management of single Member States ('National Champions'), to the massive privatization of public assets and to the birth, within the Single Market, of the 'European Champions' described in the previous chapter. On the other side, implementing the extreme version of an economic system controlled, regulated and directed almost entirely by the market has been exposed as insufficient. In a market economy, the production and the distribution of wealth must be guided by both of the two great mechanisms of social regulation – the state and the market (on the role of the state in free market economies, see, for example, Stiglitz (1989), Chang (1996), Mazzucato (2014) and Velo and Velo (2013)).

These two players, the state with its fundamental job of redistribution and the market with its responsibility for efficient allocation and use of resources, have in fact dominated the economic stage up to present day. The crisis of the welfare state and, more recently, the economic and financial crisis (which has led to a critical reflection about the difficulties of effectively regulating the market), have nevertheless raised questions about the idea of a capitalistic system that is founded exclusively on a market that pursues maximum profit and a state that is essentially relegated to redistributing resources and offering welfare services.

In recent years, a third actor has begun to take on a more starring role on the economic stage: the non-profit or 'third' sector.[1] As a matter of fact, volunteers working in civil society represent a considerable percentage of the economically active population in many developed and developing nations, arriving at 1.5 per cent in Italy, Spain and Tanzania, 1.9 per cent in Argentina and Australia, 3.5 per cent in the United States, 3.6 per cent in the United Kingdom, 3.7 per cent in France and 5.1 per cent in Sweden and the Netherlands (Salamon and Sokolowski 2004). Even more surprising is the purely economic weight that the non-profit sector has in many national economies.[2]

Considering the data and, more generally, the evident difficulty that the classic state–market binomial has had in responding to the problems that characterize modern capitalist economies, it seems clear that the non-profit sector has great importance to free-market economies and models of capitalism, a fact that has already been widely recognized by economists.

Let's return to Figure 3.1. It is true that there is something arbitrary in this two-columned division of economic institutions. Where should we place 'schools' and, more generally, the entire education system? This system does provide a vital source for equal opportunity for all members of a community. But it is equally true that 'human capital', as theories on endogenous growth have demonstrated over the last decades, represents one of the most important factors for economic growth. So while we have placed schools, for the sake of simplicity, in the first category, technical schools, vocational training and universities must also be considered as part and parcel of the second one as well.[3] The university, in fact, must necessarily be placed on both sides of our chart, given its role in formation of highly skilled human resources, and the fundamental contribution that it therefore makes in research and development (R&D), basic or applied, especially in collaboration with the business community.

Overall, the ten institutions that we have identified – and perhaps even this number is slightly arbitrary – can reasonably constitute a kind of set of variables, or a toolbox, for better understanding the 'models of capitalism' that coexist in our Western society, and for observing their evolution. There are two necessary preconditions that must precede these ten institutions in order for any model of capitalism to function well: (i) macroeconomic stability; (ii) openness to international trade.

In Europe – as has been widely discussed in the literature (for a review, Esping-Andersen 1990) – there is no single model of capitalism. It cannot be found at the financial level (stakeholder capitalism vs shareholder capitalism), or amongst the welfare systems (Nordic, Anglo-Saxon, Continental and Mediterranean). Nevertheless, an equally wide intellectual debate has taken place over the possible 'convergence' of different models.

At this point we must pose the following question: might industrial policy represent the Elysian Fields where such a convergence, incomplete though it may be, can come to pass?

Keeping in mind the distinctive characteristics of the new industrial policy (see the Prologue and Chapter 1), we now know which institutions and instruments it can depend upon for its proper implementation. A complication arises, though, from the fact that in the field of industrial policy (in its 'technological' dimension,[4] the triangle's third side treated in the previous chapters) the specific roles to be played by supranational bodies and national governments have not been well defined within the EU. It is equally true, however, that after the 'Lisbon Strategy (2000–2010)', it is now 'Europe 2020' that represents the medium- to long-term plan for the EU to carry out economic and social reforms.

Significantly, within this reform agenda, industrial policy represents one of its 'flagship initiatives'.

Europe and its 'capitalisms': separation or reconciliation?

In the beginning – it was the year 1991 – there was *Capitalism vs Capitalism* by Michel Albert (1991a) where the so-called 'neo-American' model and the 'Rhine' model squared off.

Things hadn't always been this way. It is true that only after the fall of the Berlin Wall and the dissolution of the entrenched dichotomy between free-market and centrally planned economies – or between capitalism and socialism – was it possible to have a more accurate analysis of the models of capitalism. Yet from a historical perspective, a close study of the 'dynamics of industrial capitalism' had already made its mark. We are of course referring to the work of

Alfred D. Chandler Jr, in particular the Chandler (1990) of *Scale and Scope* more than the Chandler (1977) of *The Visible Hand* (in which he analyses the 'managerial revolution in American business').

Analysing the primary institution of managerial capitalism – the modern industrial enterprise – from the 1870s to the Second World War, Chandler identified three models: the 'competitive managerial capitalism' of the USA, the 'personal capitalism' of Great Britain and the 'cooperative managerial capitalism' of Germany. Over this span of time, these three nations accounted for two-thirds of global industrial production.

In this book, one of the most important studies of business history ever published, Chandler examines the specific decision-making processes carried out by owners and managers in the 200 largest manufacturing enterprises from each of these three countries between 1870 and 1940. Of acute interest to our own comparative analysis is one of Chandler's conclusions. He writes (1990, 12):

> The German experience … was closer to the American. German entrepreneurs made the investments and created the organizational capabilities needed to form a number of major industries. But the new large enterprises in Germany were concentrated on the production of industrial goods, whereas those in the United States produced and distributed consumer goods as well. The basic difference between the two countries was, however, that industrial leaders in the United States continued to compete functionally and strategically for market share, while in Germany they often preferred to negotiate with one another to maintain market share at home and in some cases abroad. In the United States managerial capitalism was more competitive; in Germany it became more cooperative. This brand of modern industrial capitalism – *cooperative managerial* capitalism – was one aspect of the arrival in Germany of what scholars have termed organized capitalism.

The same old story, one might say: but it is only after the fall of the Berlin Wall and the 'victory' of capitalism that the theme re-emerged with all its force. Albert's book, as already noted, quickly became the classic work of reference, in which the author argued that capitalism is not a single species, but a Janus-faced creature with its 'two great, contrasting models' (i.e. neo-American and Rhine).[5]

Without embarking on a full summary of Albert's definition of these models, the 'superiority of the Rhine modal' is clearly elicited by the author, a superiority at that specific historical moment in both the 'social' and 'economic' spheres. From the latter point of view[6] and as a final result of what Albert calls the 'virtuous circle of a strong currency', the strength of industrial manufacturing in the Rhine nations comes to the fore. With a strong currency (the mark, though the same could be said of the yen during this period) – he claims – 'businesses are forced to enhance productivity – virtually the only recourse available to them to compensate for the higher cost of their goods abroad'. Moreover, a strong currency 'gives manufacturers a clear incentive to concentrate on top-of-the-range goods, where the selling point is not so much price as quality and innovation, not to mention after-sales service. This in turn requires a long-term commitment to research and development'.

In the end, it is the relative importance of financial institutions that determines the real difference between these two models. This difference, Albert notes, 'depends significantly on the modalities for financing businesses'.

Let's keep the financial system in mind for a moment, for it will take us places: it leads us, for example, to the spot where 'the Bank kneels before the Stock Exchange', to use Albert's comment on the hypothesis of a possible convergence of the two models exactly ten years after the appearance of his *Capitalism vs Capitalism* (Albert 2001).

The author evokes the image of a bank that is 'bound, at least in terms of risk assumption, to bow to the wills of the Stock Market. Europe has started to adopt the neo-American model by which the top executive (manager) becomes subordinate to the shareholder' – at least, he adds, from a 'mesoeconomic' (i.e. forms and functions of the financial system) viewpoint. While on the other side, the analysis of the two models from the 'macro' and 'microeconomic' perspectives give Albert cause for greater caution in predicting a complete convergence of the two capitalisms, given their profoundly different characteristics in the economic role of the state (macro) and the internal organization of enterprises (micro).

In so doing, a key point in Albert's new, updated analysis (Albert 2001) deals with Europe, which 'is still the continent *par excellence* for diversity; not merely historical, geographical and cultural diversity, but also economic and social diversity'.[7] Europe, he continues,

> seeks a balance between three sides of a triangle: democracy, free-market economy and social justice. Other continents only concern themselves with two of these three 'sides'. In America, democracy and the free market to the detriment of social justice. In Asia, social cohesion and the free market, to the detriment of democracy.

The final stage in the evolutionary dynamics of the two capitalisms depends primarily on 'Europe's capacity to move from the monetary union to a political union that will be able to push forward with a reestablishment of the social pact'.[8]

In the decade between Albert's two fundamental works, many events have affected the two great models, the first based on the Stock Exchange's centrality, the second on the 'mixed banking' and its large actors; or, put in a different way, the first essentially interested in the *shareholders'* value maximization, the second designed to satisfy the goals of all persons who have an abiding interest (holders), the so-called *stakeholders'* model of capitalism. These differences seemed to be absolutely accurate; they also seemed capable of determining reliable outcomes in terms of economic results. But then the 1990s came, bringing with them many rebuttals to the claims of the single models as to which one was the best and the brightest.

Adair Turner (2001) in his *Just Capital*, identified five different moments when there was a 'lead change' between these two models in the middle of the

1990s; we have seen many more of these from 2000 to today. We could continue to count the number of times that the baton has been passed from one model to the other: at least, taking Turner's lead, if we refer to the perception that the business community has based on the relative strength and performance of the single models. But we are certain that it would prove a never-ending task.

If, instead, we want to get to the root of things, it is once again the financial system that comes forth as the primary – though not the only – element that fundamentally differentiates the two models. It was against this background that Will Hutton's essay (1996) *The State We're In* enjoyed so much success in England. The nation was coming out of an almost 15-year period of Conservative government which would soon be cut short by the emphatic victory of Tony Blair and Gordon Brown's New Labour.[9] Hutton's essay, written in the tradition of political economy, became required reading for those who, from within the homeland of Anglo-Saxon capitalism (or rather, 'shareholder capitalism'), wished to examine the virtues of the 'stakeholder capitalism' of Germanic (and also Japanese) stamp. Hutton (1996, xxvii) wrote:

> The central *economic* argument is that the weakness of the British economy, particularly the level and character of investment, originates in the financial system. The targets for profit are too high and time horizons are too short. But British finance has not grown up in a vacuum. Behind the financial institutions stand history, class, a set of values and the political system.

The virtues of that 'other' capitalism are stability, long-term investment capability (both by private enterprise and governmental bodies) and social cohesion. Attaining these virtues, so the argument goes, requires both a new blueprint for the financial system and a reform (a 'democratization') of the welfare state. Once again, the financial system serves as the point of departure for moving towards an overarching vision of society, towards a reform plan that, in the words of the author, wanted to be 'neither a return to the bastardised Keynesian corporatism of the 1960s and 1970s, nor the forced march towards a wholly deregulated market'.

In truth, after the initial debates over the different forms of financial systems (bank vs stock exchange) – a debate that was perhaps necessary though not wholly sufficient for demarcating the major differences – there then followed a more general period of examination of all the various economic institutions that shape our industrialized democracies. This widened form of analysis has already been seen in the above thesis of 'shareholder capitalism' compared to 'stakeholder capitalism', even if it is only during the mid to late 1990s that we see the literature move decisively in this direction.

From the volume edited by Colin Crouch and Wolfgang Streeck (1997) we learn that the debate on convergence and diversity between forms of capitalism was already taking place in the 1960s. In fact, a quarter century had passed between the publication of Michel Albert's famous work and that of Andrew Shonfield (1965) – *Modern Capitalism* – which was the first to have applied the dominant 'theory of convergence' to the free-market model. Shonfield argued that capitalist systems have inherently the capacity to organize themselves in markedly different ways and thus to create the types of society that are most in line with collective interests, without technology and markets being seen as *deterministic*. This was the way out of the tight-fitting and stereotypical choice between liberal capitalism and state-owned economy: all countries had the need to create 'non-market institutions' that could regulate the economy.

The key concept that emerged in the literature is that of *institutional economies*: economies where the mechanisms of governance are not merely those that derive from market-driven factors and managerial prerogatives. On the contrary, these mechanisms are modified by various forms of 'social' intervention: 'co-management' (or 'co-determination'), designed to foster cooperation between groups with opposing interests (employers and trade unions); a certain practice of government interventions in the economy; the existence of informal associations and communities (the civil society).

In the 1970s and especially the 1980s, growing evidence was gathered that gave proof of the superiority of institutional economies, those capable of combining competitive behaviour with the creation of collective goods. One of the examples given by Crouch and Streeck (1997) is that of the German automotive industry's training of human capital in order to turn out high-quality vehicles, an initiative that was beyond the grasp of British industry; other equally significant examples can be found within other models of institutional economies: Japan, Sweden and so on.

Nevertheless, in the 1990s there is a change in the perception of the value of institutional economies in terms of competitiveness and performance: Japan and Germany (followed by other nations in continental Europe) entered into a severe recession with rapidly rising unemployment. On the other side, the United States embarked on what would later reveal itself to be an exceptional economic expansion throughout this same decade.

At this point, Crouch and Streeck asked the question: 'Back to convergence?' The question would lead them to discuss the decline, during these years of increasing globalization, of the capacity of the nation-state to regulate the economy: a genuine loss of sovereignty. Fortunately, the same cannot be said about the new mechanisms of governance that have been established at the international level, those of the EU among them.[10]

The final, crucial decade of the 1900s concluded, then, after countless passes of the baton from one model to the other in terms of 'superiority', with the pole position being occupied by that of 'Anglo-Saxon' capitalism: these were the years, especially in the US, of the 'New Economy', relevant here in particular because of its role as the primary cause of the stock market boom.

Before the collapse of dot.com stock values (in March 2001), an event that would effect a deep re-evaluation of the New Economy itself, Ronald Dore (2000), the author of the celebrated *Taking Japan Seriously* (1987) reconsidered the fates of the different models, which were becoming ever more 'mixed'. Dore asks if (and how) these differences were destined to survive in a world driven by the globalization of finance. Using a causal link map ('Neoliberalism and the growing predominance of the financial sector'), Dore argues that shareholder value maximization is becoming 'the only legitimate goal for business leaders'. Admittedly, there are three other 'facilitating factors' that are more directly dependent upon political will: the reduction of state-funded assistance to the elderly; a growing preoccupation with competitiveness; faith in the superiority of the 'Smithian' model for the allocation of resources. The truly important fact resides in the way – again according to Dore – that some of these tendencies are taking hold in Japan and Germany alike: tendencies that were already solidly established in Great Britain and the United States by the 'conservative revolution' of Margaret Thatcher and Ronald Reagan ever since the beginning of the 1980s.

What nations produce, and why

At the moment when the Anglo-Saxon model seemed to have triumphed definitively behind the thrust of the New Economy between the end of the twentieth century and the beginning of the twenty-first century, Michele Salvati (2002) wisely observed:

> We must take pause and reflect before declaring the death of cooperative and controlled capitalism of the kind that Michel Albert defined 'Rhine' capitalism. Perhaps the model toward which we should aspire to converge is not the pure Anglo-Saxon, and certain parts of the 'Rhine' model should be saved.

Then came the years of uncertainty that have dominated the last decades for both models. Large corporate scandals between 2001 and 2002 (above all, Enron, but also WorldCom, Arthur Andersen, Global Crossing, Qwest, Tyco, etc.) shook the foundations of the American stock markets, generating demands for new rules of corporate governance. During those same years, on this side of the Atlantic, the crisis of the large 'mixed' banks in Germany raised doubts about the stolid certainties of many German practices. Again in 2002, three of the four largest of these banks (HVB, Dresdner Bank, Commerzbank) had significant losses; what's more, the insurance giant Allianz suffered the first year of losses in its entire history, precisely because of its acquisition of Dresdner.[11]

Understandably, many things were thus destined to change in both models: Germany – having itself become the 'Sick Man of Europe' for a period of time – would react through a series of profound structural reforms that were able to change many of the economic institutions that shape its model; the wisdom of these reforms has been borne out by the successes of German corporations in international markets over the past five to six years.

On the other side, it is difficult to avoid the impression that the neo-American (or Anglo-Saxon) model during the first decade of the new century was overly enamoured with finance (not the kind beloved by Schumpeter) and short-term gains. This time, just over seven years after the Enron scandal (and others), it would be the collapse of Lehman Brothers that held the mirror up to the defects of the system and revealed the need to correct them.

What, then, has the last decade (2000–2010) left as an inheritance for the new decade we are now living in? If we set aside the arduous path of reforming the financial system in the US and the EU alike (consider all the discussion of a European 'Banking Union') given the different starting points, today the topic that seems to link the two sides of the Atlantic, more than any other, is the *revival of manufacturing* – a revival followed by the logical consequence of renewed interest in industrial policy (or for advanced manufacturing) that we spoke of in Chapter 1.

Might this shared interest amongst the EU and the US for manufacturing and industrial policy represent the catalyst to change the models where necessary, and to have them move towards a virtuous convergence? A debate on manufacturing means bringing in the voices of industries and enterprises (the structure of the former, the behaviour of the latter), while a discussion of industrial policy means pausing for reflection on the role of R&D, technological innovation and human capital.

The topic, unsurprisingly, has already been treated in the literature on models of capitalism.

In the beginning, it was once again Albert (1991a), in the chapter dedicated to 'The Economic Superiority of the Rhine Model' (Chapter 7), who asked: 'How on earth (do) they manage it?'

The answer was the following:

> Let us be clear on one point: the strength of the Rhine economies lies first and foremost in their immense industrial strength, promoted by aggressive salesmanship. That Rhine manufacturing industry is the best in the world is simply not in doubt. Moreover, it occupies pride of place within the national context: in Germany, Japan and Sweden, industry accounts for about 30 per cent of both GDP and total wage-earners; in the rest of the OECD, the figure is below 25 per cent (and in the USA it is under the 20 per cent mark). This superiority, as previously argued, is not just numerical but qualitative as well. Rhine-type countries have established leading positions in virtually every sector of manufacturing from the oldest, most traditional industries to the highest of the high-tech ... True, in certain high-tech industries, the Rhine economies still lag somewhat behind America, the leader, but for how long?

There are three main reasons, according to the author, why the industries of Rhine countries have shown such exceptional dynamism:

i   'They pay close attention to *production techniques*' (quality control, modern management methods, investments in machinery, etc.).

ii   '*Training* is a priority, not a luxury' (Albert cites the vocational education system).

iii 'Company spending on *research and development*' (at a rate of about 3 per cent of GDP). As for this final factor, Albert underlines how 'Rhine governments take a particularly active role in promoting civil R&D projects, often with generous subsidies ... primarily aimed at developing basic technology which can ultimately benefit all branches of industry.'

His conclusion is that:

> Taken as a whole, the industries of Rhine countries are a formidable dynamo, outstripping all competitors. What is more, they are backed up by some extremely effective (and aggressive) sales and marketing techniques. The Rhine countries have thus become the undisputed export champions of the world.

The emphasis on the 'real' economy (which has become popular once again in the wake of the crisis of 2008), was already quite evident in the debate on different forms of capitalism following the fall of the Berlin Wall. The interdisciplinary and wide-ranging Harvard University research project begun in 1992 called 'Varieties of Capitalism' followed similar lines as it brought together the opinions of economists, sociologists and political scientists from both America and Europe. The eponymous publication, edited by Peter A. Hall and David Soskice (2001), was given a noteworthy subtitle: *The Institutional Foundations of Comparative Advantage*.

The 'varieties of capitalism' approach can be seen as an effort 'to go beyond three perspectives on institutional variation that have dominated the study of comparative capitalism in the preceding thirty years' – that is, 'the modernization approach', 'neo-corporatism' and 'the social system of production'. As Hall and Soskice (2001, 1–68) pointed out in the first paragraph of their 'Introduction':

> We want to bring firms back into the center of the analysis of comparative capitalism. Where we break most fundamentally from these approaches, however, is in our conception of how behaviour is affected by the institutions of the political economy ... We think these approaches tend to miss or model too incompletely the *strategic interactions* central to the behaviour of economic actors ... This *varieties of capitalism* approach to the political economy is actor-centred ... The relevant actors may be individuals, firms, producer groups or governments. However, this is a firm-centred political economy that regards companies as the crucial actors in a capitalist economy. They are the key agents of adjustment in the face of technological change or international competition whose activities aggregate into overall levels of economic performance.

For the purposes of their inquiry, the authors focus on 'five spheres in which firms must develop relationships to resolve coordination problems central to their core competencies':

i   industrial relations;
ii   vocational training and education;
iii   corporate governance;
iv   inter-firm relations; and
v   their own employees.

'It follows [they argue] that national political economies can be compared by reference to the way in which firms resolve the coordination problem they face in these five spheres.'

The core distinction they draw is between two types of political economies:

i   'In *liberal market economies* (LMEs), firms coordinate their activities prim- arily via hierarchies and competitive market arrangements' (in short, 'The American Case').[12]
ii   'In *coordinated market economies* (CMEs), firms depend more heavily on non-market relationships to coordinate their endeavours with other actors and to construct their core competencies' (in short, 'The German Case').[13]

After turning the traditional postulate about the relationship between 'institu- tional structures' and 'business strategies' on its head – it is the former that drives the latter, according to Hall and Soskice, and not vice versa – their major step forwards is represented by the introduction of the concept of 'comparative institutional advantage'. If the theories of Robert J. Barro, Gene M. Grossman, Elhanan Helpmann, Paul Krugman and Paul Romer – just to name a few[14] – have helped explain phenomena like endogenous growth and/or the formation of busi- ness clusters, these same theories 'say little about why production of *that* type should be concentrated in *that* particular nation, while other nations specialize in other kinds of production'. Moreover, 'We still need a theory that explains why particular nations tend to specialize in specific types of production or products. We think that such a theory can be found in the concept of *comparative institu- tional advantage*.'[15]

This is where institutional structures come into play, affecting growth rates and technological advancement. In this context, CMEs – the authors argue (pp. 39, 40) – 'should be better at supporting incremental innovation'; on the other hand, 'the institutional framework of LMEs is highly supportive of radical innovation'.[16]

The comparison between the USA and Germany in terms of industrial specialization (making reference to fundamental data on patents) gives solid empirical evidence in support of the authors' initial hypothesis. In reference to the data on 'Patent specialization by technology classes (*United States vs Federal Republic of Germany*, 1983–84 and 1993–94)', Hall and Soskice write:

> The striking finding is that Germany specializes in technological develop- ments that are just the reverse of those in the USA ... Firms in Germany have been more active innovators in fields predominantly characterized by incremental innovation, including mechanical engineering, product handling,

transport, consumer durables and machine tools, while firms in the United States innovate disproportionately in fields where radical innovation is important, such as medical engineering, biotechnology, semiconductors and telecommunication. These patterns are consistent over time and precisely the ones our analysis would expect. There does appear to be specialization in innovation across nations, with firms in the liberal market economy specializing in radical innovation, while those in the coordinated market economy concentrate on incremental innovation.

(pp. 41–44)

Industrial specialization revisited: an update

Twenty years have passed since the above snapshot of the industrial specializations (i.e. technological levels) of Germany and the USA was taken. In the years following the fall of the Berlin Wall, these nations became the emblems of two models of capitalism (Rhine and neo-American, in Albert's terms (1991a)), and of two types of political economies (CMEs and LMEs, in the definitions offered by Harvard academics (Hall and Soskice 2001)).

Much has happened during that time on both sides of the Atlantic.[17]

Focusing our attention on the real economy, some of the most relevant changes have already been addressed in the preceding pages, where we described the results achieved by the process of European integration, the revival (or the *renaissance*) of manufacturing and the new life afforded to industrial policy. The first Communication of the European Commission, the oft-mentioned one from December 2002 (European Commission 2002), already highlighted the need for EU industry to reinforce its position in the 'Enabling Technologies', and this is the common thread that winds its way through each successive Communication until the last one of January 2014 (European Commission 2014). It is worth recalling the comparative analysis done on the more recent policy documents from the EU, from Germany and from the US, and the emphasis that all of these place on certain ground-breaking technologies (see Chapter 1, Table 1.5).

Our examination, in the previous chapter, of the big European players helped shed light on the prevailing specializations in EU manufacturing, which has become a truly changeable landscape; one of the most noticeable signs of this lies in the ongoing consolidation – via horizontal M&As – in almost all sectors of traditional specialization of European industry (automotive, chemical and pharmaceutical, fashion and luxury goods, etc.). There's more. Despite the past and present impact of the most recent financial crisis (post 2008), things are changing in an even more general way.

One of the most detailed report in the series 'EU Industrial Structure Report: Trends and Performance' (European Commission 2011) underlines, above all, 'the role and importance of the EU manufacturing sector', and describes how 'the EU plays a central role in trade of high value added goods and services'. In so doing, their two analyses (technology and trade) make it possible to update/ complete the data presented by Hall and Soskice (2001).

The report has the following to say about the first category (technology):

> The crisis has impacted on the growth potential of EU manufacturing sectors. Nonetheless, large drops in shares of value added and employment in manufacturing sectors does not mean that manufacturing industries have become less important. From a long-term perspective, manufacturing sectors have remained among the most productive in the EU economy. Labour productivity growth per person employed in industrial sectors, from 1995 to 2010, was higher than in the most productive services activities, such as wholesale, retail and financial intermediation. R&D intensity is one of the factors driving higher productivity growth in manufacturing. Among all sectors in the economy, the most R&D intensive in 2006 were manufacturing: *radio, TV and communication equipment*, followed by *pharmaceuticals, other transport equipment* and *motor vehicles*.

The full histogram, which also reflects the comparison between the EU and the US, is published in Appendix III.1. The other sectors operating at the highest level of research intensity, after the four listed above, are given here in decreasing order:[18] *scientific and other instruments, office machinery, chemicals, machinery nec.* And so, what *is* the fundamental difference between the EU and the US? The European Commission (2011, 80) data show that the difference lies not only in the well-known aggregate data ('In 2007, R&D represented 1.85% of EU GDP in comparison with 2.67% in the US')[19] but also, in a more entrenched manner, in their sectoral location; that is, the eight most-intensive R&D sectors are exactly the same – in this classification – in the EU and US, aside from a slight variation in rank.[20] The fundamental sectoral difference lies in the fact that in full seven out of eight of these sectors (the top dogs, so to speak), the level of research intensity is decidedly higher in the US. The Commission writes: 'Among the more R&D intensive sectors, there is only one sector where the EU significantly outperforms the US: chemicals.' It is only in the second part of the classification, from the ninth position down, that the EU passes the US in some industries: electrical machinery, refined petroleum, basic metals. It should be noted that once we have descended to these ranks, the general intensity is much diminished, passing from levels that range from 20 to 40 per cent in the top positions to levels no higher than 5 per cent for these mid-ranking positions.

The analysis from a technological perspective continues through the use of two indicators of patents, once again divided up by sectors. The first (PAT1, *patenting intensity*)

> reflects the number of patents in a sector relative to employment. As was the case with R&D, these vary substantially across sectors, from the highest value in two ICT sectors (office machinery and telecommunication equipment) to the near negligible value for clothing, wood and wood products, and printing and publishing.

The second indicator (PAT2) 'compares the performance of EU sectors with the same sectors in the world'. (To give its full comparative view, this diagram is also published in Appendix III.1) In general,

> the results for this indicator show that the EU performs slightly better than the world in a number of sectors. However, the EU specialisation is lower than the world average in a range of R&D-intensive sectors such as ICT industries and pharmaceuticals.

After having illustrated the results of innovation in terms of R&D expenditures ('inputs in knowledge production') and patents ('output indicators'), the 'EU Industrial Structure' (European Commission 2011) report examines, as we hinted before, a second category that is of great relevance to our task at hand: 'International competitiveness'.

First of all, the report makes a point about European leadership in this category, which is all too often ignored:

> The EU, Asia and North America account for about 84% of total world export flows in 2009. Trade among EU countries represented more than a quarter of world trade of manufactured goods in 2009. In comparison, intra-regional trade in Asia and North America accounted for 15% and 4% respectively of world trade with manufactured goods.

Next, the report presents an interesting analysis of 'competitiveness on world markets'. This 'is measured by indices of revealed comparative advantages (RCA)'. In Table 3.1 we have provided a summary of the results of the more detailed analysis by the European Commission on RCA (which will, again, be fully reproduced in Appendix III.2).

Table 3.1 RCA (revealed comparative advantages) for manufacturing, EU-27 vs US, 2009[1]

EU-27 RCA	EU-27 *Did not have any RCA*	US RCA
Printing	Computers	Chemicals
Beverages	Electronic and optical products	Pharmaceuticals
Tobacco products	Textiles	Machinery
Motor vehicles	Clothing	Other manufacturing goods
Pharmaceuticals	Refined petroleum	–

Source: adapted from European Commission (2011, 10).

Notes
1 In addition: 'Japan had high RCAs in capital equipment, particularly motor vehicles and machinery. In China, the trade specialisation profile is strongly oriented towards textiles, clothing, leather and furniture; although China also has a high RCA in sectors such as office machinery and computers' (p. 107).

Summarizing the many observations made about RCA, the Commission writes: 'Compared to the EU, the US seemed to have high revealed comparative advantages in the following groups of products in 2009: other manufacturing, computer, electronic and optical products, chemicals, refined petroleum products and machinery, and equipment' (p. 107).

Twenty years, as we said, have passed since the moment when the industrial structures of the two different 'models of capitalism' – or the two different forms of 'political economy' – were identified and explained; we mention again the 'three factors' of Albert and the 'five spheres' of Hall and Soskice. These are structures that, in spite of the significant variations that have been felt by the global economy (ceaseless technological progress, growing globalization, etc.), have shown both a certain stability and a certain resilience in their strong points. The data then and the data now seem to confirm the thesis of a frontier of technological progress that has been secured mainly by the US, while European manufacturing – with the 'Rhine model' at its core – is robust (in terms of overall value added), innovative (in its mix of industries and firms in leading positions) and competitive on the international level (in terms of its percentage of global trade).

What, then, is the road that (still) needs to be travelled in Europe?

In order for it to be successful, is there anything missing from the potential route towards convergence between the different models of capitalism that are found in the EU?

Does the rediscovery of manufacturing, after years (decades) of domination by finance and short-termism, represent the true path?

If the answer is *yes*, as we believe it to be, which of the ten economic institutions – presented above in our initial schematic view (see Figure 3.1) – must be bolstered and/or reformed in order to set out confidently in this new direction?

It is to these questions that we now turn in the concluding section of this chapter.

Towards a genuinely 'European' model of capitalism?

Contrary to the conventional wisdom, in their paper on the 'Dynamics of Scientific and Technological Research in Europe', Dosi *et al.* (2005) argued that the 'European Paradox does not exist'. The so-called 'European Paradox' – they pointed out – 'holds that European Union countries play a leading role in terms of high-level scientific output, but lag behind in their ability to convert this strength into wealth-generating innovations'. Again:

> There is little evidence of a 'European excellence' based on analysis of patenting activity, R&D expenditures, and a range of bibliometric measures of scientific strength. At the same time, one finds evidence of widespread corporate weakness – as demonstrated, e.g., by trade performance and shares of international production in high-tech industries.

Finally:

> Belief in this paradox has led to a situation where European Union support to basic research is virtually non-existent. This correction of the accuracy of the 'European Paradox' leads to suggestions about European Union policy – e.g., less emphasis should be put on various types of networking, and more emphasis on strengthening 'frontier' research and strengthening corporate actors.

In light of the analyses made in the preceding section on R&D and patents, the thesis presented by Dosi *et al.* holds water nearly *in toto*. Is the EU's solution to overcoming these limitations sufficient, founded as it is on the two corner-stones of the 'Europe 2020 Strategy' and the 'Multiannual Financial Framework (MFF) 2014–20'? This is the key question for the years to come.

In the Strategy, as they note at the Bureau of European Policy Advisers (BEPA) of the Barroso Commission, many measures are trying to have a direct impact on the competitiveness of European industry: 'To equip people with the right skills, labour market reforms, setting standards, fostering innovation, embracing new resource efficiency standards.' The MFF, approved by the European Parliament in 2013, contains within it the 'Horizon 2020', the new tool that replaces from 2014 onwards the 'Framework Programmes' (in their seventh edition for 2007–2013) for implementing the provisions of 'Europe 2020', the Bureau rightly argued. But the funds earmarked for 'competitiveness' are precisely those which were cut during the debate on the budget that took place, during the first months of 2013, between the European Commission and the European Parliament. This does not seem to be an auspicious beginning for breaking away from the status quo, and the EU budget – lacking a fiscal capacity, even a limited one, for the Union – seems once again to be a problem. Given its importance, we will return to this topic in the next two chapters.

Pausing for another minute on R&D and more general knowledge-based investments, we have three observations to make. First, we must reiterate this is not merely an issue of financial resources; governance has its role to play as well: who does what in which field and under which authority (from the supranational to the regional or local level, including national governments). Our own proposals for a strengthening of *technology policy* (in a broad sense) support a decisive move upwards in terms of responsibility.

Second, a consolidation of public–private cooperation, in particular for the development of so-called 'general purpose technologies', should be the result of the industrial policy proposals that the European Commission has made since 2002 to the present date – the most recent in particular (2012 and 2014), with its emphasis on the new 'Six Priority Lines'.

Third, in the oligopolistic structure of global industry, the top European companies already play an important role in R&D investments (Joint Research Centre and European Commission 2012, 37–39). Amongst the *Top 1500*, the EU percentage is 28.3 per cent, second only to the US (34.9 per cent) and higher than that of Japan (21.9 per cent). This percentage owes much to Germany, which by itself accounts for 10 per cent of R&D investments in the *Top 1500 companies* world-wide. There is a scale effect in R&D activity that we must always keep in mind: this is what motivated our thoughts on the big players and European Champions. But we should also add that an important contribution can come – bearing in mind the structure of European industry previously depicted – from SMEs, especially wherever they are grouped into industrial districts or clusters (see Boxes 2.1 and 2.2). As we had already pointed out at the end of Chapter 2, the subject of indus-trial localization is hardly new: it gets its origins in Alfred Marshall's (1890) work on England at the end of the 1800s (the 'Marshallian districts'); the subject has since been revisited and updated countless times, notably by Paul Krugman (1991) and in the work of Michael E. Porter (1990) who formulated it in terms of 'com-petitive advantage'. In all of these variants, as is well known, the pressing eco-nomic question lies in the agglomeration economies (a particular kind of scale effect, 'external' to enterprises), while the SMEs that operate as isolated units never seem to be able to reach the same levels of efficiency. As a result, a greater focus by European industrial policy on districts or clusters could represent a useful com-plement to the actions of the big players.

It is difficult, if not impossible, to predict whether or not the famous '3 per cent' objective (R&D/GDP ratio) will be achieved by the EU by 2020, especially since the EU already missed its target in the first round (by 2010, the end of the 'Lisbon Strategy'). What is more certain is the direction that it must continue to move in. If the steps that we have drawn here eventually lead to a happy ending, we will find ourselves inside a model of European capitalism which, with its 'Economic institutions that guarantee the proper and efficient functioning of markets' (the right-hand column of Figure 3.1), will finally have its full integrity, moving even the fourth institution ('Public–private system for basic and applied R&D) to the EU level.[21] This would eventually mean, as it did in the other cases, simply a more rational division of labour with the other levels of government.

The fifth institution on the right-hand side of Figure 3.1, 'University/II: links with the business community' has important connections also with the left-hand side: 'Economic institutions that support and protect citizens'. Do these con-tribute, or *could* these contribute (given the necessary reforms), to the formation of the type of European capitalism we are proposing here, one that is able to meld the best of our traditions? This is the most fascinating and dynamic of the challenges ahead, for it touches the lives and employment opportunities of all our young people of talent. We are only at the beginning (the steps taken so far by European politics on higher education have been inferior to those on R&D and innovation), but it is a challenge that must be met if we are to build a society that embraces the beneficial effects of efficiency and equity.

This is also a challenge that promises reasonable chances for success when we consider the potential within the EU of qualified human capital, an element that tends to get overlooked in political debate. It was the professors from the Harvard Business School, Gary P. Pisano and Willy C. Shih (2012), who offered Table 3.2 in their above-cited book on the need for a 'manufacturing renaissance' in America. Read from a European point of view, it seems rather significant.

Table 3.2 University degree (first) by country in science and engineering, 2004

Country	Science and engineering graduates (total)	Engineering graduates
United States	455,848	64,675
European Union (total)	617,469	212,267
Germany	108,730	26,662
United Kingdom	109,940	19,780
Japan (2005)	349,015	97,931
Taiwan	85,891	46,870
India (1990)	176,036	29,000
China	672,463	442,463
Brazil (2002)	92,040	28,024
Russia (2006)	293,729	131,688

Source: Pisano and Shih (2012, 34).

In their chapter dedicated to the blueprints for a 'National Economic Strategy for Manufacturing', the authors (Pisano and Shih 2012, 130–133) write:

> The United States can only rebuild its industrial commons if it has the right kind of human capital to attract complementary investments in physical, financial and technological capital ... Let's start with the workforce in the areas of science, technology, and engineering ... The data paints a dark picture of how well America is doing producing this kind of human capital. As of 2008 (the latest year for which data is available), the United States produced 10 per cent of the world's undergraduate degrees in science, and 4 per cent in engineering; by comparison, the European Union's respective share was 18 per cent and 17 per cent ...[22] Government policy makers have a mind-set that manufacturing is a good sector for people with less education and training. As a result, the United States – unlike, say, Germany – spends little on training in the specialized skills required for manufacturing. This has to change.

These considerations should not lead us to ignore the fact – as the authors themselves say – that 'the US university system has an extraordinary capacity to train scientists and engineers ... Yet many young Americans are not going into these fields.... The United States has become a net importer of foreign human capital.'

This is a fair assessment of the facts, just as it is safe to say that American universities have cemented their role as leaders in all of the major rankings of the best universities in the world (among the Europeans, needless to say, the best results are achieved by British universities). But this does not cancel out the positive data about the EU as a whole. Rather, a European flaw comes forth from the data above, because they depend primarily on a simple summation of national results, where there is very little actual European role (in the supranational or Community sense).

Along these same lines, Joe Ritzen and Luc Soete (2011, 15) in a wide-ranging and visionary paper argue that:

> Higher education has remained first and foremost a nationally organized and funded activity even though the curricula, the evaluation and accreditation of an increasing number of study fields became internationally organised. Over the last decades students in Europe and beyond have become partially mobile thanks to the Erasmus programs and the Bologna reforms which have made the study load involved in courses and degrees more transparent thanks to the allocation of a common framework of study points. Yet, student mobility and cross-border flows in studies – which are limited in terms of admissions only in a couple of Member states (Austria-Germany, Flanders-The Netherlands, Wallonia-France) – has remained low with the exception of the inflow students in the UK and Ireland.

This being said, it is clear that higher education reforms in Europe are absolutely critical.

Indeed, a European Higher Education Area would provide a positive upward spiral of competition between universities across borders, and would lift trans-national mobility above the very low levels that we find at the moment.

The largest area for which the authors make their recommendations is that of 're-thinking public action on "knowledge investment" ' – i.e. research and higher education. And it is especially in the latter that, in their opinion, the most inno-vative ideas are needed, though they recognize that the issue of research also has its weak points. Ritzen and Soete's proposal for this issue lies in a 'Common Research Policy' as the end goal of an evolution that goes as far back as the ECSC.[23] A common policy that we have described here through the idea of a fully fledged 'third side' of the 'triangle'.

All of this may not be enough – so goes the reasoning that refers to the previous work done by Ritzen (2010a, 2010b) – if the advances made on the research side do not go hand in hand with similarly important advances on the teaching side. The authors (Ritzen and Soete 2011, 16–17) make reference to 'the empowerment of European universities manifesto', which is founded on at least two principles: (i) 'the creation of a European Statute for universities in Europe';[24] (ii) 'a second avenue could be to reward countries if their universities are able to attract students from other EU countries, in such a way that a net inflow of foreign EU students would be compensated for through European funds.... These different proposals should have as final goal to increase higher education student mobility needs to the 20% level "promised" in the Bologna agreement.'

This way, even this fundamental institution (the university) which we have placed on the left-hand side of our graph will come to be managed in an relevant manner at the supranational level through appropriate multi-level governance mechanisms. Moreover, many nations in the EU have chosen to watch and take note of the German example on technical education and vocational training, which has set the true benchmark in Europe. The other socio-economic institutions on this side (pensions, social work, labour markets and industrial relations) by their very nature are deeply rooted in the historical and social traditions of each Member State. It is therefore natural to expect in the near future a coexistence of multiple 'models', especially as regards the welfare state, even though we should not ignore the movement towards 'convergence' in the labour market that is coming about due to the implementation of large-scale programmes of structural reform designed by many EU Member States.

For many years (decades, in truth), the most successful theory by policymakers and economists alike has been the following: 'The main industrial policy of the EU is the completion of the Single Market.' No one wishes to deny the validity of this thesis, though in the light of history it does perhaps seem a bit overly reductive. Nevertheless, this is what we have been trying to demonstrate throughout our book. And so the attempt to recuperate a genuinely European vision of the 'triangle of industrial policy' represents, to our view, the primary objective. The weakest side – as we have shown time and again in these pages – is the third, the side of *technology policy*, seeing as how the other two (trade policy and competition policy) have been part and parcel of the *acquis communautaire* for many years.

This *technology policy*, into which we have tried to install all of the necessary elements, can be broken down into the following terms:

i   a pan-European R&D policy;
ii   a pan-European Higher Education policy;
iii a pan-European policy for structural change, which today means a policy that favours key production technologies (such as the so-called *enabling technologies*) rather than a policy for specific industries.

The first two policies – ever more critical in markets that are not 'perfect', but where the role of endogenous technical change prevails – would thus become truly supranational. The third should also be handled at the Community level, as the European Commission Communications have been proposing for more than a decade (2002–2014), ever since the Commission justly returned industrial policy to the top of its policy agenda. The rationale is to overcome the relative weakness of European industry in technological progress, even though the EU boasts a manufacturing capacity that still plays a leading role on the global level (both in terms of its percentage of total production and for its leading position in many sectors that demand medium to high levels of technological competency).

If we can reasonably expect a growing consensus in favour of the first two policies, the third policy remains a more complicated issue where battles – ideological above all – between those in favour and those against industrial policy are destined to be fought. The lesson of Ha-Joon Chang (1996) is worth recalling. The Cambridge professor offered his own definition of industrial policy, motivated by a methodological consideration: avoiding definitions that 'tend to be too overloaded'. Chang wrote (1996, 60):

We propose to define industrial policy as a policy aimed at *particular industries* (and firms as their components) to achieve the outcomes that are *perceived by the state* to be *efficient* for *the economy as a whole*. This definition is close to what is usually called 'selective industrial policy' (for example, by Lindbeck, 1981).

In today's world, can we replace 'particular industries' with 'enabling technologies' (or 'general purpose technologies'), and 'the state' with 'the EU'? If the answer is *yes*, we will have taken a step forward towards the construction (or reinforcement) of the third side. This goal no doubt demands the greater emphasis that is given today (compared to nearly 20 years ago) to investments in education; investments that at that time were excluded from the definition of 'selective industrial policy', but which together with R&D spending make up the knowledge-based investments of today.

Figure 3.2 – the 'triangle' with details on the three components of *technology policy* – maps out the recommended course.

This entire project remains partially unresolved, though, due to the problem of resources, which is no small matter. The relevant document is the 'MFF 2014–2020', about which the European Parliament adopted a resolution on 3 July 2013 by a wide majority. In the words of the Barroso Commission's Financial Programming and Budget Commissioner, J. Lewandowski: 'Today ... the European Parliament has opened the way for putting in place a seven year

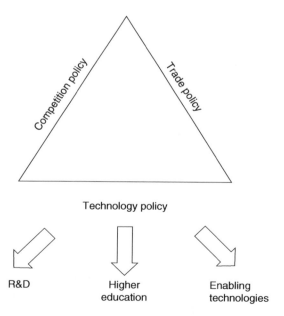

Figure 3.2 The European industrial policy 'triangle': strengthening the 'third side'.

growth and jobs fund worth almost 1,000 billion Euros for the next 7 years' (European Commission 2013). It is no easy task to wade quickly through this complicated document, and a deeper analysis will be needed in the near future in order to identify all of the means by which the investments and programmes listed above will be financed.

Nevertheless, the opinions on this new 'MFF 2014–2020' have not been particularly sanguine, starting immediately after the European Council of February 2013 during which, after the usual marathon rounds of negotiations, the heads of state came to an agreement about the budget. Some of the most important observers of European affairs – three Brussels-based think-tanks – made the following judgements: (i) Bruegel spoke of the 'same old Europe' and of the deal as a 'missed opportunity' (Marzinotto 2013); (ii) the CEPS of 'a smaller EU budget: Less is not more' (Ferrer and Gros 2013); and, finally, (iii) the EPC of an 'agreement, but at a price' (Zuleeg 2013). These initial analyses have also shed light on the amount of funds destined, on one side, to 'competitiveness' (an umbrella topic for many of the items directly linked to the 'Europe 2020 Strategy') and, on the other, to 'rural funds' and 'cohesion funds'. Overall – they argued – agriculture once again absorbs the majority of the budget.

These analyses beg us to make one additional comment: breaking away from the status quo is a truly difficult task in the Europe of our times. And yet, in order to resolve Europe's growth problem, the one we have been trapped in for many years (decades), this is exactly the kind of courage that we need. In a word: getting past the status quo through reforms that are geared towards, as examples: re-launching the 'Sapir Report' of 2003, giving the EU its own 'fiscal capacity', allowing for the emission of 'Eurobonds', at least in the nations of the euro area.

We will take up these issues in the next chapter.

Notes

1 It is not possible to identify within the existing literature a universally accepted criterion that allows us to clearly define the third sector and the organizations by which it is comprised. Various studies and research have offered proposed definitions of the non-profit sector. Along these lines, the study conducted by the researchers at the Center for Civil Society at Johns Hopkins University (see: www.jhu.edu/~cnp/) is of particular importance. In general, the definitions that characterize the third sector in individual nations are the result of different histories and traditions that led to the birth of non-profit sectors in different contexts. Among the various phrases used to express the concept of *non-profit sectors* (itself the prevailing term in the North American context) are: *charitable sector* (terminology developed in England); *philanthropic sector* and *independent sector* (primarily in the United States); *informal sector* (common in the Anglo-Saxon world, this term refers primarily to less-structured organizations of the third sector); *voluntary sector* (Anglo-Saxon nations, Great Britain in particular); and *intermediary system* (Germany).

2 The research carried out by Salamon *et al.* (1999), which takes into account 22 nations both European and non-European shows that the non-profit sector accounts for an average of 3.5 per cent of GNP. According to more recent estimates (Salamon *et al.* (2007) for the period 1999–2004) on eight countries (Canada, United States, Japan, Belgium, New Zealand, Australia, France and Czech Republic) this percentage rises

to 5 per cent. The non-profit sector also showed a rate of growth that was higher than that of the economic system in general (Salamon *et al.* 2007). Within the multi-faceted world of non-profits, a significant portion is made up of cooperatives and social enterprises (e.g. Borzaga and Defourny 2001). These organizations represent a relevant component of many national economies. In 2005 in Italy, where the phenomenon is particularly advanced (Degli Antoni and Portale 2011), there were 7,363 active social cooperatives that employed roughly 244,000 workers and generated roughly €6.4 billion.

3 This line of reasoning for schools can be applied to almost all of the institutions in the left-hand column, such as welfare and the labour market. Inherently important to the idea of equity, they both have an effect at the level of efficiency (consider the relationship between the unequal distribution of wealth and economic growth). Again, the logical place for competition policy (i.e. *antitrust*, state aids, control of concentrations) is on the right-hand side of our chart. It is notoriously the model of perfect competition that guarantees the maximization of efficiency, while monopolies lead to sub-optimal allocation of resources. Nevertheless, how can we forget that *antitrust* legislation was born in the USA at the end of the 1800s when the justly celebrated 'Sherman Act' of 1890 was passed with the expressed goal of protecting citizen consumers?

4 As has already been noted, the situation is different for the other two dimensions of European industrial policy: competition policy and commercial (trade) policy.

5 *Il Mulino*, the Italian leading political and cultural journal, published one of the first in-depth examinations of these contrasting 'models' with essays by Albert (1991b) and Romano Prodi (1991).

6 In particular, the 'economic superiority' is described in chapter 7 (Albert 1991a, 127–146).

7 'Can one therefore speak of a 'European model' as such?', Albert asked himself ten years earlier. His own answer was as follows:

> Everything would seem to point in that direction: the European Community has been under construction for over 30 years; it takes the form of an essentially economic union, regardless of the current debate over political, social, diplomatic or military ties; it is a concrete reality with its own dynamics. And yet there is no single, consistent European economic model.
>
> (Albert 1991a, 17)

8 The evolution also depends on what Albert called – passing to the other side of the Atlantic – 'the sustainability of the American economic miracle'.

9 Highly influential for the evolution of British politics under the Labour government of the 1990s and 2000s, was the book written by Anthony Giddens (1998) on the 'third way'.

10 Other research follows similar lines, confronting the theme of the *convergence–divergence* between capitalisms from different perspectives, such as the case study of Japan (Dore 1987), the institutions of the labour market (Freeman 2000), the allocation of capital (Porter 1992) and business ownership structures (Gros-Pietro *et al.* 2001).

11 The acquisition of Dresdner Bank by Allianz (2001) was followed by the sale of the same German bank (2008–2009) to its 'rival' Commerzbank and a subsequent fusion with the latter.

12 The authors' more complete list of LMEs includes the following: Australia, Canada, Ireland, New Zealand, UK and United States.

13 The authors' more complete list of CMEs includes the following: Austria, Belgium, Denmark, Finland, Iceland, Germany, Japan, Netherlands, Norway, Sweden and Switzerland.

14 For an original account of the revolution in trade theory of the 1980s and the most recent decade, see Helpman (2011).

15 More in depth:

> The basic idea is that the institutional structure of a particular political economy provides firms with advantages for engaging in specific types of activities there. Firms can perform some types of activities, which allow them to produce some kinds of goods more efficiently than others because of the institutional support they receive for those activities in the political economy, and the institutions relevant to those activities are not distributed evenly across nations.
>
> (p. 37)

16 As already noted, the key distinction they draw is between 'radical innovation' and 'incremental innovation' (pp. 38–39): the former 'entails substantial shift in product lines, the development of entirely new goods, or major changes to the production process'; the latter is 'marked by continuous but small-scale improvements to existing product lines and production processes'.

17 We should stress the fact that the Atlantic no longer represents the sole fulcrum of global growth today in the age of rising BRICs and emerging nations. During the 'Asian Century', the one we are currently in, the Pacific has taken on a starring role. For a look at these changes in the global economic geography of development, see the analysis presented in the previous chapters based on data released by OECD, Goldman Sachs, etc.

18 On R&D intensity, the European Commission points out that 'In order to estimate and compare the intensity of innovation efforts in different sectors, R&D expenditure were divided by value added generated in the sector.'

19 The Commission continues: 'The gap [is] mainly explained by private investment in R&D. To analyse R&D expenditure, an aggregate was formed (an EU sample of 17 countries) representing more than 80% of total R&D expenditure in the EU.' So, the different graphs EU vs US published in Appendix III.1 will focus on

> the gross domestic expenditure on R&D (GERD) financed by industry; they do not reflect the sectoral R&D effort by governments. In order to estimate and compare the intensity of innovation efforts in different sectors, R&D expenditures were divided by value added generated in the sector.
>
> (p. 80)

20 As an example, *scientific and other instruments* is the US sector with the highest R&D, while it is only fourth in the EU ranking; another example is office machinery, which comes in fourth in the US and sixth in the EU.

21 The first two institutions in this schematic view of 'models of capitalism' are already involved in the important decisions being taken by the EU on the 'Banking Union', as well as (in international forums: the G20 and others) on the rules of 'Corporate governance'; the third, 'Competition policy', has been supranational ever since the Treaty of Rome.

22 China's respective share – they added – 'was 18 percent and 34 percent, and the rest of Asia was 26 percent and 17 percent'.

23 They mention as European achievements/instruments on the 'research side': the (subsequent) European Framework Programmes, the European Science Foundation, the European Research Council and the European Institute of Technology.

24 Under such a scheme (a Statute) 'around 10% of the universities of individual member countries of the EU would be governed and financed through European funds and by EU legislation by 2020'.

References

Albert M. (1991a) *Capitalisme contre Capitalisme*, Paris, Seuil (US edition: *Capitalism vs. Capitalism: How America's Obsession with Individual Achievement and Short-term Profit has led it to the Brink of Collapse*, New York, Four Wall Eight Windows, 1993).

Albert M. (1991b) 'L'economia dopo la fine della storia', *il Mulino*, 1, 14–20.

Albert M. (2001) 'Capitalismo contro capitalism: Dieci anni dopo', in V. Castronovo (ed.), *Storia dell'economia mondiale*, vol. 6, *Nuovi equilibri in un mercato globale*, Roma-Bari, Laterza (259–276) (see also: *il Mulino*, 3/2001, 383–395).

Borzaga C., Defourny J. (eds) (2001) *The Emergence of Social Enterprises*, London, Routledge.

Chandler A. Jr (1977) *The Visible Hand: The Managerial Revolution in American Business*, Cambridge, MA, Harvard University Press.

Chandler A. Jr (1990) *Scale and Scope: The Dynamics of Industrial Capitalism*, Cambridge, MA, Harvard University Press.

Chang H.-J. (1996) *The Political Economy of Industrial Policy*, Basingstoke, Macmillan.

Crouch C., Streeck W. (1997) *Political Economy of Modern Capitalism: Mapping Convergence and Diversity*, London, Sage.

Degli Antoni G., Portale E. (2011) 'The Effect of Corporate Social Responsibility on Social Capital Creation: An Empirical Study on Participation in Social Cooperatives', *Nonprofit and Voluntary Sector Quarterly*, 40, 566–582.

Dore R. (1987) *Taking Japan Seriously: A Confucian Perspective on Leading Economic Issues*, London, Athlone Press.

Dore R. (2000) *Stock Market Capitalism: Welfare Capitalism: Japan and Germany versus the Anglo-Saxons*, Oxford, Oxford University Press.

Dosi G., Llerena P., Sylos Labini M. (2005) 'Science–Technology–Industry Links and the 'European Paradox': Some Notes on the Dynamics of Scientific and Technological Research in Europe', Pisa, Sant'Anna School of Advanced Studies, May (www.lem.sssup.it).

Esping-Andersen G. (1990) *The Three Worlds of Welfare Capitalism*, Cambridge, Polity Press.

European Commission (2002) 'Industrial Policy in an Enlarged Europe' (COM (2002)714), Brussels, December.

European Commission (2011) 'EU Industrial Structure Report: Trends and Performance', Directorate-General for Enterprise and Industry, Luxembourg, Publications Office of the European Union.

European Commission (2013) 'Parliament adopts Resolution on MFF 2014–2020: Statement by Financial Programming and Budget Commissioner Janusz Lewandowsky', Memo/13/646, Brussels, 3 July.

European Commission (2014) 'For a European Industrial Renaissance' (COM (2014) 14), Brussels, 22 January.

Ferrer J. N., Gros D. (2013) 'A Smaller EU Budget: Less is not More', *Editorial – CEPS News*, Centre for European Policy Studies, Brussels, 26 February (www.ceps.eu).

Freeman R. B. (2000) 'Single Peaked vs. Diversified Capitalism: The Relation between Economic Institutions and Outcomes', NBER Working Paper No. W7556, February (www.nber.org).

Giddens A. (1998) *The Third Way: The Renewal of Social Democracy*, London, Polity Books.

Gros-Pietro G. M., Reviglio E., Torrisi A. (2001) *Assetti proprietari e mercati finanziari europei*, Bologna, Il Mulino.

Hall, P. A., Soskice D. (eds) (2001) *Varieties of Capitalism: The Institutional Foundations of Comparative Advantage*, Oxford, Oxford University Press.

Helpman E. (2011) *Understanding Global Trade*, Cambridge, MA, Belknap Press of Harvard University Press.

Hutton W. (1996) *The State We're In*, London, Vintage.

Joint Research Centre and European Commission (2013) *EU R&D Scoreboard: The 2012 EU Industrial R&D Investment Scoreboard*, JRC and D-G for Research and Innovation, Luxembourg, Publications Office of the European Union (www.jrc.ec.europa.eu/).

Krugman P. (1991) *Geography and Trade*, Cambridge, MA, MIT Press.

Marshall A. (1890) *Principles of Economics*, London, Macmillan.

Marzinotto B. (2013) 'Same old Europe', *Prospect Magazine*, 14 February (www.bruegel.org).

Mazzucato M. (2014) *The Entrepreneurial State: Debunking Public vs. Private Sector Myths*, revd edn, London, Anthem Press.

Pisano G., Shih W. (2012) *Producing Prosperity: Why America needs a Manufacturing Renaissance*, Cambridge, MA, Harvard Business Review Press.

Polanyi K. (1944) *The Great Transformation*, New York, Rinehart.

Porter M. E. (1990) *The Competitive Advantage of Nations*, Basingstoke, Macmillan.

Porter M. E. (1992) 'Capital Disadvantage: America's Failing Capital Investment System', *Harvard Business Review*, 70, 5, 65–82.

Prodi R. (1991) 'C'è un posto per l'Italia fra i due capitalismi?' *il Mulino*, 1, 21–33.

Ritzen J. (2010a) *A Chance for European Universities*, Amsterdam/Chicago, IL, Chicago University Press.

Ritzen J. (2010b) 'Manifesto: Empower European Universities', Brussels, Expert Group on European Universities Meeting, 15–16 June.

Ritzen J., Soete L. (2011) 'Research, Higher Education and Innovation: Redesigning Multi-level Governance Within Europe in a Period of Crisis', United Nations University (UNU-MERIT), Working Paper Series, #2011-056.

Salamon L. M. and Sokolowski S. W. (2004) *Global Civil Society: Dimensions of the Nonprofit Sector*, vol. II, Bloomfield, CT, Kumarian Press.

Salamon L. M., Anheier H. K., List R., Toepler S., Sokolowski S. W. and Associates (1999) *Global Civil Society: Dimensions of the Nonprofit Sector*, Baltimore, MD, Johns Hopkins Center for Civil Society Studies.

Salamon L. M., Megan H. A., Sokolowski S. W., Tice H. S. (2007) 'Measuring Civil Society and Volunteering: Initial Findings from Implementation of the UN Handbook on Nonprofit Institutions', CCSS-WP-23.

Salvati M. (2002) 'È la rivincita del modello "renano"?' *la Repubblica*, 21 July, 12.

Sandel M. J. (2012) *What Money Can't Buy: The Moral Limits of Markets*, New York, Farrar, Strauss & Giroux.

Shonfield A. (1965) *Modern Capitalism: The Changing Balance of Public and Private Power*, Oxford, Oxford University Press.

Stiglitz J. (1989) *The Economic Role of the State*, Oxford, Blackwell.

Turner A. (2001) *Just Capital: The Liberal Economy*, London, Macmillan.

Velo, D. and Velo, F. (2013) *A Social Market Economy and European Economic Monetary Union*, Bern, Peter Lang AG.

Zuleeg F. (2013) 'The EU Multiannual Financial Framework (MFF): Agreement but at a Price', 'Commentary', European Policy Centre, Brussels, 11 February (www.epc.eu).

4 Drawing the third side of the triangle

Reshaping EU 'technology policy'

No matter how accurate the idea of a gap may or may not be, it has a political effect that should not be underestimated: it is on this basis that new forces in European society are pushing for the creation of a federal authority capable of planning at the continental level the development of industrial production and scientific research, of creating a vast market of public procurements in industries on the cutting edge of technology, and of soliciting and controlling the growth of large firms on an international scale.

The same European industrial leaders, availing themselves of the pessimistic image of Europe's future that has been given credit through the widespread story of the gap, is today ready for an evolution of the original concept of the common market as a customs union toward a political entity that can delineate supranational planning policy over European economies. The importance given to the financing of industrial research and the creation of a market for products of science-based industries by the American federal government has led to a more serious examination of the negative consequences of the existence of a plurality of procurement policies by national administrations, policies that give rise to an inefficient profusion of research efforts in individual nations, and that slow the growth of market sizes.

(Andreatta 1968)

Introduction

The 'Europe 2020 Strategy' is not the first example of the European Union launching an ambitious economic and social reform programme that lays particular emphasis on research and innovation (R&I). The 'Lisbon Strategy' (European Commission 2000) pushed forward by the EU over the previous decade (2000–2010) had already made notable strides in this direction, even allowing for some of its low points. And how could we forget, looking further back to the 1990s, the White Paper on 'Growth, Competitiveness, Employment' (European Commission 1993) written at the behest of Jacques Delors and left to us almost as a sort of intellectual inheritance from the great French president of the Commission?

The previous chapter concluded with a schematic breakdown of the 'Triangle of Industrial Policy' as a whole; in the current chapter, we will pause for greater investigation and reflection upon the third side of that triangle – the aforementioned *technology policy* – which represents the missing link for a complete and contemporary industrial policy.

We will undertake this in the following manner: first (in the next section), we will summarize the issues relevant to this policy coming from two antecedent programmes of the EU, the 1993 White Paper and the later Lisbon Strategy. In the following two sections, we will look into the structure of the new programme for research and innovation – the oft-cited Horizon 2020 programme – and then into a few particularly crucial aspects of the European productive system. Last, we will try to fuse these two analyses: the former of the institutional, governmental side; the latter of the real economic situation. At this point we will have arrived at a final question: does the industrial structure of the EU (its manufacturing, in particular) deserve a genuinely European policy (in the sense of it being supranational) in the field of R&I? The final section of this chapter will be dedicated to this question, though we can safely say here at the outset that the answer will be an affirmative one.

Two fundamental landmarks on the European road map to economic reforms

The Delors White Paper of 1993

In the 'Preamble' of the White Paper in question, the following is written:

> We are convinced that the European economies have a future. Looking at the traditional bases of prosperity and competitiveness, Europe has preserved its chances. It possesses assets which it has only to exploit – assets such as its abundant non-physical capital (education, skills, capacity for innovation, traditions), the availability of financial capital and highly efficient banking institutions, the soundness of its social model, and the virtues of cooperation between the two sides of industry.

It goes without saying that time and tide wait for no man, and that everything that was true yesterday – more than 20 years ago – may no longer be so today, especially when the economic crisis of 2008 and the great recession that followed it is found in the midst of these events. Nevertheless, the introduction to the White Paper is still compelling for the extent to which it was able to pinpoint essential sources for growth, not to mention its extraordinary prescience in making proposals that would invigorate competitiveness and create jobs.

Let it be clear: Western Europe (Maddison 2001; Eichengreen 2007)[1] at that time no longer represented an area where growth in *real gross domestic product per capita* hovered around the exceptional level of 4.0 per cent (*average annual compound rate*), as it had during its pre-eminent period of the first two decades of European integration (1950–1973), when the growth rate went so far as to touch 5.0 per cent in places like Germany and Italy.

Compared to this Golden Age – once again using the calculations made by Eichengreen (2007) on the widely read *Millennial Perspective* by Angus Maddison (2001) – growth in Western Europe in terms of GNP per capita fell to

1.8 per cent as an annual average during the following three decades (1973–2000), less than half its previous value.

The White Paper entitled 'Growth, Competitiveness, Employment', which had an equally engaging subtitle ('The Challenges and Ways Forward into the 21st Century'), was published by the European Commission at a moment when high unemployment (11 per cent)[2] had forced its way to the top of the policy agenda for the Copenhagen European Council in June; it was from this meeting that the Delors Commission was given the task of drafting a White Paper that would lay out a medium-term strategy.[3]

Two fundamental stages in the process of European integration had been accomplished in 1992, just one year before the Delors White Paper. These were: the principle that is most commonly known as 'One Market, One Currency', which was the keystone in the construction of the common market with its four freedoms, itself set into motion by the Delors Commission with its 1985 White Paper (European Commission 1985); and the signing of the Maastricht Treaty, with its indication of the three essential phases for economic and monetary Union that had to be met no later than 1 January 1999. Emboldened by these two accomplishments (which would be followed by a third, the enlargement of the Union to the East, which was at the time only on the horizon), the time seemed right for a frontal attack on the economic challenges of 'competitiveness and job creation', as the White Paper called them.

It is literally impossible in the brief space allowed here to summarize all of the proposals contained in this document, and even less realistic to explain the rationales behind the proposals. For the sake of simplicity, we will stick to two considerations.

The first is that the Delors White Paper is still today an instructive read for anyone – policy-makers, entreprenuers, scholars, etc. – whose business it is to grapple with questions of a European dimension, and, more viscerally, who take the destiny of the 'real economy' – as it has become known since the big crash – as a gravely serious matter. The second consideration is that some of the proposals deserve mention here on a case by case basis because of the lasting relevance or extraordinary importance that they had, not to mention for the forward-looking vision that they still inspire.

It would be naive to suggest that technologies have not changed during this period, nor would it be overly exaggerated to claim that the field of information and communication technology (ICT) in particular has trained our contemporary society to accept (and expect) lightning fast, radical changes over the past ten to 15 years. No matter how visionary the White Paper's position on the 'information society' appears to be from a contemporary perspective (and we shall see in Table 4.1b an illuminating quotation on this score), it was probably impossible for it to predict what has actually happened with the explosion of the Internet and mobile telephony, with the digital revolution that we all are living through and adapting to our existence. These are technologies that, after having changed the lives of people, are already evolving in the direction of an 'Internet of Things' (IoT), a new technological revolution of extraordinary industrial potential.

Taking due notice of this caveat, we now being to take a new look at this White Paper, and we find ourselves in the company of policy proposals that envisioned both tangible (physical) and intangible networks/assets that had the capacity to 'bind' (in the sense of connecting more thoroughly) the economies of the then 12 Member States of the Union, which were shortly to become 15 in 1995: partners who already shared a Single Market (the famous 'Objective 92'), and who were bracing themselves to share – after the signing of the Maastricht Treaty one year earlier – a common currency.

The policy proposals formulated at the time, and which are closer to the core of the subject matter of the present work, can be schematized in the manner shown in Table 4.1a, b and c.

We could obviously cite numerous other chapters from the White Paper, but the extracts summarized in Table 4.1 give ample evidence of a sort of parallelism between some of the most important recommendations of the Delors Commission and that which today is commonly called the 'new' European industrial policy.

This new policy – about which we have spoken at length in previous chapters of this work (Chapters 1 and 3 in particular) – is primarily designed to stimulate 'knowledge-based investments' (R&D, human capital), just as it tries to fuel the creation/diffusion of 'enabling technologies'. Looking closely, those are exactly the investments and technologies that the White Paper called for in now-distant 1993. On the other hand, those same Trans-European Networks (TENs) in the field of transports, energy and telecommunications are of crucial importance in terms of connecting the various protagonists (states, local communities, citizens and firms) of a borderless economic area that has, in the meantime, grown enormous (28 countries with more than 500 million inhabitants). Unfortunately, this same economic area is often fragmented when the time comes to consider the inherent development goals of the TENs. To give a recent example, just think of the uncertainties that have come to the fore in the political life of the EU as a result of the 2014 crisis between Ukraine and Russia, with all of its myriad

Table 4.1a The 1993 White Paper

	Networks	*Priorities*
Development theme I	Information network	Promote the use of *information tech*; provide basic trans-European services; create an appropriate regulatory framework; develop training on new tech; improve industrial and tech performance
Development theme II	Trans-European transport and energy network	(a) *Transport*: combined transport; roads; inland waterways; conventional rail infrastructure; airport infrastructure; seaport (b) *Energy*: reduction of costs by making better use of existing capacities; enhancing security of supply

Table 4.1b The 1993 White Paper: a focus on 'competitiveness'

	Instruments and means	Main aims
Trans-European Networks (Title XII of the Treaty)	(a) Transport infrastructures: *'A financing problem'*. (b) Energy transport infrastructure: *'Towards better utilization of capacities'*. (c) Telecommunications networks: *'Creation of new markets'*.	(a) 'An initial list of projects which are both of Community interest and have the potential to mobilize private economic operators must quickly be drawn up.' (b) 'What tends to be the problem is that private sectors investments are often hampered by administrative constraints. These constraints are above all the consequence of exclusive import and export rights, transport monopolies, limited possibilities to construct and operate gas pipelines and transmission lines.' (c) 'In the not too distant future, the telecommunications networks will be capable of instantly transporting and processing voice traffic, text and images between any location, be they homes, offices or businesses, thanks to digitization techniques and electronic processing of information. These networks will therefore constitute the nervous system of the economy, and more generally of tomorrow's society.'
Research and technological development	Measures by the Member States: • tax credit schemes for research; • to encourage companies to fund research by universities. Community measures and concerted action: • 4th Framework Programme 1994–1998 (research consortia, support for Eureka projects); • new large-scale research projects.	'Research and technological development (RTD) can contribute to renewing growth … A series of conditions must be satisfied: an adequate level of funding; an appropriate range of research activities; and effective mechanism for transferring the results.'
The changing society, the new technologies	(a) The information society. (b) Biotechnology and its diffusion. (c) The audiovisual sector.	(a) 'A common information area' (i.e. information itself, hardware and software, the physical infrastructure, the basic TLC services, the applications, users). (b) 'The creation of new products and highly competitive processes in a large number of industrial and agricultural activities.' (c) 'The audiovisual sector … has an economic importance that is often underestimated as compared to its unquestionable cultural significance.'

Table 4.1c The 1993 White Paper: a focus on 'employment'

	Instruments	Main aims
Adaptation of education and vocational training systems	'*Training – the catalyst of a changing society*' (e.g. Germany and Japan: 'the countries with the highest level of general education and training are the least affected by the problems of competitiveness and employment').	'To develop human resources throughout people's working lives; to develop systems and formulas which provide sound adequate basic training and establish the link between school education and working life; formulas of apprenticeship and in-service training in businesses which allow people to gain skills in the world of work should be developed; cooperation between universities and the business world; to anticipate skill needs correctly and in good time by identifying the developing areas and the new economic and social functions to be fulfilled, as well as the skills required for them.'

Source: adapted from European Commission (1993).

consequences in tow, foremost of which is the safeguarding of energy supplies for many European nations (Italy and Germany amongst them).

Staying with the theme of the TENs, there was another decidedly innovative aspect to the White Paper that deserves mention and that, in fact, is still awaiting its moment to be taken up and implemented: the modalities of financing. It was on this precise occasion that, regardless of the amounts in play at the time (which are inevitably different from what they can or should be today), the European Commission pushed forward for the very first time the idea of Union Bonds. In terms of what should have been, at least in theory, 'Community financing of the Trans-European Networks', alongside the normal financing that came from the total budget of the Community (the 'Structural and Cohesion Funds'), the Delors Commission called for three other sources, which we cite here verbatim: '*EIB (loans); Union Bonds (esp. transport and energy); Convertibles guaranteed by EIF (esp. telecoms)*'[4] (European Commission 1993, 33–34).

For some years now – as we shall see at the end of the final chapter – 'Eurobonds' have been on everyone's lips, which, given the existence of a real single currency, would represent the natural evolution of the Union Bonds along the road of the mutualization of debt – at least at the level of the eurozone. Moreover, during the years immediately following the crisis – an economic tempest in the midst of which the EU, in truth, still finds itself – the idea of strengthening even the role of the European Investment Bank (EIB) is widely shared.

All of these rapidly summarized facts are good reasons for 'returning to Delors' and to the inspiration behind this famous White Paper.

In truth, with the *Jobs Summit* in Luxembourg in November of 1997 – which itself followed upon the heels of a similar initiative undertaken at the G7 level in Detroit – the EU seemed to have reopened the discussion, dedicating this unique summit to the problem of unemployment, which was stuck at a very high level (around 11–12 per cent on average among EU nations), especially when compared to the (barely) 5 per cent level found in the US at that same time.

In line with what had been written in the final Communiqué of the Detroit G7, small- and medium-sized enterprises (SMEs) took their rightful place – which was a positive new development – in the *Presidency Conclusions* of this special summit as well (European Council 1997): within this document, there was even discussion of 'Developing Entrepreneurship' (sections 61–68 of the 'Conclusions').[5] Emphasis was given to the idea of the creation of an administrative, fiscal and social security branch that would encourage the birth of new SMEs.[6] To this end, dedicated funds were made available at the EU level: an allocation on a three-year basis, decided by the European Parliament, of support to innovative SMEs that created new jobs; the funds that the EIB makes available under different forms, among which particular mention should be made of those dedicated to the 'risk capital' of these businesses.

But in the flurry of activity of a united Europe, something had to get lost in the shuffle: the White Paper of President Jacques Delors, which in the years following its publication never received the attention it deserved. Was it because it got necessarily overshadowed by the hefty dossiers related to the birth of the

EMU? Was it because the political and cultural climate – starting from the dominant ideas in the American and European academic worlds – had already started its move towards the *pensée unique* of the 'Washington Consensus'? Was it a combination of the two?

Whatever it may have been, that brief reopening of the debate at the *Jobs Summit* of Luxembourg was never allowed to arrive at its concluding remarks, and the question of the real economy never found enough widespread support to make its rise to the top of the EU policy agenda.

Patience would be necessary. Between 2–3 May 1998 and 1 January 1999 the third (and final) phase of the EMU reached its conclusion, as delineated by the terms of the Maastricht Treaty: the launch of the euro.

Macroeconomic stabilization – or fiscal discipline, however we wish to call it – represents a policy decision that is of absolute consensus within the Union and, in particular, among the Member States that share the common currency (this, in any event, is the way things were during those years; later years certainly tell a different story, but one that would take us too far afield from the work at hand). Fiscal discipline, fixed exchange rates, low interest rates and modest inflation – in other words, a healthy macroeconomic climate – these are what appeared to be the prerequisites for returning to growth and to investments (considering, as regards the latter, how low interest rates can help). This virtuous cycle – balancing the federal budget and boosting growth through new investments – was exactly what had taken place in America under the two Clinton Administrations (so-called 'Clintonomics').

In March 2000, the European Union, at the inaugural edition of what would become a series of 'Spring Summits' dedicated to questions of work and growth, launched the Lisbon Strategy – envisioned for the entire decade of 2000–2010 – which had the ambitious goal of making Europe the 'most competitive and dynamic knowledge-based economy in the world'.

'The Lisbon Strategy' (2000–2010)

It is no simple task to summarize what the Lisbon Strategy has meant for the European Union over the past decade: its ultimate goals, not to mention the hopes for change that it ushered in; the peaks and valleys of its journey through individual Member States and Brussels. A practically limitless literature has already been published on the subject, which we heartily recommend for further reading.[7]

Here, however, keeping in line with the analysis of the White Paper that was undertaken in the previous section, we will limit our discussion to a single, specific topic: can we discover the trail of breadcrumbs that leads from one of these two important economic and social reform programmes to the other?

Let us start from the fact that the gulf in terms of economic performance between the US and the EU, which was already significant at the time of the White Paper, had grown wider, from the level of unemployment (11 per cent vs 6 per cent) to the discrepancy in R&D, in which investments were blocked, even then, at the average European level of less than 2 per cent of GDP.[8] Most importantly, it was the critical indicator of growth in productivity that showed signs of weakness on this side of the Atlantic. In 2001, if the labour productivity level in the US was established at 100, the EU average rose no higher than 78 (see Table 4.2 (European Commission 2002)).[9] Things had not always been this way, though. Table 4.2, in fact, tells a very different story: for a long period of time (1975–1995) the growth in labour productivity in the EU surpassed that of the US, which would only regain supremacy in the mid 1990s, thanks to the role of ICT and the New Economy.

Faced with these data, the Directorate-General for Enterprise and Industry of the European Commission (2002) made a statement in its 'Competitiveness Report' about the widening of the 'productivity gap' between the EU and the US. The CEPS (2002) – a respected think-tank based in Brussels – had come to the same conclusion a couple of years earlier when it spoke about the 'great slowdown of productivity' in Europe. At the macroeconomic level, the primary effect of these dynamics of productivity is – as we know from the analysis in Chapter 1 of the 'Sapir Report' (Sapir *et al.* 2003) – the decisive slowing down of the growth rate of the European economy; at a more detailed level, since the beginning of the 1980s, there has been a complete halt in the process of narrowing the gap between EU pro-capita GNP and its American counterpart.

After productivity, there are two other 'roots' of economic well-being: distribution of wealth and levels of employment/unemployment (see the illuminating analysis by Krugman 1990). The road map for the reforms desired by the EU could not, therefore, remain entirely bound to the New Economy, important as that may be; much less so to a New Economy that for many was synonymous with the (variable) fortunes in the stock market during the dot.com era.

A quick, panoramic look back to this programme – recommended by the European Commission led by Romano Prodi on the cusp of the first Spring Summit – should be sufficient to grasp the much larger plan (European Commission 2000). Table 4.3, by and large, evokes more than one of the typical institutions of a 'model of capitalism' – institutions that we have already seen in Figure 3.1 presented at the beginning of Chapter 3. We can state that the two great general objectives and the relative priorities of the 'renewal programme' launched by Europe in Lisbon, manage to embrace both *competitiveness* and *social cohesion* simultaneously – in other words, both *efficiency* and *equity*.

Table 4.2 Labour productivity in EU Member States, US and Japan, 1975–2001 (average annual growth of GDP/employed person (%), ranked according performance in 1995–2001)

	1975–1985	*1985–1990*	*1990–1995*	*1995–2001*	*2001*	*Labour productivity in 2001 (US = 100)*
EU-15	2.2	1.9	1.9	1.2	0.5	78
US	1.2	1.0	1.2	1.9	1.2	100
Japan	2.9	3.8	0.6	1.2	−0.3	67

Source: taken from European Commission (2002, p. 21, table 1.4).

Table 4.3 A programme for economic and social renewal in Europe

The two great general goals	Priorities
I Conduct economic reform in a manner that makes way for the *knowledge-based economy*	• *e*Europe – a society of digital information for everyone. • Internal market – necessary progresses. • Total integration of financial markets by 2005. • Entrepreneurial Europe. • A European area for research and innovation. • Re-examining the financial instruments of the Community (together with the EIB and EIF).
II Modernizing the *European social model* by investing in human resources	• Build on the values of the European social model. • Employment – our key goal. • Education and training – the best investment. • Social inclusion, not exclusion. • Social dialogue.

Source: adapted from the European Commission's contribution to the special European Council, Lisbon, 23 and 24 March 2000.

The 'Presidency Conclusions' of the European Council in Lisbon (European Council 2000) followed the Commission's lead, adding its own contributions, in particular:

i   the strategic objective for the new decade 2000–2010 was described in terms of 'Employment, Economic Reform, and Social Cohesion';[10]
ii   the 'transition to a competitive, dynamic, and knowledge-based economy' was established as the first and fundamental priority (sections 8–23, 'Presidency Conclusions');
iii and established as the second priority, 'modernizing the European social model by investing in people and building an active welfare state' (sections 24–34, 'Presidency Conclusions').

This is a strategy that is grappling with policy areas that are much more difficult to apply under stringent quantitative limits than things like, for argument's sake, the internal market (directives that must be legally undertaken by each Member State within a certain deadline) and the EMU (five Maastricht parameters that must be respected, once again within a deadline). With regard to the implementation of the Lisbon Agenda, we are speaking of an 'open method of coordination': a softer method compared both to the 'community method' and to the dispositions available to the Treaties.

Nevertheless, some early quantitative targets were established. One of the first of these concerned the labour market and the employment rate, where the strategy called for an increase – we cite directly from paragraph 30 of the 'Presidency Conclusions' (European Council 2000) – 'from an average of 61% today to as close as possible to 70% by 2010'.[11]

A second target was placed for R&D, which was now fixed with greater precision thanks to the work done at the third Spring Summit which took place in Barcelona on 15 and 16 May 2002. At that meeting, the EU decided to significantly increase its efforts

> in order to close the gap between the EU and its major competitors [as is stated in paragraph 47 of the 'Presidency Conclusions' (European Council 2002)] there must be a significant boost of the overall R&D and innovation effort in the Union, with a particular emphasis on frontier technologies. The European Council therefore: agrees that overall spending on R&D and innovation in the Union should be increased with the aim of approaching 3% of GDP by 2010. Two-thirds of this new investment should come from the private sector.[12]

And so, at the beginning of the new century, ten years after the White Paper, the gap with the US had not yet narrowed, nor could it have been otherwise: the R&D investment to GDP ratio that – on average among the 15 nations – was still shy of 2 per cent (1.94) compared badly to a ratio close to 3 per cent in the US (2.7), not to mention the exactly 3 per cent in Japan.[13] Sweden and Finland were the only two Member States that had passed the goal of 3 per cent (3.78 and 3.67, respectively); making it above the mark of 2 per cent were two large nations like Germany (2.52) and France (2.13), as well as Denmark (2.07) and the Netherlands (2.02); two other nations traditionally tied to the German economy turned in respectable numbers in Belgium (1.96) and Austria (1.86); the UK was stagnant (1.86), followed distantly by Ireland (1.21); the Mediterranean nations took up the rear, all of them – with the exception of Italy (1.04) – below the 1 per cent mark: Spain (0.97), Portugal (0.76) and Greece (0.67).[14]

Moving along quickly in our brief excursus, we already know that the EU–US gap will not even have been filled by the end of the decade to which the Lisbon Strategy was dedicated (see the analysis in Chapter 1, as well as Table 1.10, in this context). Its economic and social reform objectives will merge together initially during the so-called 'Lisbon 2' (2005–2010), which focused more heavily on 'growth and employment'[15] to then be picked up afterward, from 2010 on, by the new 'Europe 2020' strategy. Among those objectives, once again we find the 3 per cent ratio of R&D to GDP.

Pisani-Ferry and Sapir (2006), in one of their oft-cited 'Bruegel Policy Briefs', provide an excellent explanation of the failings of governance in 'Lisbon 1' and the new elements introduced into 'Lisbon 2' thanks to the 'Kok Report' (European Commission 2004) – elements that the authors nevertheless consider insufficient to the task.[16]

If we remain on the subject of 'motives for acting jointly', there are two reasons that push countries to coordinate their structural reform policies (Pisani-Ferry and Sapir 2006, 2, emphasis mine):

First [they write] interdependence may render independent decision-making undesirable. This can be either because of spillover effect of national decisions, or because EU policies and national policies complement each other. *Spillovers are clearly at work for research and development*, whose benefit do not remain confined to the spending country.... The second main reason for coordination is that governments and civil societies learn from the experiences of others.

'The *lack of coordination at various levels* of the research and technological development activities, programmes and strategies in Europe' was the second weakness discovered (next to the insufficient level of resources, both financial and human, invested in the Community): a weakness that had been expressly stated in the 1993 White Paper as well. 'There is', the argument continues, 'lack of coordination between the *national research policies*',[17] which is another way of stigmatizing the missed opportunity in Europe for spillovers from the field of R&D.

At the conclusion of the decade, the CER (Centre for European Reform) posed the following question in its tenth and final 'Lisbon Scorecard' (Tilford and White 2010, 3): 'What remains of the Lisbon agenda?' The answer is twofold:

Most countries are closer to most of their Lisbon targets now than they were in 2000. Progress has unquestionably been made ... On the whole, however, the level of progress has been underwhelming. Few member-states have come close to hitting the targets they set themselves in 2000, and the gap between the best and the worst performing countries is arguably wider in 2010 than it was in 2000.

That same year, the London think-tank also compiled its final 'Lisbon League Table' (Tilford and White 2010) as it had done every year since its inaugural 'Lisbon Scorecard I' (Bannerman 2001), and which we reproduce here in Table 4.4a and b).[18] As can be seen, the demarcation line between the 'strong performers' and the 'laggards' is found unsurprisingly between the northern and southern nations, the former already well on their way towards the transition to a knowledge-based economy (as well as being renowned for inclusive and modern welfare states).[19]

Three further comments will help us more fully understand the results of this 'Scorecard' (Tilford and Whyte 2010, 6–7): first, 'If one country stands out as the "chief hero" of the CER's Lisbon scorecard it is the Netherlands. It is the only EU country to combine very high levels of productivity with a high employment rate'; second, 'Two of the new member-states also rank as strong performers: the Czech Republic and Slovenia'; third, 'Every EU member-state could do better.'

Table 4.4a The Lisbon process = C–

Heroes	Austria, Denmark, Sweden, Netherlands
Villains	Greece, Italy, Spain

Table 4.4b The Lisbon league table: overall Lisbon performance

	Rank 2009	Rank 2008
Sweden	1	1
Austria	2	4
Denmark	3	3
Netherlands	4	3
Finland	5	5
Germany	6	8
Ireland	7	6
UK	8	7
France	9	10
Czech Republic	10	9
Slovenia	11	14
Luxembourg	12	12
Belgium	13	13
Cyprus	14	15
Estonia	15	11
Lithuania	16	17
Latvia	17	16
Slovakia	18	18
Spain	19	19
Portugal	20	21
Poland	21	24
Greece	22	20
Hungary	23	23
Italy	24	22
Bulgaria	25	25
Romania	26	26
Malta	27	27

Source: taken from 'The Lisbon Scorecard X' (Tilford and Whyte 2010, 10–11).

Summing up, we can say that the EU enters the second decade of the new century (and millennium) lugging the baggage of a paradox – probably not merely one – which is this: we have an EU that, despite its successes in achieving great things like the Single Market, the euro and Eastern enlargement, is incapable of reaching its potential as a knowledge-based economy. Will the new 'Europe 2020' programme finally be the key for making the leap forward that first the Community and then the Union have been trying to make since at least the early 1990s?

This is the theme to which we will turn our attention in the next section.

'Europe 2020' and 'Horizon 2020'

Within 'Europe 2020: A European Strategy for Smart, Sustainable, and Inclusive Growth', one particular programme stands out above the rest: 'Horizon 2020: The EU Framework Programme for Research and Innovation' (European Commission 2011), as its full title reads.

Europe 2020 represents – in our reconstruction of the facts – the third stage in the process of economic reform, after the White Paper and the Lisbon Strategy, which we analysed in the previous section of this chapter, examining both their high and low points. Even though they are different creatures, not least because of their differing legal statutes, we can claim for both of them that while they do an excellent job of identifying priorities and the needed tools for achieving those priorities, both strategies then suffered in terms of insufficient implementation, at least whenever those priorities spoke of increasing efforts for R&D in Europe and narrowing the gap in this field with traditional competitors (the US and Japan, to which we must today add China). In turn, this insufficiency could be traced back to problems of governance (i.e. who does what, who controls 'ownership' of the process, what is the working method), of available resources (the EU budget) and of politics (the respective roles of the European Commission and the Member States).

Under closer examination, the decade of the Lisbon Strategy – as we showed in the previous section – could itself be divided into two parts (Lisbon 1 and Lisbon 2) insofar as how at the midpoint of the decade, following the 'Kok Report' (European Commission 2004) and an ongoing revision, the EU opted for laying greater focus on its goals of 'growth and employment'. This was the second stage that we summarized above; it is now time to turn to the third, 'Europe 2020'.

As usual, the subtitle of the programme indicates a quite wide-ranging, multi-directional European strategy: 'smart, sustainable, and inclusive growth'. As with the previous stages, we will focus on the priorities and the instruments that are most closely tied to the subject of New European Industrial Policy. It is precisely for this reason that Horizon 2020 emerges as the core subject of this section.

As documented in countless Community publications,[20] Horizon 2020:

> is the biggest EU Research and Innovation programme ever with nearly €80 billion of funding available over 7 years (2014–2020) – in addition to the private investment that this money will attract. It promises more breakthroughs, discoveries and world-firsts by taking great ideas from the lab to the market.

Next: 'Horizon 2020 is the financial instrument implementing the Innovation Union, a Europe 2020 flagship initiative aimed at securing Europe's global competitiveness.'

Finally:

> The EU Framework Programme for Research and Innovation will be complemented by further measures to complete and further develop the European Research Area. These measures will aim at breaking down barriers to create a genuine single market for knowledge, research and innovation.

These short extracts have enough details to allow us to begin to describe this third stage – which in itself calls into play other Community dossiers – and bring our excursus full circle from the 1990s to today.

Our starting point – sticking, as always, to the strictly economic facets of this strategy – is the re-proposal on the part of the Commission of the famous, important 'EU headline target' on research: by 2020, '3% of the EU's GDP should be invested in R&D'. Other targets of Horizon 2020 involve issues such as employment, climate and energy, education and social inclusion.[21]

The choice of method, after establishing the three priorities (those of the sub-title) and subsequent targets (which are 'representative' but 'not exhaustive', as the Commission reminds us), was that of 'putting forward seven flagship initiatives to catalyse progress under each priority theme'. We have already met one of these flagship initiatives in Chapter 1, under the title of 'An industrial policy for the globalisation era', which was primarily concerned with improving European competitiveness on the global scale (European Commission 2010, 15–16).[22]

In this section, though, we must look more thoroughly at another flagship initiative, the one called Innovation Union (IU), which can be found within the first priority of Europe 2020 ('Smart growth – an economy based on knowledge and innovation'). The IU is designed 'to improve framework conditions and access to finance for research and innovation so as to ensure that innovative ideas can be turned into products and services that create growth and jobs' (European Commission 2010, 9–12).[23]

From this perspective, Horizon 2020 – as already mentioned – is the financial tool created to implement the Innovation Union.

Based on the various presentations made by the European Commission,[24] at first glance there appear to be two primary characteristics to its financial aspects:

> the already-cited (*in current prices*) roughly €80 billion in funding for the seven years between 2014 and 2020, equal to the remarkable figure of €70.2 billion *in constant prices or real terms*: this means a 30 percent increase compared to what was found in the last Research Framework Programme (FP7: 2007–2013)[25]

and compared to past FPs, this case offers, 'a single programme bringing together three separate programmes/initiatives'.[26]

A closer examination, still in line with the explanations provided by the Commission itself, reveals the truly distinguishing characteristic of Horizon 2020: the subdivision of its budget into three tracks ('Excellent science', 'Industrial leadership' and 'Societal challenges'). Figure 4.1 shows this budget breakdown, while a table of greater detail is available in Appendix IV.[27]

The analysis of the new EU framework programme for research and innovation (Horizon 2020) could at this point head off in multiple directions (the involvement of stakeholders, rules for participation, international cooperation, etc.). For everything that pertains to the procedural aspects of the new programme (and related *calls for tender*) there is already a wide series of

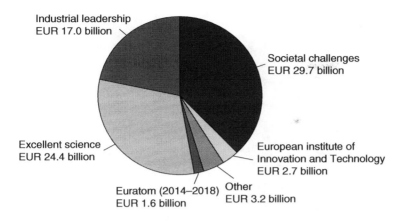

Industrial leadership
EUR 17.0 billion

Societal challenges
EUR 29.7 billion

Excellent science
EUR 24.4 billion

European institute of
Innovation and Technology
EUR 2.7 billion

Euratom (2014–2018)
EUR 1.6 billion

Other
EUR 3.2 billion

Figure 4.1 Horizon 2020 budget (in current prices) (source: European Commission 2014b).

Community publications which we recommend for review. In this section, we will limit ourselves to the link – if one truly exists – between one flagship initiative (the Innovation Union) and another that has piqued our interest (an industrial policy for the globalization era), seeing as how the thesis that we are trying to prove is this: in order for a truly 'new' European industrial policy to come to fruition, the third side of the triangle – technology policy (R&D, innovation, human capital, etc.) – must be completed.

Let's take a step back to Chapter 1, when we looked at programmes such as the American 'Advanced Manufacturing', Germany's 'High-Tech Strategy' and the series of Commission Communications on 'Industrial Policy in an Enlarged Europe' since 2002. Each and every one of these programmes gives a privileged role to certain new technological developments: no longer the (old) industrial sectors of the past, so much as the (new) enabling technologies. No longer, therefore, an industrial policy based on the idea of 'picking the winners' so much as an industrial policy based on the principle of strengthening the scientific and technological capacities of a country (or group of countries, as in the case of the EU). Not even a strictly horizontal industrial policy based on the conviction that the proper functioning of the internal market was in and of itself both necessary and sufficient for bringing about industrial reorganization.

The good news is that the same emphasis on new technological developments can also be found throughout Europe 2020, and therefore from the Innovation Union to Horizon 2020 and even the European Research Area (ERA) itself.[28] In Table 4.5 – much as we have done in the previous sections – we try to summarize the main issues under discussion, beginning from the fundamental documents (first column) and highlighting in each case the relevant new challenges or new technologies (second and third columns), the latter seen either in

Table 4.5 R&D and innovation: the way forward

EU's documents/decisions	New challenges	New technologies
Europe 2020: Flagship Initiative 'IU' (2010)	• Climate change. • Energy and resource efficiency. • Health and demographic change.	—
Horizon 2020 (2011)	7 priority 'societal' challenges:[3] • health and well-being; • food security; • secure, clean and efficient energy; • smart, green and integrated transport; • climate action; • Europe in a changing world; • secure societies.	(i) Frontier research (ERC).[1] (ii) Future and emerging tech.[1] (iii) World class infrastructure (e.g., high powered lasers, high-tech airplanes).[1] (iv) Key enabling and industrial tech (e.g. ICT, advanced materials, biotechnology and nanotechnologies).[2] European companies leading position in key tech such as: (i) health; (ii) food; (iii) renewable energies; (iv) environmental tech; (v) transport.
Research and Innovation as Sources for Growth (2014)	—	—
A Reinforced European Research Area Partnership (2012)	• An open labour market for researchers (the 'fifth freedom' of free circulation). • Optimal circulation, access to and transfer of scientific knowledge.	—

Source: adapted from European Commission (2010, 2011, 2012, 2014a).

Notes
1 From the first priority of Horizon 2020: 'Excellent science'.
2 From the second priority of Horizon 2020: 'Industrial leadership'.
3 From the third priority of Horizon 2020: 'Societal challenges'.

terms of technological developments that should be pushed further, or as fields in which the best European firms already hold positions of primacy.

If these priorities make sense (as they indubitably do) and if there is any consistency between the two flagship initiatives of Industrial Policy and the Innovation Union, then we must think once again about the resources that are effectively available for achieving these ends. We have already seen the budget breakdown of Horizon 2020 for its entire period (2014–2020). Nevertheless, if we want to understand fully the allocation of resources for the third side of our triangle, then we must add to the funds of Horizon 2020 also those that come from other budgetary tracks, such as: (i) Competitiveness of enterprises and SMEs (COSME), (ii) Education, Training, Youth, and Sport (Erasmus+) and (iii) Competitiveness.[29]

An example of this can be located in the current MFF – Multiannual Financial Framework 2014–2020 – for the year 2014. From an official publication of the Commission (2013), written during the mandate of the Barroso Commission and signed by Commissioner Lewandowski, we have pulled the numbers summarized here in Table 4.6.

What should we say in the face of figures that mark such a clear increase compared to even the recent past? First of all, that the Community funds we identified for New Industrial Policy (in its broadest sense, within the budget entry called 'Smart and inclusive growth') are equal to 13.05 per cent of total commitment appropriations.

Second, making a nod to the spirit of the 1993 White Paper, we can also add – from Heading 1a – funds for Large Infrastructure Projects (€2.4171 billion) and for the CEF (Connecting Europe Facility) (€1.9762 billion); the total, though, would not be significantly changed.

Third, the total *would* change dramatically if we added the Cohesion Fund (a subset of Heading 1b with a value of €8.9224 billion).

There remains, though, a final comparison to be made that shows exactly how far things still need to go for real reform: the two funds destined for Agricultural

Table 4.6 Knowledge investment: the basic figure

'Smart and inclusive growth'	€ million[1]	% (of the total)
Heading 1a: *Competitiveness for growth and jobs*	(16,484.0)	(100.0)
• Horizon 2020	9,330.9	56.6
• COSME	275.3	1.7
• Erasmus+	1,555.8	9.4
Heading 1b: *Economic, social and territorial cohesion*	(47,502.3)	(100.0)
• Competitiveness	7,403.4	15.6
4 programmes from 1a + 1b	**18,565.4**	–

Source: adapted from European Commission (2013, 2014b).

Note
1 Commitment appropriations.

Policy (EAGF and EAFRD)[30] in the 2014 budget are valued at a total of €57.7691 billion, a figure that is 40.62 per cent of the total budget and roughly three times the value that we calculated in Table 4.6.

Without taking anything away from the gains made, thanks especially to the increase in the Horizon 2020 budget compared to that of FP7,[31] the least that can be said is that the recommendations of the 'Sapir Report' still remain out of reach. One of the principles, seen in Chapter 1, dealt specifically with the 'mobilizing' of the EU budget, starting from the realization that at the beginning of the current century, the CAP (still) consumed more than 40 per cent of available resources compared to a modest 4 per cent for R&D. Hence why André Sapir and his co-authors proposed to make a significant paradigm shift from the (then) status quo. In fact, they proposed to merge the budget expenditures of the EU 'into three new instruments (or funds)', organized in the following way: a *'Fund for economic growth'* (in percentage of EU GNP: 0.45); a *'Convergence fund'* (0.35); a *'Restructuring fund'* (0.20).[32]

The soundness of the European production systems

Looking at things from a historical perspective, as we have tried to do in the previous sections, a few constant elements emerge. Two in particular: a consistent gap between the US and Europe in terms of total investment (public and private) in R&D; and a growing effort within the EU to set up and implement a pan-European policy in R&I, an effort that has been ongoing since the 1980s.[33]

In this section, we are going to change our point of view in order to look at what is currently happening, now, in the world of European enterprises. From the rankings published in both Chapter 1 and Chapter 2 we learned that all of the main players in the EU – manufacturing countries and European Champions – have maintained their positions amongst the important global producers, though the growth of emerging nations remains undeniable.

We can add another level of performance to this of manufacturing: merchandise exports. Both levels are in fact – as can be seen in Figure 4.2 – excellent for the EU as a whole: its portion of the total is still above one-third, even if the world economic geography has changed dramatically in the last years (and decades) and problematic questions of a related matter certainly still exist.[34]

It is time to dive into an analysis of productive structures (in the broad sense) in order to understand better the position of European nations on the new international scene; with this in mind, we now present three other rankings, all three quite recent: 'The Global Competitiveness Report 2014–2015' (World Economic Forum 2014); 'Doing Business 2015' (World Bank Group 2014); and the 'World Investment Report 2014' (UNCTAD 2014).

The first report – as is widely known – 'assesses the competitiveness landscape of 144 economies, providing insight into the drivers of their productivity and prosperity'. Since 2005, the World Economic Forum has based its analysis on the 'Global Competitiveness Index (GCI)', which brings together both micro and macroeconomic aspects – an index that groups its numerous components

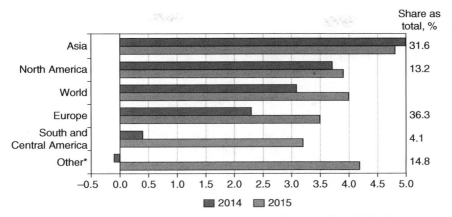

*Africa, Commonwealth of Independent States and the Middle East

Figure 4.2 'World merchandise exports. Forecasts, % change on a year earlier' (source: WTO (quoted in *The Economist*, 27 September 2014, p. 85)).

into the '12 pillars of competitiveness'.[35] The EU boasts five positions within the top ten, as can be seen in Table 4.7; the number one position is itself held by another European nation, Switzerland. It is worth mentioning that the same nations held the same positions in the previous edition of the GCI as well.

European performance continues to be positive even beyond the top spots; after Norway's 11th place, there are three more EU nations in the top 20: Denmark (13th), Belgium (18th) and Luxembourg (19th), all three of which have a score above five. A more controversial position is occupied by France

Table 4.7 The Global Competitiveness Index 2014–2015 rankings (and 2013–2014 comparisons): top 10

Countries[1]	Rank (out of 144)	Score (1–7)	Rank among 2013–2014 economies
Switzerland	1	5.70	1
Singapore	2	5.65	2
United States	3	5.54	3
Finland	*4*	*5.50*	*4*
Germany	*5*	*5.49*	*5*
Japan	6	5.47	6
Hong Kong SAR	7	5.46	7
Netherlands	*8*	*5.45*	*8*
United Kingdom	*9*	*5.41*	*9*
Sweden	*10*	*5.41*	*10*

Source: taken from World Economic Forum (2014, 13).

Note
1 EU countries in italics.

(23rd), while once again it is the Mediterranean nations that are underperforming: Spain (35th), Portugal (36th), Italy (49th) and Greece (81st). Amongst the new Member States from Central and Eastern Europe, we find Estonia (29th), followed by Lithuania (41st), Latvia (42nd) and Poland (43rd), while the others – Cyprus and Malta included – all fall between 47th and 70th place.

Moving along to our second report, 'Doing Business' (World Bank Group 2014), once again in its most current available edition (2015, data referring to 2013/2014), we immediately note its subtitle: 'Going Beyond Efficiency'. This report, which is compiled by the World Bank and is now in its 11th edition, 'assesses regulations affecting domestic firms in 189 countries and ranks the economies in 10 areas of business regulation, such as starting a business, resolving insolvency, and trading across borders'.[36] Does the EU measure up in this ranking as well? Yes, but not with the same strength as in the previous GCI (see Table 4.7); here we need to look at the top 20 in order to have a complete view of the performance of EU Member States. There are a full seven representative economies of the EU in the top 20, a number that rises not insignificantly if we take into account other European nations as well.

Table 4.8 Ease of doing business ranking: top 20

Rank	Economy[1]	DTF score[2]
1	Singapore	88.27
2	New Zealand	86.91
3	Hong Kong SAR, China	84.97
4	*Denmark*	*84.20*
5	Korea, Rep.	*83.40*
6	Norway	82.40
7	United States	81.98
8	*United Kingdom*	*80.96*
9	*Finland*	*80.83*
10	Australia	80.66
11	*Sweden*	*80.60*
12	Iceland	80.27
13	*Ireland*	*80.07*
14	*Germany*	*79.73*
15	Georgia	*79.46*
16	Canada	79.09
17	*Estonia*	*78.84*
18	Malaysia	78.83
19	Taiwan, China	78.73
20	Switzerland	77.78

Source: taken from World Bank Group (2014, 3 and 14).

Notes
1 EU countries in italics.
2 'The distance to frontier score (DTF score) shows how far on average an economy is at a point in time from the best performance achieved by any economy on each *Doing Business* indicator since 2005. The measure is normalized to range between 0 and 100, with 100 representing the frontier.'

Germany, which is among the strongest nations in the world in the rankings on manufacturing and GCI (not to mention its remarkable trade surplus), finds itself *only* (so to speak) in 14th place, followed by Estonia at 17th, leader amongst the Eastern nations. The majority of the Member States are found between 21st and 33rd place, with higher rankings being attained in more than one case by the Eastern European nations compared to those of Western Europe.[37]

We should keep in mind the fact that this study has the express purpose of evaluating, step by step, the 'regulatory reforms making it easier to do business', with indicators that are focused primarily 'on measuring efficiency, such as by recording the procedures, time, and cost to start a business or transfer property'. Given this, it is in the very nature of the study to reward emerging or developing nations worldwide, all of which are in the midst of a profound economic transition.[38] In the category of advanced nations, on the other hand, leadership tends to be found among Nordic and Anglo-Saxon countries, who have long been enacting a vast structural reform process – as was seen from similar results in the Lisbon Agenda mentioned above in the second section of this chapter.

The 'World Investment Report' (UNCTAD 2014) is the third and final document placed under our magnifying glass, and in this case, like the others, our goal is to evaluate the position of EU nations against a global backdrop; in particular, their role in the global flow of foreign direct investment (FDI). The numbers involved in global FDI are astounding, along the lines of $1.5 trillion in 2013, and UNCTAD foresees a steady increase over the next three years.[39] Given the nature of FDI, it is necessary for us to look at the flows in two directions, as the rankings in Table 4.9a and b show.

The report sheds light on the gigantic reshuffling of the cards in FDI flows that took place in recent years on the global scale. The explanation lies, on one hand, in the consequences of the economic crisis (being particularly severe in developed countries) and, on the other, in the continuing economic rise of developing nations (not to forget those in transition). Two summary facts, among the many presented here, can help us get a clearer view.

First, 'Developing economies maintain their lead in 2013', UNCTAD writes.

> FDI flows to developed countries increased by 9 per cent to $566 billion, leaving them at 39 per cent of global flows, while those to developing economies reached a new high of $788 billion, or 54 per cent of the total. The balance of $108 billion went to transition economies.

Second, again according to UNCTAD,

> *Inflows to developed countries resume growth but have a long way to go....* The recovery in FDI inflows in developed countries to $566 billion, and the unchanged outflows, at $857 billion, leave both at half their peak level in 2007. Europe, traditionally the largest FDI recipient region, is at less than one third of its 2007 inflows and one fourth of its outflows. The United States and the European Union saw their combined share of global FDI inflows decline from well over 50 per cent pre-crisis to 30 per cent in 2013.[40]

Table 4.9a FDI inflows: top 20 'host' economies, 2012 and 2013 ($ billions)

	Economy ('recipient')[1]	2013	2012
1	United States	188	161
2	China	124	121
3	Russian Federation	79	51
4	Hong Kong, China	77	75
5	Brazil	64	65
6	Singapore	64	61
7	Canada	62	43
8	Australia	50	56
9	*Spain*	*39*	*26*
10	Mexico	38	18
11	*United Kingdom*	*37*	*46*
12	*Ireland*	*36*	*38*
13	*Luxembourg*	*30*	*10*
14	India	28	24
15	*Germany*	*27*	*13*
16	*Netherlands*	*24*	*10*
17	Chile	20	29
18	Indonesia	18	19
19	Colombia	17	16
20	*Italy*	*17*	*n.a.*

Note
1 EU countries in italics (=$210 billion).

If this is indeed the situation, with FDI flows that are a contributing factor to solidifying the new paths opened up by the globalization of markets, then a comparison of the EU with the US can provide once again crucial information. Amongst the developed economies – or, if we prefer, the industrialized Western nations – there is a neck-and-neck race between the US and the EU. First, the FDI inflows from 2013, where the $188 billion recorded by the US come up against the $210 billion of the seven EU nations that rank in the top 20 (see Table 4.3a), a figure that rises to $246 billion if we include the entire EU.[41]

Let's now turn to FDI outflows where, in 2013, developed economies have a striking lead in terms of foreign investment compared to developing economies ($857 vs $454 billion). The United States (see Table 4.3b) tops the charts with $338 billion, followed at a distance by Japan and China. Nevertheless, the EU still remains the only real contender to the American title: the Union reaches the important figure of $264 billion when we total the investments of all nine Member States that rank in the top 20.[42]

In conclusion of our analysis of these three particularly relevant aspects to the European productive system – respectively, 'Global Competitiveness Index', 'Doing Business' and 'FDI flows' – we can say that each of them shows the fundamental soundness of the productive structures of a large majority of the EU nations. It is certainly true that in more than one case it is the largest and most powerful of these countries that leads the pack – Germany – but this is neither

Table 4.9b FDI outflows: top 20 'home' economies, 2012 and 2013 ($ billions)

	Economy ('investor')[1]	2013	2012
1	United States	338	367
2	Japan	136	123
3	China	101	88
4	Russian Federation	95	49
5	Hong Kong, China	92	88
6	Switzerland	60	45
7	*Germany*	*58*	*80*
8	Canada	43	55
9	*Netherlands*	*37*	*n.a.*
10	*Sweden*	*33*	*29*
11	*Italy*	*32*	*8*
12	Republic of Korea	29	31
13	Singapore	27	13
14	*Spain*	*26*	*(−4)*
15	*Ireland*	*23*	*19*
16	*Luxembourg*	*22*	*3*
17	*United Kingdom*	*19*	*35*
18	Norway	18	20
19	Taiwan Province of China	14	13
20	*Austria*	*14*	*17*

Source: UNCTAD (2014, 4–5).

Note
1 EU countries in italics (=$264 billion).

always nor necessarily so. Fine results have been achieved, frequently enough, by medium-sized nations, and good news also blows in from Eastern Europe and the most dynamic *newcomers* of the enlarged Union.

Conclusion

The overall analysis of all three rankings in the previous section seems to suggest the following conclusion: the Member States of the EU who have the best results are almost always the same. We can go deeper: these results seem to reflect the performance of the nations in the more fundamental ranking, previously cited, of R&D (public and private) intensity in the Member States. For the record, we recall here that – given the goal of a 3 per cent ratio of R&D–GDP and the current European average of 2 per cent – the EU nations can be divided up in the following manner:[43]

1 The two Scandinavian nations, Finland and Sweden, with their 3.5 per cent, are well above the target value, superior to that of the US, and rank almost as high as the best performers from South-East Asia (South Korea and Japan).
2 Denmark and Germany are both quite close to reaching the target.
3 Slightly behind them, around 2.7/2.8 per cent, we find Austria and Slovenia.

4   Belgium, France, Estonia and the Netherlands are all above the EU average, around 2.2/2.3 per cent.
5   Slightly below the 2 per cent average we find the Czech Republic and the two Anglo-Saxon nations (UK and Ireland).
6   With the exception of Luxembourg, all other EU nations that fall between 0.5 and 1.5 per cent are either Mediterranean (all of them, Italy included, around 1.4 per cent) or part of Eastern enlargement (including Cyprus and Malta).

Considering the pivotal role that is undoubtedly played by 'R&D intensity of the Member States' in determining many other results by individual nations (not only the three presented by the rankings, but also, going further back, productivity levels and economic growth figures), the fundamental question of *policy* that has guided us from the first pages of this book comes once again to the fore.

In fact, that which we have previously defined as the *fundamental soundness of European productive structures* – seen, though, primarily in their individuality – could gain immensely from a genuinely European industrial policy, where *industrial policy* should be understood as the completion at the Community level of the third side of the triangle (*technology policy*: R&D, human capital, enabling technologies) to complement the already-existing other two sides (*commercial policy* and *competition policy*).

In the preceding chapters, but also in the present one (in particular, in the previous section), we have seen how the EU has taken some important steps

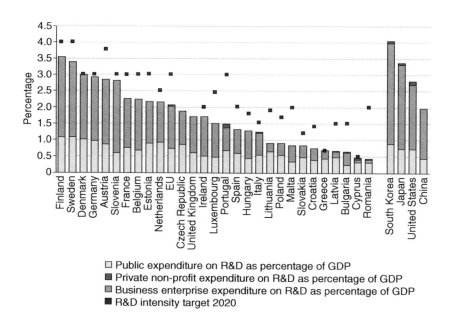

□ Public expenditure on R&D as percentage of GDP
■ Private non-profit expenditure on R&D as percentage of GDP
▨ Business enterprise expenditure on R&D as percentage of GDP
■ R&D intensity target 2020

Figure 4.3 Public and private R&D intensity in 2012 in the Member States, EU and third countries (source: European Commission 2014c).

forward in recent years, while others still remain to be implemented. We mention, in way of an incomplete summary, the Europe 2020 strategy, which has among its flagship initiatives the IU (Innovation Union); the Reinforced European Research Area Partnership; the launch of Horizon 2020, the new project for research and innovation from 2014 to 2020; the final approval of the Unitary Patent; the new Erasmus programme (Erasmus+), etc.

The scientific and technological strengths of Europe, coupled with its traditional cultures, are such as to make speaking with a 'single voice' in this field – even at the global level – an absolute goal that we may hope will be reached within five years' time.

The empirical evidence brought forward here as in other chapters should have demonstrated that the productive and manufacturing base of Europe remains strong and solid, regardless of the growing role of emerging nations and the extreme difficulties faced in the post-2008 crisis period. The industrial policy that the European Commission has tried to encourage through its numerous Communications from 2002 to 2014 runs the risk, however, of remaining nothing more than moral suasion. Like other Community policy areas, what the 'new' EU industrial policy needs most is the the transfer of responsibilities and resources to the supranational level, thereby overcoming the fragmented nature of the individual Member States (responsibilities and resources that often get further fragmented by national and local offices within each country). If there is a single field in our economies – alongside that of capital flows – where megatrends show no regard for national boundaries, that field is in manufacturing: competition in this field is truly global (consider both trade and the FDI flows). All of the rankings we have looked at say the same thing: no single nation within the EU (with the partial exception of Germany from the perspective of quality manufacturing) can face, all at once, the renewed American challenge and the new Asian challenge. But taken together, summing their individual results, the European Union certainly takes its place as a major global leader.

An example can help illuminate the importance of moving responsibilities and resources for business policies – currently in the hands of Ministries of Industry and/or Institutes controlled by single Member States – upwards to the EU level. A European problem that reaches us from the distant past is the inadequate communication between the worlds of research and industry. The Delors White Paper (European Commission 1993, 87) spoke with typical clarity about it. After identifying the insufficient level of spending in research and technological development (RTD) and the lack of coordination between various levels of scientific and technological activity, the Paper writes, 'The greatest weakness of Europe's research base, however, is its comparatively limited capacity to convert scientific breakthroughs and technological achievements into industrial and commercial successes.'

The advancements made so far in terms of *research in Europe* need more than to be simply completed. The impression given is that they also require complementary actions that can be developed in terms of *businesses in Europe*, which, as is well known, are predominantly made up by SMEs, which are themselves often organized locally into Marshallian industrial districts and/or clusters *à la* Porter.

From this perspective, the *Small Business Act (SBA) for Europe* initiative, called for by the EU in 2008,[44] should evolve into something with greater structure, otherwise it runs the risk of remaining mired at the level of a statement of principle (at the Community level) without having the necessary degree of coordination to put into practice the high number of programmes dedicated to SMEs (at the national and local level).[45]

If we play a slight word game with the acronym, the goal should be to transform/evolve the European SBA into something more similar to the American SBA, the Small Business Administration, a federal agency created back in the 1950s. In Mariana Mazzucato's excellent book, she dedicates a part of chapter 4 ('The US Entrepreneurial State') to the timely reconstruction of an exceedingly important SME programme (Mazzucato 2014, 79–83). She observes, crucially, that one of the most significant events of the 1980s was

> the signing of the Small Business Innovation Development Act by Reagan in 1982, setting up a consortium between the Small Business Administration and different government agencies like the Department of Defense, Department of Energy, and Environmental Protection Agency. The act was based on a National Science Foundation (NSF) pilot programme initiated during the Carter Administration.

Mazzucato then goes on to describe this pilot programme, 'the Small Business Innovation Research (SBIR)', which,

> required government agencies with large research budgets to designate a fraction (originally 1.25 per cent) of their research funding to support small, independent, for-profit firms. As a result, the programme has provided support to a significant number of highly innovative start-up firms (Lerner 1999; Audretsch 2003). In addition, the network of State and local institutions that worked in partnership with the federal programmes was expanded.[46]

Notes

1 Maddison (2001) and Eichengreen (2007) give their definition of the 'Twelve Western European Countries' as the following: Austria, Belgium, Denmark, Finland, France, Germany, Italy, Netherlands, Norway, Sweden, Switzerland and the United Kingdom. Their list then continues with the 'Five Countries of European Periphery' (Greece, Ireland, Portugal, Spain and Turkey) all of which were destined, with the notable exception of Turkey, to become Member States of the European Union; the data show, moreover, that these five countries also experienced wondrous growth during the first period (5.1 per cent annual average from 1950–1973), which would then be cut in half during the subsequent years of 1973–2000 (2.5 per cent).

2 In its analysis of the problem, the Commission wrote:

> On present trends, a stabilization of the rate of unemployment cannot be expected before the end of 1994. By that date, more than 18 million citizens could be out of work ... The difference between the unemployment rates currently experienced in the major global economic areas – 11% of the civilian labour force in the

Community against rates of about 7 and 2.5% in the USA and Japan respectively – has given rise to questions about the existence of a specific European unemployment problem ... No hasty negative conclusions ought to be drawn.

(European Commission 1993, 40)

3 In the analysis that follows on the 1993 White Paper we will focus on the aspects that regard competitiveness, so as to remain true to our work at hand. To be thorough, though, we should say that the strategy put forward by the Commission was already based,

> on three inseparable elements: (a) the creation and the maintenance of a *macro-economic framework* which instead of constraining market forces, as has often happened in the recent past, supports them; (b) determined actions in the structural area aimed at increasing the *competitiveness* of European industry and at removing the rigidities which are curbing its dynamism and preventing it from reaping the full benefits of the internal market; (c) active policies and structural changes in the *labour market* and in the regulations limiting the expansion of certain sectors (notably the service sector) which will make it easier to employ people and which will therefore increase the employment content of growth.
>
> (European Commission 1993, 47)

It is not without relevance to note that the necessary balance between these three elements has been lost along the way, to the primary advantage of the first (though also to the third): an unbalance that has since led the entire eurozone – independent of the starting conditions of each single nation – to an excessive emphasis on budget austerity, while the results of the structural reforms of the labour market are more debatable, not to mention very much at the whims of actions by each individual Member State.

4 In the words of the European Commission (1993, 34), the

> *Union Bonds* for growth would be issued on tap by the Union for long maturities to promote major infrastructure projects of strategic interest covering the trans-European networks plus cross-border projects with EFTA, Central and Eastern Europe and North Africa. The beneficiaries would be project promoters (public sector agencies, private companies) directly involved in TENs. The EIB would be invited to appraise and advise the Commission on the overall structure of the financial arrangement and act as agent for individual loan contracts.

5 Along with this, we find three other suggestions in the 'Presidency Conclusions': 'Improving employability', 'Encouraging the adaptability of enterprises and their employees' and 'Reinforcing policies of equal opportunity'.

6 As regards this particular subject (SMEs), it is relevant to note a 'Joint Declaration' – sent to Jean-Claude Junker, who was presiding over the Summit – by the Italian Prime Minister Romano Prodi, the Swedish Prime Minister Goran Persson and the British Prime Minister Tony Blair.

7 In the literature, see as representative works: Rodrigues 2009; the papers of the London think-tank CER (Centre for European Reform) (www.cer.org.uk), which published annually 'The Lisbon Scorecard' in which it divided EU nations into 'heroes' and 'villians' (for the tenth and final edition of the series, see Tilford and Whyte 2010).

8 In chapter 4 of the White Paper (from p. 86 on), we learn that

> the Community invests proportionately less than its competitors in research and technological development (RTD). In 1991, for example, its total public, private, civil and military spending on RTD stood at some ECU 104 billion, compared with ECU 124 billion for the USA and ECU 77 billion for Japan. This was equivalent to an average of 2% of GDP in the Community, 2.8% in the USA and 3% in Japan ... The Community has also proportionately fewer researchers and engineers: 630,000 (4 out of every 1000 of the working population) compared with 950,000 (8 per 1000) in the USA and 450,000 (9 per 1000) in Japan.

9   Breaking down the data, we should add that only a single, small nation, Luxembourg, with an index number of 108, beat the Americans, and that only three others – themselves small to medium sized – scored between 90 and 100: the Netherlands, Ireland and Belgium. The four big nations had less than brilliant showings: UK 73, Germany 74, Italy 83 and France 87.

10 The text from section 5 of this 'Presidency Conclusions' would later become a rallying cry, practically a mantra:

> The Union has today set itself a *new strategic goal* for the next decade: to become the most competitive and dynamic knowledge-based economy in the world capable of sustainable economic growth with more and better jobs and greater social cohesion.
>
> (European Council 2000)

11 The objective continued as follows: 'And to increase the number of women in employment from an average of 51% today to more than 60% by 2010.'

12 After the Barcelona Summit, two Communications by the European Commission were crucial for defining the strategy: 'More Research for Europe: Towards 3% of GDP' (COM (2002), 499 final, Brussels, 11 September 2002); 'Investing in Research: An Action Plan for Europe' (COM (2003), 226 final, Brussels, 4 June 2003).

13 In absolute terms – as the Commission explains in greater detail in the two Communications cited above – this gap in percentage of the R&D investment–GDP ratio is equivalent to an advantage for the US over the EU-15 that 'is already more than €120 million and is rapidly increasing'.

14 All data, both for the three macro-areas (EU, US, Japan) and for the single Member States of the EU-15, refer to the years 2000–2001 and come from the 'Sapir Report' (Sapir *et al.* 2003, 34).

15 This is the second stage of the Lisbon Strategy, following the independent review conducted in 2004 by the 'High Level Group' headed by Wim Kok, nominated by the Commission at the request of the European Council (European Commission 2004).

16 The authors give the following summary opinion about the new system of governance (Pisani-Ferry and Sapir 2006, 1):

> Of the three key changes advocated in the Kok Report, only National Reform Programmes (NRPs) drawn up by the member states made it off the drawing board. The proposals to provide appropriate EU funding to support the Lisbon goals, and 'name and shame' poor performing member states were rejected. The driving force of Lisbon 2 is thus 'ownership' of the reforms.

17 The data presented on this occasion speak for themselves:

> The Community's research budget accounts for only 4% of research spending by the 12 Member States. Even adding the resources allocated to joint European RTD activities in other frameworks (e.g. under Eureka, ESA, CERN, EMBL, etc.), the budget amounts to only 10% or so of the total.
>
> (European Commission 1993, 86–87)

18 'For the purposes of the scorecard we have grouped the main targets under five broad headings: *Innovation, Liberalisation, Enterprise, Employment and social inclusion, Sustainable development*' (Tilford and White 2010, 13).

19

> Those countries that already meet many or most of the Lisbon targets are awarded '*hero*' status, as are those that are catching up at a fast pace. Those that lag seriously behind or have made slow progress are designated as '*villains*'.
>
> (Tilford and White 2010, 5)

20 For example, European Commission (2014b) and, more in detail, 'What is Horizon 2020?' all available online (http://ec.europa.eu/programmes/horizon2020/).

21 In the language of the Commission, the following are the 'EU headline targets' that should be reached by 2020:

> 75% of the population aged 20–64 should be employed. The '20/20/20' climate/ Energy targets should be met. The share of early school leavers should be under 10% and at least 40% of the younger generation should have a tertiary degree. 20 million less people should be at risk of poverty.
>
> (European Commission 2010, 3)

22 We should mention that this is one of the initiatives that gives teeth to the second priority ('Sustainable growth – promoting a more resource efficient, greener and more competitive economy'), along with the one relating to energy ('Resource efficient Europe').

23 The other two initiatives that fall under the umbrella of 'Smart growth' are the following: 'Youth on the move' and 'A digital agenda for Europe'. Rounding out the seven flagship initiatives are the two which remain from 'Inclusive growth': 'An Agenda for new skills and jobs' and 'European Platform against Poverty'.

24 See once again: http://ec.europa.eu/programmes/horizon2020/.

25 The increase when expressed *in current prices* is more than 40 per cent.

26 For example, the 7th Research Framework Programme (FP7), innovation aspects of Competitiveness and Innovation Framework Programme (CIP), EU contribution to the European Institute of Innovation and Technology (EIT).

27 We must immediately point out that the budget, alongside the three primary tracks that are worth more than 90 per cent of the total, also has 'Other' tracks for funds (Figure 4.1 and Appendix IV) related to 'Spreading excellence and widening participation', 'Science with and for society', the role of both the 'Joint Research Centre (JRC)' and the 'European Institute of Innovation and Technology (EIT)'; then there are also the funds that the MFF 2014–2020 continues to set aside for Euratom.

28 The ERA's main purpose is to create a single market for knowledge research and innovation (European Commission 2012), and it will be complemented by Horizon 2020 (e.g. boosting support to ERA priorities such as population ageing, energy security, mobility, environmental degradation, infrastructures, knowledge transfer, policy learning, etc.; stronger partnerships with Member States and private sector to invest more efficiently; taking account of gender, ethical issues, researcher careers and open access to results).

29 Greater detail can be found in Appendix IV.

30 Respectively, 'European Agricultural Guarantee Fund (EAGF) – market related expenditure and direct payments' (€43.7781 billion) and 'European Agricultural Fund for Rural Development (EAFRD)' (€13.991 billion).

31 Over the long haul (1984–2020), growth for the 'framework Programme Funding' has been consistent: from the few billion euros of FP1 (1984–1987) to the more than 50 billion of FP7 (2007–2013). Recent years have shown real acceleration if we consider that prior to FP6 (2002–2006), the level of 20 billion had never been reached.

32 Total 'economic and social measures': 1 per cent of EU GNP.

33 In the year 1984 the first FP was established.

34 *The Economist* commented on the data from the WTO:

> The World Trade Organisation has lowered its forecast for growth in world trade this year from 4.7% to 3.1%, and from 5.3% to 4% for 2015. It blames weaker than expected economic growth and increased geopolitical risk. Both factors have hit Europe, which accounts for a third of global exports, especially hard. Commodity exports from South and Central America are likely to be squeezed as demand from China continues to decline. Although the WTO expects growth in global trade to pick up next year, it will still be below its historical average rate of

5.2%. Continued conflicts in the Middle East and Ukraine, and the Ebola health crisis, pose the biggest near-term risks to global commerce.

(27 September 2014, p. 85)

35 Summing up, the 12 pillars of the 'GCI' are the following (World Economic Forum 2014, 9): (1) institutions, (2) infrastructure, (3) macroeconomic environment, (4) health and primary education (i.e. *basic requirements subindex*); (5) higher education and training, (6) goods market efficiency, (7) labour market efficiency, (8) financial market development, (9) technological readiness, (10) market size (i.e. *efficiency enhancers subindex*); (11) business sophistication, (12) innovation (i.e. *innovation and sophistication factors subindex*).

36

Doing Business continues to focus on regulations that affect domestic small and medium-size enterprises, operating in the largest business city of an economy, across 10 areas: starting a business, dealing with construction permits, getting electricity, registering property, getting credit, protecting investors, paying taxes, trading across borders, enforcing contracts, resolving insolvency ... This year's report introduces a change in the basis of the ranking, from the percentile rank to the distance to frontier score. The distance to frontier score benchmarks economies with respect to a measure of regulatory best practice – showing the gap between each economy's performance and the best performance on each indicator.

(World Bank Group 2014, 2)

37 Italy, among the large EU nations, is once again the one with the worst results, coming it at 56th (Luxembourg, Greece and Cyprus being among the very few who did worse).

38 Not to forget one of the main conclusions of the 2015 edition, a year in which 230 business reforms were recorded worldwide:

Among the 21 economies with the most reforms making it easier to do business in 2013/14, 10 stand out as having improved the most in performance on the *Doing Business* indicators: Tajikistan, Benin, Togo, Côte d'Ivoire, Senegal, Trinidad and Tobago, Azerbaijan, Ireland and the United Arab Emirates. Together, these 10 top improvers implemented 40 regulatory reforms making it easier to do business.

(World Bank Group 2014, 5)

39 As a matter of fact,

in 2013 FDI flows returned to an upward trend. Global FDI inflows rose by 9 per cent to $1.45 trillion in 2013 ... Global FDI stock rose by 9 per cent, reaching $25.5 trillion. UNCTAD projects that global FDI flows could rise to $1.6 trillion in 2014, $1.75 trillion in 2015 and $1.85 trillion in 2016.

(UNCTAD 2014, 1)

40 The values of the outflows still reflect the hierarchy of nations in terms of wealth and productive-financial potential, equal to $857 billion for developed economies (61 per cent) – as the above quotation already pointed out – and $454 billion for developing economies (32 per cent), with the remaining $99 billion for transition economies (7 per cent).

41 The EU has a decided superiority in this FDI flow compared even to each of the BRIC nations, all of which are ranked within the Top 20. The story changes – as has already been mentioned above in our second summary fact – when we analyse, following UNCTAD's example, the so-called 'megaregional groupings'. From this perspective, in 2013, 'developing Asia continues to be the region with the highest FDI inflows, significantly above the EU, traditionally the region with the highest share of global FDI' (UNCTAD 2014, 1).

42 Once again, the EU FDI outflow is higher than both BRIC nations (China and Russian Federation) that rank in the top 20. Moreover, if we add the FDI outflows of the two European nations that are not members of the EU – Switzerland ($60 billion) and Norway ($18 billion) – to the EU value of $264 billion, we reach a total of $342 billion, which would launch Europe into first place globally, just ahead of the US. A true photo-finish, so to speak.

43 The data referring to 2012 come from the recent Communication on R&I by the European Commission (2014a), cited above, which uses the DG Research and Innovation database.

44 The European Commission (2008, 4–5) points out that

> the symbolic name of an 'Act' given to this initiative underlines the political will to recognise the central role of SMEs in the EU economy and to put in place for the first time a comprehensive policy framework for the EU and its Member States through: a set of 10 principles to guide the conception and implementation of policies …; a set of new legislative proposals which are guided by the 'Think Small First' principle …; a set of new policy measures which implement these 10 principles according to the needs of SMEs both at Community and at Member State level.

45 In spite of the emphasis given to the (necessary) ten principles (e.g. 'Create an environment in which entrepreneurs and family businesses can thrive and entrepreneurship is rewarded; Ensure that honest entrepreneurs who have faced bankruptcy quickly get a second chance; Adapt public policy tools to SME needs: facilitate SMEs' participation in public procurement and better use State Aid possibilities for SMEs'), it is difficult not to come to the conclusion that this is nonetheless a poorly structured initiative, and that it leaves too much space to the individual Member States to make decisions (including those on relative financial resources). It thus seems to make the same mistakes – little Community method, much room for an intergovernmental approach – that we have seen before when we examined the most recent Commission Communications related to the European Research Area (2012) and R&I (2014a).

46 The three other examples cited by Mazzucato in chapter 4 (2014, 73) are: 'The Defense Advanced Research Projects Agency (DARPA)', 'The Orphan Drug Act' and 'The National Nanotechnology Initiative'. With these, plus the experience of the SBA-SBIR in the citation above, the author is trying to demonstrate how, 'despite the perception of the US as the epitome of private sector-led wealth creation, in reality it is the State that has been engaged on a massive scale in entrepreneurial risk taking to spur innovation.' In the same vein, Chapter 5 of her book is dedicated to 'The State Behind the iPhone'.

References

Andreatta N. (1968) 'Tecnologia ed economia nella controversia sul divario fra America ed Europa', *il Mulino*, XVII, 184, 109–130.

Bannerman E. (2001) 'The Lisbon Scorecard: The Status of Economic Reforms in Europe', London, CER (Centre for European Reform), 2 March.

CEPS (2000) '4th Annual Report of the Ceps Macroeconomic Policy Group', Brussels, June.

Economist, The (2014) 'World Merchandise Exports', 27 September.

Eichengreen B. (2007) *The European Economy Since 1945: Coordinated Capitalism and Beyond*, Princeton, NJ, Oxford, Princeton University Press.

European Commission (1985) 'Completing the Internal Market', White Paper from the Commission to the European Council, Milan, 28–29 June (www.europa.eu).

European Commission (1993) 'Growth, Competitiveness, Employment: The Challenges and Ways Forward into the 21st Century', White Paper (COM (93)700), Brussels, 5 December.

European Commission (2000) 'Contribution to the Special European Council, Lisbon, 23 and 24 March', Brussels.

European Commission (2002) 'European Competitiveness Report 2002', Directorate-General for Enterprise and Industry (SEC (2002)528), Brussels.

European Commission (2002) 'More Research for Europe: Towards 3% of GDP', Brussels, 11 September.

European Commission (2003) 'Investing in Research: An Action Plan for Europe', Brussels, 4 June.

European Commission (2004) 'Facing the Challenge: The Lisbon Strategy for Growth and Enlargement', Report of the High Level Group chaired by Wim Kok, Brussels, November.

European Commission (2008) ' "Think Small First": A "Small Business Act" for Europe' Communication from the Commission (COM (2008)394), 25 June.

European Commission (2010) 'Europe 2020: A European Strategy for Smart, Sustainable and Inclusive Growth', Communication from the Commission (COM (2010)2020), Brussels, 3 March.

European Commission (2011) 'Horizon 2020: The Framework Programme for Research and Innovation', Communication from the Commission (COM (2011)808), Brussels, 30 November

European Commission (2012) 'A Reinforced European Research Area Partnership for Excellence and Growth', Communication from the Commission (COM (2012)392), Brussels, 17 July.

European Commission (2013) 'Multiannual Financial Framework 2014–2020 and EU Budget 2014: The Figures', Publication Office of the European Union, Luxembourg.

European Commission (2014a) 'Research and Innovation as Sources of Renewed Growth', Communication from the Commission (COM (2014)339), Brussels, 10 June.

European Commission (2014b) 'Horizon 2020 in Brief: The EU Framework Programme for Research and Innovation', DG for Research and Innovation, Brussels.

European Commission (2014c) Directorate-General for Research and Innovation on data from Eurostat, OECD, Member States.

European Council (1997) 'Extraordinary European Council Meeting on Employment. Luxembourg, 20 and 21 November, Presidency Conclusions' (www.consilium.europa.eu).

European Council (2000) 'Lisbon European Council 23 and 24 March: Presidency Conclusions'.

European Council (2002) 'Barcelona European Council 15 and 16 March: Presidency Conclusions'.

Krugman P. (1990) *The Age of Diminished Expectations: US Economic Policy in the 1990s*, Washington, DC, Washington Post Company.

Pisani-Ferry J., Sapir A. (2006) 'Last Exit to Lisbon', 'Bruegel Policy Brief', March.

Maddison A. (2001) *The World Economy: A Millennial Perspective*, Paris, OECD.

Mazzucato M. (2014) *The Entrepreneurial State*: *Debunking Public vs. Private Sector Myths*, revd edn, London, Anthem Press.

Rodriguez M. R. (ed.) (2009) *Europe, Globalization and the Lisbon Agenda*, Cheltenham, Edward Elgar Publishing Ltd.

Sapir A., Aghion P., Bertola G., Hellwig M., Pisani-Ferry J., Rosati D., Viñals J., Wallace H. (eds) (2003) 'An Agenda for a Growing Europe: Making the EU Economic System

Deliver', Report of an Independent High-Level Study Group established on the initiative of the President of the European Commission, Brussels, July (then published by Oxford University Press, 2004).

Tilford S., Whyte P. (2010) 'The Lisbon Scorecard X: The Road to 2020', CER–Centre for European Reform, London.

UNCTAD (2014) 'World Investment Report 2014: Investing in the SDGs: An Action Plan', Geneva, June (www.unctad.org).

World Bank Group, The (2014) 'Doing Business 2015: Going Beyond Efficiency', Washington, October (www.doingbusiness.org).

World Economic Forum (2014) 'The Global Competitiveness Report 2014–2015', Geneva, September (www.weforum.org).

5 State and market in today's Europe

A journey across the EU and nation-states

In seeking to promote innovation-led growth, it is fundamental to understand the important roles that both the public and private sector can play. This requires not only understanding the importance of the innovation 'ecosystem' but especially what it is that each actor brings to that system. The assumption that the public sector can at best incentivize private sector-led innovation (through subsidies, tax reductions, carbon pricing, technical standards and so on), especially but not only in the face of the recent crisis, fails to account for the many examples in which the leading entrepreneurial force came from the State rather than from the private sector.

(Mazzucato 2014)

Introduction

In the previous chapters we focused our attention on the new European industrial policy. While the goals and instruments have at least partially changed compared to the old policy, we are still talking about one of the most important areas of state intervention. The 'market failure' argument is pertinent here, but there are others as well: think of the reorganization of sectors/countries, of the information problem, of the R&D spillovers, etc. These aspects have all been dealt with – to go back to Chapter 1 – by Jacquemin and Rodrik, as well as by other distinguished scholars.

The theory of State Intervention is an old issue (for a review see Chang 1996) that immediately brings to the fore the relationship between state and market.

We will turn our attention to this grander view in our conclusions, and will do so by looking in particular at what the EU has gone through since the 2008 crash. It is a good test case, for many a reason.

In fact, an essential question enlivens today's debate concerning economic policy around the globe: once the crisis is (hopefully) over, and following the actions taken by individual governments to manage the emergency, where will the boundary between the state and the market lie?

This thorny question becomes even more complex when asked about Europe, since the sovereignty of the European Union Member States is limited by the authority given to the supranational government by the Treaties. It follows that in seeking a way out of the crisis – something we all hope will occur imminently – every EU country is faced with the question of achieving the proper balance between public and private sectors of the economy, and also that of re-establishing a suitable division of responsibility between national and supranational governments.

But it is when these questions on the state–market boundary and on the distribution of competencies between different governmental levels get entwined with business-promoting policies that the debate becomes truly heated.

Many voices in the years since the crash have talked about a return to 'Colbertism', a multifaceted concept (whose many aspects will be briefly summarized below) which at first glance evokes the idea of direct and widespread state intervention in the economy, putting special emphasis on the productive system. Is this really the characteristic feature of the new governmental actions which to some extent are occurring in all EU countries? And supposing this to be the case, does 'more *state* intervention' really mean 'more *national*' or 'more *Brussels-based*' intervention?

Before trying to answer this question, it is necessary to take a step back. All things considered, and taking an eminently political inspiration as our starting point, it is within the economic domain that we can trace the basic path of the European integration process. We need only think of the happy advancements of the Single Market, the Monetary Union and Eastern enlargement. But then, September of 2008 came along (Krugman 2009).

It was precisely in confronting this crisis, which rapidly transformed from financial to economic in all sectors, that a united Europe – the EU – revealed its shortcomings.

Are we facing an apparent or a true paradox? We believe that the latter is the case: what we have is a union of sovereign states which has made the economy its cohesive strength, yet it cannot offer a common solution to the damage caused by the most serious economic crisis since the Second World War; or, at the very least, one that is *sufficiently* common.

It is not that work on appropriate reforms (economic governance, community budgets, etc.) had not begun in the preceding years or that far-sighted working hypotheses had not been brought into play; indeed, as we will see, it is quite the opposite. To the purpose of this work, it is worth mentioning that among the novelties of the first decade of the 2000s was the far-reaching impulse given to industrial policy by the European Commission through its Communication of December 2002 entitled 'Industrial Policy in an Enlarged Europe', which was shortly followed by many others – as we showed in Chapter 1.

The fact is that all these reforms and working hypotheses have not had the necessary backing actually to reach their objectives or develop further because of continual national vetoes. Is there a way to overcome these uncertainties, this gap between what is and what would be necessary to enhance the competitiveness of the European productive system?

This chapter is organized as follows. In the next section we will provide a brief overview of the extraordinary results achieved over more than 50 years of integration by what is today known as the EU. The mayhem which followed the

Lehman Brothers crash, in principle, revolutionized the policy programme: macroeconomic stabilization became – once again – a categorical imperative. In the third section we will therefore try to summarize the ways in which the EU tackled the crisis. Moving on from there, in the subsequent section, we shall try to understand whether the Union is doomed to remain at the status quo or whether, by regaining the letter and the spirit of some reforms which have been left by the wayside, it can take on the role it deserves in the twenty-first century. In the final section we will make some concluding remarks.

The three successful ideas behind Europe's success story

Without leaving aside several key community decisions made in Brussels (as well as in other important international meetings in which EU Member States play a significant and active part), it was the individual countries which were instrumental in helping to change the balance of economic power in Europe. Between the end of 2008 and the beginning of 2009, there was an evident withdrawal from the 'Anglo-Saxon model'. From this point of view, *The Economist*'s cover story dated 9 May 2009, with its customary efficacy and irony, gave a picture of what was happening. Under the title: 'Europe's New Pecking Order', the London weekly wrote:

> At the April G20 summit in London, France's Nicolas Sarkozy and Germany's Angela Merkel stood shoulder-to-shoulder to insist pointedly that this recession was not of their making. Ms Merkel has never been a particular fan of Wall Street. But the rhetorical lead has been grabbed by Mr Sarkozy. The man who once wanted to make Paris more like London now declares laissez-faire a broken system. Jean-Baptiste Colbert once again reigns in Paris. Rather than challenge *dirigisme*, the British and Americans are busy following it: Gordon Brown is ushering in new financial rules and higher taxes, and Barack Obama is suggesting that America could copy some things from France, to the consternation of his more conservative countrymen. Indeed, a new European pecking order has emerged, with statist France on top, corporatist Germany in the middle and poor old liberal Britain floored.
>
> (p. 13)

Of course, *The Economist* itself adds that this new balance of economic power cannot be expected to last long. However, going back to the picture on the cover which shows President Sarkozy ('Le modèle français') standing tall on the podium, Prime Minister Brown ('The Anglo-Saxon model') struggling to keep his head above ground and, between them, Chancellor Merkel ('Modell Deutschland') firmly on her feet, one question in particular comes to mind: wasn't it precisely the need to achieve macroeconomic stability that proved the most fertile ground for reintroducing – at higher government levels – the teachings of Jean-Baptiste Colbert, with the EU, rather than its Member States, experimenting with 'neo-Colbertism' where necessary?

Needless to say, the ideal conditions for the reintroduction of 'Colbertism' can be found also in another part of the Community framework: there where the Treaties and the European Commission's power of initiative have laid the foundations for a ('new') industrial policy. This essentially means, as we have seen, a true EU-level policy for research, innovation and human capital. But let us analyse these issues one by one, beginning with what has already been accomplished during the short history of the EU.

The Single Market, first and foremost. In the wake of the indications contained in the truly remarkable Treaties of Rome, but also by virtue of the helping hand given by the Delors Commission (think of the 'White Paper' for the completion of the Single Market (European Commission 1985)), the Single Market can be considered the first successful example of great European ideas.

The second successful economic idea is, of course, the Monetary Union and the advent of the euro. It clearly emerges that, from a certain point on, the two ideas overlap, as if to complete each other – this is what the Community documentation at that time put together under the title 'One Market, One Currency'.

To complete our list, the third successful idea was the Enlargement to the East, considered here from an economic point of view (i.e. as a further extension of the internal market). It is a process which essentially required a decade of intense diplomatic negotiation, going from the first summit in Copenhagen (June 1993) – which established the three criteria (political, economic and the transposition of the *acquis communautaire*) that candidate countries are required to meet – to the second summit in Copenhagen (December 2002), during which eight Central-Eastern European countries were given the green light for entry into the EU on 1 May 2004 (Romania and Bulgaria gained entry in 2007; and Croatia in July 2013). The 'economic criterion', in particular, means the existence of a functioning market economy, as well as the capacity to deal with competitive pressure and the market forces operating within the EU market.

To summarize this point, the three successful ideas have benefitted from the use of three extremely sound and effective institutional mechanisms: respectively, (i) the 'community method'; (ii) the five 'convergence criteria' set out by the Maastricht Treaty; (iii) the three Copenhagen 'membership criteria'.

In achieving this, can we affirm – going back to the cover story of *The Economist* mentioned above – that a certain 'Mr Colbert' acted at the Community level? Naturally, we must first clarify what is meant in today's modern world by 'Colbertism' (or 'New Colbertism', as may be preferred). In truth, it is rarely an easy task to transpose ideas or practices from the past, whether recent or not, into other historical eras, though this would not appear to be the case with 'Colbertism', at least if we consider the number and reliability of the definitions that can be found even today when surfing the net or consulting other sources.[1]

Despite the variety of definitions provided for this theory – a veritable idea of government – two aspects in particular are raised by all the authors: first and foremost, government control exercised towards certain industrial sectors (including subsidies provided for industries and businesses, such as the 'Manufacture royale');

second, the protectionist policies of the national economy, implemented through duties and other instruments.

It thus becomes possible to attempt to formulate an answer, albeit partial and provisional, to our question above. If 'Colbertism' is intended to mean direct intervention by the state in the economy, the answer is no, a certain 'Mr Colbert' did not move to Brussels to create those three successful ideas. On the contrary, they share a common basis, despite their differences: a skilful combination of 'rules of the game' and economic dynamics. Moreover, competition policy and commercial policy have become two of the most essential policy areas in the European Community. Colbert-style policies continued to exist, within certain limits and above all until the 1980s, in the individual European countries, primarily in France; the whole biography of 'National Champions' and so-called 'high-tech Colbertism' comes to mind (Cohen 1992). Perhaps the only case of that era which could be classified as 'Colbertism' exercised by Brussels is that of the sector-based strategies (the steel and synthetic fibre industries), started in the early 1980s and aimed at a concerted reduction in production capacity.

The skilful combination of rules of the game (aimed at creating a so-called 'level playing field') and economic dynamics has resulted in an extraordinary performance: the EU has become the world's biggest economy.[2] If we look beyond the crisis for a moment, it was best not to rest on one's laurels: the world economy was already in a rapidly changing phase, as we discussed in the first two chapters of this book.

For the EU, the challenge is essentially to achieve more economic growth. As the crisis developed in the US and then rapidly spread to this side of the Atlantic, the reforms envisaged in Lisbon for 'Growth and Employment' (2000–2010) – discussed in the previous chapter – were inevitably placed on the back burner, overcome by the economic emergency which had arisen.

The real question now is: what kind of response did Europe give to the emergency? Was it able, strengthened by the economic successes achieved during its history, to find within itself the vision and resources with which to give a decisive and shared response? Or did nationalism, with everything it entails, prevail? In short, does 'Mr Colbert', who in previous decades rarely (if ever) went to Brussels, now 'make his home' – so to speak – in the EU capital?

The EU in the face of the crisis: some facts

It will be the task of tomorrow's historians to create a detailed reconstruction of the various stages which led to the EU's response (or *non*-response) to the crisis, as well as to draw a parallel with the decisions – both rapid and consistent – taken by the US, the epicentre of the crisis. In this chapter, we can merely recall some facts.

First, the Paris summit held in early October 2008 between the four key EU players and, around the same time, the interest rate reduction made by the ECB in Frankfurt in agreement with the major central banks worldwide.

During the first period of the crisis, the ECB reduced the interest rate from 4.25 per cent (July 2008) to 1 per cent (May 2009). Moreover, under president Jean-Claude Trichet the ECB started the measure of the Securities Market Programme (May 2010). However, it was only when Mario Draghi arrived at the Eurotower in Frankfurt that the ECB changed its approach in terms of implementation of an expansive monetary policy, with the interest rate that reached a historic low (0.05 – September 2014) and the adoption of various unconventional measures, such as the Long Term Refinancing Operation (LTRO), the Targeted Long Term Refinancing Operation (TLTRO), the Outright Monetary Transactions (OMT) and the announced purchase of Asset-backed securities (Abs) from European banks (for an appraisal of ECB policy, see: Pill and Reichlin).[3] This was then followed by further decisions made by the ECB – the rightly famous 'quantitative easing' (QE) – which has provided a considerable cash injection into the market since March 2015.

Second, the decision to create on 9 May 2010 the European Financial Stability Facility (EFSF), and subsequently the European Stability Mechanism (ESM) which started its operations on 8 October 2012: a temporary and a permanent crisis resolution mechanism respectively. The aim of EFSF is to protect financial stability in Europe by providing loans to the Member States of the euro area with a view towards macroeconomic adjustments. The ESM was established through an intergovernmental treaty on 2 February 2012. In line with the EFSF's objectives, the ESM was created as a permanent rescue mechanism, which provides financial assistance to euro area Members States, with a maximum lending capacity of €500 billion.

Third, the financial crisis made it clear that a deeper integration of the banking system could not be postponed. That's why in June 2012, heads of state and government agreed to create a Banking union by establishing a Single Supervisory Mechanism (that gives to the ECB the responsibility of supervising banks in countries belonging to the euro area – this new role of ECB started 4 November 2014) and a Single Resolution Mechanism (concerning the management of bank bailouts). The European Banking Union applies to countries belonging to the euro area, even though also non-euro area countries can join the Union. The objectives are to make banks safer, to ensure that any problems can be managed as quickly as possible by supervisors and to increase the ability to manage bank crisis effectively.

Fourth, the gradual development of 'national approaches' to the handling of the financial crisis, although fortunately this was partially counterbalanced by several decisions taken by Ecofin. What was (and is) essentially at stake is the integrity of the Single Market.

Fifth, at the end of November 2008 the European Commission's approval of 'A European Economic Recovery Plan' (European Commission 2008) for – quoting directly from the title of the press release (IP/08/1771) – 'the benefit of growth and employment, aimed at increasing demand and restoring faith in the global economy'. As a whole, the impact of 'budget support' decided by Brussels – support that is to be 'timely, targeted and temporary' – seemed impressive: €200 billion, equal to 1.5 per cent of the EU GDP. Shortly after-wards, however, we were to learn that around €170 billion (1.2 per cent of the GDP) were resources which came via the national budgets of the individual Member States, whilst only €30 billion (0.3 per cent of the GDP) were appar-ently released from the budgets of the EU and the European Investment Bank.

The plan refers to the 'protection and creation of jobs' and even to 'intelligent investment' (education, training and requalification), and also highlights the link with the reforms that had already begun with the Lisbon Strategy for growth and employment. Yet it is hard to ignore the impression that the essence of the plan is represented by decisions taken by the individual Member States, and that they thus become subject to diverse political sensibilities, strategic capacities and actual available budgets.

Sixth, the participation of the four key players in Europe at the G20 meeting held in London on 2 April 2009 and attended by President Obama. Focusing on our specific theme (Europe's response to the crisis), the key point concerns the size of the fiscal stimulus packages. The 'Leaders' Statement' made at the summit in London reminds us, first of all, of the unprecedented 'concerted fiscal expansion', which – according to the G20 – will amount to $5 trillion at the end of next year. How are these colossal amounts distributed among countries? On this point, we may refer to the document issued by the International Monetary Fund (IMF 2009) for the G20 summit of the Ministers of Finance and of the Governors of the central banks, held in London on 13 and 14 March, i.e. on the eve of the 'G20 summit' of the Heads of State. The data featured in Table 5.1 on the so-called 'discretionary fiscal measures' speak for themselves.

Responses at national levels have clearly been at least as important as responses at the European level predominant within the EU. Could things have gone differently, with a coherent and more active response from the EU? The statement made by Jean-Claude Juncker on 15 July 2014 in the European Parlia-ment on the willingness 'to mobilize up to € 300 billion in additional public and private investment in the real economy over the next three years' suggests that the crisis has affected the idea of the role European central institutions should have in tackling the crisis by stimulating 'private investment in the real economy' (European Commission 2014).

A relevant role for public sector institutions in promoting economic growth and revolutionary investments through a proactive intervention in the market economy is not only auspicated by many prominent scholars – the Nobel laure-ates Paul Krugman (2012) and Joseph Stiglitz (2010) represent significant exam-ples – but also verified in recent analyses (e.g. Mazzucato 2014).

After the remarkable achievements culminating in the completion of the Single Market (1986–1992), the adoption of the euro (1992–2002) and the enlargement to the East (1993–2004), is the EU to some degree condemned to a situation of status quo?

We shall attempt to provide a preliminary answer to these questions in the next section.

Table 5.1 G20 countries: estimated cost of discretionary measures (in % of GDP, relative to 2007 baseline)

	2008	2009	2010
Argentina	0.0	1.5	–
Australia	1.2	2.5	2.1
Brazil	0.0	0.6	0.5
Canada	0.0	1.9	1.7
China	0.4	3.1	2.7
France	0.0	0.7	0.8
Germany	0.0	1.6	2.0
India	0.6	0.6	0.6
Indonesia	0.0	1.4	0.6
Italy	0.0	0.2	0.1
Japan	0.3	2.4	1.8
Korea	1.1	3.7	1.2
Mexico	0.0	1.5	–
Russia	0.0	4.1	1.3
Saudi Arabia	2.4	3.3	3.5
South Africa	2.3	3.0	2.1
Spain	1.9	2.3	–
Turkey	0.0	0.8	0.3
UK	0.2	1.5	0.0
US	1.1	2.0	1.8
Total (PPP-weighted average)	0.6	2.0	1.5

Source: IMF, *IMF Staff Position Note 'Fiscal Implications of the Global Economic and Financial Crisis'*, June 9/2009, p. 15 (www.imf.org).

Condemned to status quo? Some talking points

The crucial event – the 'crash' of autumn 2008 – which caught the EU partially unprepared, became increasingly complex and challenging as the impact of the crisis on the one hand was transferred from the financial world to the production system and, on the other, became a contributing factor in the deterioration of the public finances of individual countries. Extending our view as far as possible to the whole European framework, it would appear to us that nowadays it is struggling with at least six missing features. Let us examine each one briefly:

i   The EU (or, at least, the euro area) has neither a common economic policy able to represent the second arm of the monetary policy led by the ECB in Frankfurt (in fact, there is no central governing authority able to take appropriate decisions of a fiscal nature), nor a pan-European financial supervisory authority able to counterbalance the European financial players operating well beyond their national boundaries. It is time to act on both fronts, and something new and concrete seems finally to be on the rise; at least, after the severe macroeconomic crisis of 2008–2009, there is a new awareness of the need to fill these gaps.

ii   Nor does the Union possess an integrated and consistent 'foreign economic policy'. The outlines of this policy are described in an interesting study by Bruegel (Sapir 2007): the two main areas of interest for the EU, considering the evolution of its neighbours (see Table 2.1) are identified by the authors in 'the guarantee of energy supplies and security in immigration'. The basic idea is to replicate at the supranational level – speaking with 'one voice' – the type of governance existing in Europe in fields such as trade (it is the EU which takes part in negotiations with the WTO), monetary policy and exchange rates (the responsibility of the ECB, as already mentioned), competition policy (it is the European Commission, to quote just one of the most famous cases, which carried out the investigation into Bill Gates's Microsoft for 'abuse of a dominant position').

iii   The EU budget is not aimed at growth, as was pointed out by the 'Sapir Report' – 'An Agenda for a Growing Europe' – requested in 2002–2003 by the then President of the European Commission, Romano Prodi (Sapir *et al.* 2003). Recognizing that over 40 per cent of budget resources went to CAP and only one-tenth to R&D, the report proposed 'mobilising the Union's budget' (ch. 12, section 2) by means of a radical reform, concentrating 'expenditure on economic and social sectors where it can make a more significant contribution to growth and solidarity in Europe'. These are therefore the three new instruments (or funds) proposed: 'Growth Fund' (subdivided between R&D, innovation, education and training, infrastructure); 'Convergence Fund' allocated to low-income countries in order to help them catch up (two chapters: strengthening the institutions, and capital goods and human capital); 'Restructuring Fund' (also in two chapters: aid for the agricultural sector and all categories of redundant workers). The simulation for the financial period 2007–2011 outlined by the authors provided for the allocation, in percentages of the EU GDP, of 0.45 to Growth, 0.35 to Convergence and 0.20 to Restructuring. From the point of view of expenditure, these far-reaching changes would have required, according to Sapir and his co-authors a corresponding and consistent modification with regard to revenues, 90 per cent of which is currently covered by national contributions.[4]

iv   Much of the great networks identified by the prescient Jacques Delors in his 1993 'White Paper': 'Growth, Competitiveness, Employment' (European Commission 1993) still needs to be completed. The setting-up of the 'trans-European infrastructure networks' (in transport, energy, information companies) was seen – quoting directly from the Introduction written by President Delors himself to the Italian edition (Delors 1994):

> not so much as a neo-Keynesian measure but instead as a way of providing this great economic expanse [the Single Market] with the means to circulate more quickly and at a lower cost and to have at its disposal an increasing number of instruments of the industrial society's latest feature, i.e. information.

Naturally, much has changed since then: some networks have been created and, consequently, not everything that was provided for in the White Paper can still be considered necessary (the information technology and communications revolution come to mind). Yet the continual enlargement of the internal market (from 12 to 15 and then to 25 to 27), the technological progress and the challenges associated with energy and the environment make important parts of that White Paper more pressing than ever.[5]

v   After the 'Lisbon Strategy' – with all its strengths and weaknesses – it is now time for 'Europe 2020: A Strategy for Smart, Sustainable and Inclusive Growth', as we already know from the analysis carried out in Chapter 4. The new ten-year strategy focuses on three priorities: 'An economy based on knowledge and innovation; Promoting a more resource-efficient, greener and more competitive economy; A high-employment economy.' It is worthy of notice that among the so-called 'Flagship Initiatives' of the second priority is the following: 'An Industrial policy for the globalisation era', which, with an approach defined as modern, aims 'to support entrepreneurship of Europe's primary, manufacturing and service industries and help them seize the opportunities of globalisation and of the green economy' (European Commission 2010, 15–16).

vi Finally, 'A New Strategy' is required also 'for the Single Market': this was the title of the report to the President of the European Commission written by Mario Monti (2010). Starting from the statement of fact that the Single Market was, and still is, the 'cornerstone' of the European integration process, the report on one hand outlines the challenges it has to face, and on the other puts forward a new strategy. Among the initiatives explicitly mentioned in the report's third chapter ('Building Consensus on a Stronger Single Market'), is the following significant case: 'the potential for an active Industrial policy based on sound competition and state aid policies'; this is quoted from the Executive summary, whereas later (section 3.7) it is explained that 'the word [Industrial policy] is no longer taboo',[6] and its relationship with competition policy – which is complementary and not antagonistic – is underlined. In the words of Monti, a former competition Commissioner: 'A sound competition and state aid policy is not in contrast with a sound industrial policy. The opposite is true: competition is necessary to create the varieties, comparative advantages and productivity gains on which growth and innovation flourish' (pp. 86–87). Xavier Vives (2008, 419–469) has analysed the effects of competition on process innovation and product introduction, obtaining 'robust results'.

From this initial six-point list, the Union's 'fiscal capacity' and 'Eurobonds' are explored further in Box 5.1, while the British position deserves special attention (see Liddle 2014).

Box 5.1 Eurobonds and the EU's fiscal capacity

In the severe economic crisis the EU is facing, there are two open questions on the tables of the European institutions, both at the supranational level and at the Member State level: Eurobonds, and the fiscal union. Are these going to proceed on parallel tracks to infinity, as if the solution to one of them could (or should) exclude the other, or is a more thorough reform viable?

A seemingly endless crisis has highlighted the complete inadequacy of the European economic governance at the time of the euro; that is, a Monetary Union that is not counterbalanced by a common budget policy has long been known for its weaknesses. Of course, the crisis that burst in the autumn of 2008 has worsened the situation, but the need to complete the European construction in a reasonable way is not new at all. Hence the two questions mentioned above, which can be posed as follows:

First, does the EU consider the time ripe for an initial offering of Eurobonds, or does it want to consign this idea – which is almost 20 years old (as you know, it was suggested by Jacques Delors in his White Paper of 1993) – to the 'book of dreams'?

Second, which areas of national sovereignty are the EU countries ready to give up (to a higher level, that is to the supranational government) in order to start a real fiscal union?

Considering these questions in their totality, there is a strong temptation to consider them hopelessly unsolvable: one doesn't know where to start putting the pieces together. Today this risk must be avoided at all costs, given that Europe is coming out of months (not to say years) of hesitation. If on one hand we have seen nothing come of many a summit, on the other hand, recent practices have been able to introduce some relevant changes. Think of the many purchases by the ECB in Frankfurt of government bonds issued by eurozone countries in difficulty (Italy among them), first under the chairmanship of Trichet and then of Mario Draghi.

However, a sea change is a long way off, and seeing our European countries at the daily mercy of international financial markets is in no way a point of pride. The 27-member EU, with a GDP of €13.5 trillion (which becomes 9.5 for the 18 members of the euro area), is still the largest economy in the world today (the United States remains at 12.3).

How come such a grand economic power cannot find in itself the inspiration and the will to overcome the state of uncertainty in which it is trapped? It should be noticed that the crisis has come to such a point that, all around the world, many are talking about a likely end of the euro and, what is worse, are betting on it.

As we said, a sea change is needed. From this perspective, two proposals are particularly noteworthy. The first is the one on 'EuroUnionBonds' launched by Alberto Quadrio Curzio and Romano Prodi (2011, 2012); the second is that on the 'fiscal union' elaborated by the Bruegel think-tank in a paper written by Benedicta Marzinotto, André Sapir and Guntram B. Wolff (2011).

- In short, Prodi and Quadrio Curzio's original proposal on Eurobonds focuses on the institution of a European Financial Fund (EFF) with a capital of €1,000 billion constituted by the 'gold reserves of the European System of Central Banks (ESCB)' and by 'other assets like bonds and shares assessed at real market values and not at devalued market values'. At this point, it is argued, 'the EFF with 1,000 billion of paid up capital could issue 3,000 billion of EuBs with a leverage of 3 and a 10-year (and beyond) duration at an interest rate of 3%'. Finally, the capital thus raised by the EFF should be divided in two parts; quoting the original article:

> in order to bring the average debt-to-GDP ratio of the EMU from the current 85% to 60%, the EFF should buy out €2,300 billion of State bonds from EMU member states.... The remaining 700 billion of this issue would go to investments in large European projects aimed at unifying and helping continental companies in the energy, telecoms and transportation sector, of which the EFF would become a shareholder, grow.

- On the other hand, Bruegel published an interesting paper entitled 'What Kind of Fiscal Union?'. In it, Marzinotto *et al.* propose 'a limited fiscal union', including the creation of a euro-area finance ministry, with a minister with veto rights over national budgets that could threaten euro-area sustainability. The institutional innovations required by this very current proposal – in many instructional meetings and summits the fiscal union has been amply discussed – are manifold and significant. In short: the introduction of a tax levied at the European level, that is, 'the availability of fiscal resources at the federal level' by taxing directly the European taxpayers given that – the authors argue – 'all successful currency areas have a sizeable federal budget'. Their proposal implies a smaller budget, with the new euro-area finance ministry having a taxing capacity of about 2 per cent of the GDP of the selfsame area. Another required institutional innovation regards the appointment of the new euro-area finance minister, who should be 'elected by the European Parliament and the Council by the normal majority rule'. The proposal of the Bruegel scholars also includes the supervision and regulation of the euro-area financial system, with the institution – with the help of the above-mentioned ministry – of a new Authority (EDIC, Euro-area Deposit Insurance Corporation), especially needed to supervise the large banks operating at the continental level and that therefore elude the control of national authorities.

The proposals on UnionEuroBonds and on the fiscal union both require changes to the Treaties. Both would help solve the issue of the ECB mission, which could finally buy – so to speak – 'federal European' bonds. Obviously, these proposals are quite different, but still they have something in common: they help us look forward, towards a renewed European pact.

It is up to our politicians to decide where to start in order to solve this apparent puzzle.

All in all, the list mentioned above leads us to point out that not everything is lost in Europe. In this perspective, the step forward in the banking union – with the 130 major European banking groups that from 4 November 2014 are under the direct supervision of the ECB – is particularly significant. The banking union is a determinant element also for an effective monetary union.

When the crisis is definitively over, the EU will find that it must deal with the unfinished business of the European integration process. We have just seen that there is much work to be done. As we recalled in the first paragraph to the introduction of this chapter, the crucial question, which justifiably echoes back to the debate on economic policy at national, European and international levels, is as follows: once it is possible to see the proverbial light at the end of the tunnel, *will we have more state or more market*? And, in the former, would it be a stronger national state or stronger supranational institutions (the EU above all)?

In short, where will the pendulum stop? To my mind, there cannot be one clear-cut solution to this question; the great 'crash', among other things, has also brought down a number of certainties on dominant theories and should have taught us that when a theory becomes the one and only truth (one is put in mind of the so-called 'Washington Consensus') then something is not quite right.

All this is true *a fortiori* for industrial policy. Indeed, if there is an area of public policy that more than others needs to be redefined both in its theoretical and in its practical aspects, it is precisely industrial policy, which had basically disappeared in the golden age of the 'Washington Consensus'. Now something has definitely changed and the perspective embraced by the European Commission (the pioneering Communication of 2002, the integrated approach of 2005 and this year's acceleration) is clear evidence of this.

Conclusions

Combining what has been and is yet to be done, it will not be too long – as we have tried to demonstrate – before a genuinely European 'construction' can be achieved. Yet, as with any building equipped with solid foundations (the enlarged Single Market, the ten years of the euro) and solid pillars (the Treaties), a roof is also clearly needed (the public policies that cover strategic areas at the pan-European level such as R&D, TENs, energy, competitiveness, macroeconomic stabilization, and so on). Otherwise we run the serious risk of non-completion: without a roof, the rain gets in.

If we go back to the image at the beginning of this chapter (something like 'The life and work of the contemporary Mr Colbert'), we can venture to say that there is something to learn from this legacy ('Colbertism'), obviously if reinterpreted by the right degree of pragmatism. The spirit of the times must be taken into account, encouraging the political elite to fight against nationalism (or economic 'patriotism').

The emphasis placed on the opening up of markets is undoubtedly a 'no' to 'Colbertism', as is the commitment undertaken by the world's largest economies to once again take up the Doha Round negotiations on the freedom of world trade so as to conclude them by the end of 2010. As we recall, 'protectionism' was one of the two main constitutional elements at the basis of the governmental intervention usually attributed to the controller-general of finances and the minister to the royal family during the reign of King Louis XIV.

And what about the other constitutional element, the 'economic control' of sectors and businesses? The question now becomes: does the 'new' industrial policy mean the foundation of a genuine European policy for R&D, technology and innovation, tertiary education and human capital mobility? And also: can we find in the approach of the European Commission the seeds – the buds – of a policy aimed, according to Rodrik's thinking, at 'economic restructuring'? If the answer to these questions is affirmative, then it is a *yes* to '(New) Colbertism'.

We have a 'no' to protectionism and a 'yes' to smart interventions in favour of business, in line with the guidelines we have tried to illustrate (industrial policy with an integrated horizontal-vertical approach, consistency between this industrial policy and competition policy, new strategies for the Single Market, 'knowledge-based' investments increasingly made at the supranational government level, etc.).

What is certain is that the sum of many national 'Colbertisms' no longer adds up, not unless our goal is to jeopardize what has already been constructed through European integration.

Notes

1 Without intending to provide a complete list, the following definitions were consulted (or found on the Internet): 'Colbertism', in *Routledge Dictionary of Economics*, 2nd edn (www.bookrags.com/tandf/colbertism-tf/); Jean-Baptiste Colbert, in *Encyclopaedia Britannica* (www.bookrags.com/eb/colbert-jean-baptiste-eb/) as well as an entry from Wikipedia (http://it.wikipedia.org/wiki/Jean-Baptiste_Colbert).

2 See for example ECB (2014): GDP at PPP (€ trillions): EU 13.5; US 13.0; Japan 3.6, China 12.5.

3 The Securities Markets Programme (SMP) has been adopted in order to reduce tensions in certain market segments that created difficulties to the correct transmission of monetary policy. It consists of purchasing government securities in favour of countries hit by the crisis. LTROs are long-term open market operations aimed at refinancing the financial sector. They have been proposed between December 2011 and February 2012 in two tranches (as a whole more than €1,000 billion). Moreover, the maturity of this type of operation has been raised from the standard three months (before the crisis) to three years (at the end of 2011). The TLTROs – €82.6 billion allotted in the first operation in September 2014 – are long-term refinancing operations aimed at favouring bank lending to the real economy. The OMT essentially substitutes the SMP, and consists of the possibility to purchase government securities of eurozone Member States.

4 Starting from the ideas proposed in the 'Sapir Report', Santos and Neheider (2009) have already taken a step forward by recently publishing a new proposal (a 'two-stage negotiation').

5 With regard to the financing of these trans-European networks, some European leaders have on a number of occasions put forward their proposals suggesting that 'Eurobonds' be issued.

6 The same holds true for the US: 'The concept of industrial policy is not alien to the American past and present', argue Di Tommaso and Schweitzer (2013) in their timely book.

References

Chang H.-J. (1996) *The Political Economy of Industrial Policy*, Basingstoke, Macmillan.

Cohen E. (1992) *Le colbertisme high-tech: Économie du grand project*, Paris, Hachette.

Delors J. (1994) 'Il libro bianco', Preface to *Crescita, competitività, occupazione: Le sfide e le vie da percorrere nel XXI secolo*, Milano, Il Saggiatore.

Di Tommaso M. R., Schweitzer S. O. (2013) *Industrial Policy in America: Breaking the Taboo*, Cheltenham, Edward Elgar.

ECB (European Central Bank) (2014) 'Statistics Pocket Book', September (www.ecb. europa.eu).

Economist, The (2009) 'Europe's New Pecking Order', 9 May (www.economist.com).

European Commission (1985) 'Completing the Internal Market: White Paper from the Commission to the European Council (Milan, 28–29 June 1985)' (COM (1985)310), Brussels, June.

European Commission (1993) 'Growth, Competitiveness, Employment: The Challenges and Ways Forward into the 21st Century', White Paper (COM (1993)700), Brussels, 15 December.

European Commission (2002) 'Industrial Policy in an Enlarged Europe', Communication from the Commission (COM (2002)714), Brussels, December.

European Commission (2008) 'European Economic Recovery Plan', Communication from the Commission to the European Council (COM (2008)800), Brussels, 26 November.

European Commission (2010) 'Europe 2020: A European Strategy for Smart, Sustainable and Inclusive Growth' (COM (2010) 2020), Brussels, March.

European Commission (2014) 'A New Start for Europe: My Agenda for Jobs, Growth, Fairness and Democratic Change', Political Guidelines for the Next European Commission – Opening Statement in the European Parliament by Jean-Claude Junker, Strasbourg, 15 July.

IMF (International Monetary Fund) (2009) 'Fiscal Implications of the Global Economic and Financial Crisis', *IMF Staff Position Note*, 9 June, p. 15 (www.imf.org).

Krugman P. (2009) *The Return of Depression Economics and the Crisis of 2008*, New York, W. W. Norton & Company.

Krugman P. (2012) *End This Depression Now!* New York, W. W. Norton & Company.

Liddle, R. (2014) *The Europe Dilemma: Britain and the Drama of EU Integration*, Policy Network Book, London, Tauris I.B.

Marzinotto B., Sapir A., Wolff G. B. (2011) 'What Kind of Fiscal Union?' *Bruegel Policy Brief*, 2011/06, November (www.bruegel.org).

Mazzucato M. (2014) *The Entrepreneurial State*: *Debunking Public vs. Private Sector Myths*, revd edn, London, Anthem Press.

Monti M. (2010) 'A New Strategy for the Single Market: At the Service of Europe's Economy and Society', Report to the President of the European Commission – J. M. Barroso, Brussels, 9 May.

Pill H., Reichlin L. (2014) 'Exceptional policies for exceptional times. The ECB's response to the rolling crises of the Euro Area, and how it brought us towards a new grand bargain', London, Centre for Economic Policy Research (www.cepr.org).

Quadrio Curzio A., Prodi R. (2011) 'EuroUnionBond, Here is What Must be Done', *Il Sole-24 Ore*, 23 August (www.ilsole24ore.com)

Quadrio Curzio A., Prodi R. (2012) 'EuroUnionBond, Why are We Proposing Them Again?' *Il Sole-24 Ore*, 23 August (www.ilsole24ore.com).

Santos I., Neheider S. (2009) 'Reframing the EU Budget Decision-Making Process', Bruegel Working Paper 3, Brussels.

Sapir A. (ed.) (2007) *Fragmented Power: Europe and the Global Economy*, Brussels, Bruegel Book.

Sapir A., Aghion P., Bertola G., Hellwig M., Pisani-Ferry J., Rosati D., Viñals J., Wallace H. (eds) (2003) 'An Agenda for a Growing Europe: Making the EU Economic System Deliver', Report of an Independent High-Level Study Group established on the initiative of the President of the European Commission, Brussels, July (then published by Oxford University Press, 2004).

Stiglitz J. E. (2010) *Freefall: America, Free Markets, and the Sinking of the World Economy*, New York, W. W. Norton & Company.

Vives X. (2008) 'Innovation and Competitive Pressure', *Journal of Industrial Economics*, 56, 3, 419–469.

Epilogue

The time of coincidence

Something has truly changed in the world of economics, we wrote in the Prologue at the very beginning of our journey.

Before allowing ourselves the luxury of some concluding statements, it would be worthwhile to look back for a moment, both at the process of European integration and the way in which it evolved, in order to understand better what was successful and what may still be in need of improvement.

Indeed, it is hoped that the development and evolution of influential theories (when they are accurate, we should add) will influence policy decisions and, consequently, the economy and society at large.

Sixty years of European integration have built common institutions, rules and policies that play a role in our shared lives. At the very beginning of the 1950s, the united Europe was born with the high, noble goal of establishing a lasting peace between European nations – Germany and France, above all – after centuries of internecine war. The nature of those first Community institutions (ESCS, EEC, Euratom) and the reality of unforeseeable 'accidents of history' (such as the unsuccessful plan for the European Defence Community – EDC) created circumstances that made Europe achieve its greatest successes in the field of the economy.

Both the difficulties that the EU is currently going through and, in spite of these, the far from marginal role that the EU plays in the global economy give us reason to pause at this precise point: the EU's economic architecture, as we might call it.

The growing role of microeconomic policies

The EU, as the sum of over 60 years of development and integration, is a complex institutional being with powers that cover a wide range of responsibilities. It is therefore no mistake that in the literature on 'New Regionalism',[1] the EU is considered the most natural and compact example: the only one among the five existing global economic partnerships (the EU, NAFTA in North America, MERCOSUR in Latin America, ASEAN in South-East Asia, and SADC in Southern Africa) that has attained a developmental level of great complexity compared to mere free-trade zones or compared to customs unions. A panoramic view of economic integrations schemes (El-Agraa 2001) shows just this (see Table E.1).

Table E.1 Schematic presentation of economic integration schemes

Scheme	Free intrascheme trade	Common commercial policy	Free factor mobility	Common monetary and fiscal policy	One government
Free trade area	Yes	No	No	No	No
Customs union	Yes	Yes	No	No	No
Common market	Yes	Yes	Yes	No	No
Economic union	Yes	Yes	Yes	Yes	No
Political union	Yes	Yes	Yes	Yes	Yes

Source: El-Agraa (2001, 2).

Based on this chart, Ali El-Agraa (2001, 1–2) made the observation that 'the EU is heading in this direction' by which he meant the fourth type of economic integration scheme. Complete economic unions are, in the author's words, 'common markets that ask for complete unification of monetary and fiscal policies, i.e. the participants must introduce a central authority to exercise control over these matters so that member nations effectively become regions of the same nation'.[2]

If we stay with this fourth category for a moment, we can add that the *macroeconomic* setting is, by and large, a given fact. As just a short list of examples, think of the entire corpus of norms established around the convergence criteria required by the Maastricht Treaty and by the Stability and Growth Pact; of the regulations of the more recent Fiscal Compact; of the objective of prices stability, the essential part of the ECB's mandate. It would be equally possible, though, to present a counter-argument claiming that there are still some important macroeconomic elements missing from the whole, such as a truly federal budget, larger powers for the ECB – in particular in terms of promoting economic growth and employment, and not just inflation, like the American Federal Reserve – and so on.

Given the interests of this book, and for the sake of simplicity, let us take the macroeconomic setting for granted. Is it accurate to claim that a twenty-first century *economic union*, *à la* El-Agraa is fully formed solely by virtue of its 'common monetary and fiscal policy'? If we go back to those elements that were the source of economic growth for any given country at the beginning of this century (millennium), it would be fair to respond in the negative to the question we are asking ourselves. In order completely and truly to bring about this *economic union*, it absolutely must develop its own microeconomic dimension as well. After all, was this not the essential message of the 1993 White Paper on 'Growth, Competitiveness, Employment' and, more recently, the Lisbon Strategy and Europe 2020?

Alongside the necessary macroeconomic stability, other factors of competitiveness come barging to the fore; in a word, those factors that shape a 'model of capitalism' and that, as we know from our analysis in Chapter 3, distinguish each of these models from the others.[3]

In a European perspective, where different 'models' have always been in place, we must not forget that from a historical perspective, the Single European Act (SEA, 1986), then the Maastricht Treaty (1992) and the Amsterdam Treaty (1997) all contributed to giving responsibilities to the Community in terms of policy that were not present in the original Treaties of Rome (1957) – where there was, however, a competition policy laid out in the famous formerly Articles 85 and 86.[4]

We can also state that these revisions to the Treaties of Rome concerned not only macroeconomic issues (a common currency was not part of the foundational act of the EEC), but also *microeconomic* ones. Over time, in fact, articles related to employment, industrial policy, technological R&D, economic and social cohesion and so on, including those on the environment and infrastructural networks,[5] and even those – which we have mentioned more than once – on completing the single market, came to be an integral part of the *acquis communautaire*.

Table E.2 highlights some of the most innovative articles to be found within the modifications made to the Treaties of Rome in 1986, 1992 and 1997.

If, now more than ever, a 'common monetary and fiscal policy' cannot be the definitive form of an *economic union*, then where is it to be found? Going back to El-Agraa's chart, we could perhaps uncover something in the step between the fourth and fifth categories (see Table E.1, rows) an intermediate wraith between *economic union* and *political union*. This intermediary, in its own right, implicates – from the perspective of governance (see again Table E.1, columns) – an expansion of the 'common monetary and fiscal policy' without having necessarily to arrive at the final destination of 'one government'. It is precisely here, in this expansion of classical macroeconomic policies towards more micro-economic ones, that we find the missing nexus of the EU of our times – policies which are most commonly referred to, both in academic and political circles, as *structural reforms*.

Reforms of the labour market, of social security and of the welfare state in general, by common consent fall within this sphere of structural reforms. Our own analysis has tried to advocate the thesis that any 'new' industrial policy must itself be subject to structural reforms. In fact, as we already know from nearly all of the previous chapters, the focus of European industrial policy (keeping in mind the triangle's third side) is on *knowledge-based investments* – i.e. R&D and human capital – and on *enabling technologies*. Investments and technologies that put into play national systems of research, of innovation and of training.

To our mind, these are systems that should fall under the category of those 'that require the establishment of supranational institutions', as Mario Draghi (2014) put it during his commemoration of Tommaso Padoa-Schioppa and his contributions to building a strong Europe.

In his memorial lecture the President of the ECB took up at length the debate on policy vis-à-vis its proposal for 'community-level governance' not only of fiscal policy or the banking union, but also for structural reforms. Mario Draghi (2014) stated:

Table E.2 The evolution of 'microeconomic' policies in the treaties

Year	New 'acquis communautaire'	TFEU title/article	Text
1986	Single European Act	TITLE XVIII – ECONOMIC, SOCIAL AND TERRITORIAL COHESION Art. 174 TFUE ex Art. 158 TEC	'In order to promote its overall harmonious development, the Union shall develop and pursue its actions leading to the strengthening of its economic, social and territorial cohesion. In particular, the Union shall aim at reducing disparities between the levels of development of the various regions and the backwardness of the least favoured regions.'
1986	Single European Act	TITLE XIX – RESEARCH AND TECHNOLOGICAL DEVELOPMENT AND SPACE Art. 179 TFUE ex Art. 163 TEC	'(1) The Union shall have the objective of strengthening its scientific and technological bases by achieving a European research area in which researchers, scientific knowledge and technology circulate freely, and encouraging it to become more competitive, including in its industry, while promoting all the research activities deemed necessary by virtue of other Chapters of the Treaties. (2) For this purpose the Union shall, throughout the Union, encourage undertakings, including small and medium-sized undertakings, research centres and universities in their research and technological development activities of high quality; it shall support their efforts to cooperate with one another, aiming, notably, at permitting researchers to cooperate freely across borders and at enabling undertakings to exploit the internal market potential to the full.'
1992	Maastricht Treaty	TITLE XVII – INDUSTRY Art. 173 TFUE ex Art. 157 TEC	'The Union and the Member States shall ensure that the conditions necessary for the competitiveness of the Union's industry exist. For that purpose, in accordance with a system of open and competitive markets, their action shall be aimed at: • speeding up the adjustment of industry to structural changes; • encouraging an environment favourable to initiative and to the development of undertakings throughout the Union, particularly small and medium-sized undertakings; • encouraging an environment favourable to cooperation between undertakings; fostering better exploitation of the industrial potential of policies of innovation, research and technological development.'
1997	Amsterdam Treaty	TITLE IX – EMPLOYMENT Art. 145 TFUE ex Art. 125 TEC	'Member States and the Union shall, in accordance with this Title, work towards developing a coordinated strategy for employment and particularly for promoting a skilled, trained and adaptable workforce and labour markets responsive to economic change with a view to achieving the objectives defined in Article 3 of the Treaty on European Union.'

Source: excerpts from the 'Consolidated version of the Treaty on the Functioning of the European Union (TFEU)', 2007.

I think there is a case for some form of common governance over structural reforms. This is because the outcome of structural reforms – a continuously high level of productivity and competitiveness – is not merely in a country's own interest. It is in the interest of the Union as a whole ... Markets can be opened through EU legislation. But it is only through structural reforms that firms and individuals can be enabled to take full advantage of that openness.

Full implementation of a new pan-European industrial policy is an essential part of the 'governance of structural reforms' and should as such be made in the image of 'fiscal governance'.

We feel that a European SBA (Small Business Administration) similar to that in the United States is one of the possible actions to undertake; another could be the creation of a network of Fraunhofer Institutes, using as their model the one currently operating successfully in Germany in the field of applied research and pre-competitive development of products. Then there's the entire Horizon 2020 programme, by which Europe's role in new technological trajectories is strengthened; and there would also be room for improvement in the *modus operandi* of the EIB. There are centres of excellence that need to be created and/or supported in the field of education via supranational cooperation between universities, and which could take advantage of Community programmes such as the Marie Curie Fellowships (which is found within Horizon) and Erasmus+.

There is no shortage of concrete proposals – those which we have seen in the pages of this work as well as others that with every passing week are presented by researchers, policy-makers and think-tanks. But what Europe desperately needs before any of those is a marked and widespread two-pronged change in mentality by its ruling class. First, that manufacturing matters, and that there is definite need for a 'new' industrial policy oriented towards technological advances. Second, this policy must be placed within the category of structural reforms that require 'community-level governance'.

The primary beneficiaries of this policy would be European firms – from the European Champions to the SMEs to the Clusters – from which, upon final analysis, would be sown concrete possibilities for growth and employment in the EU in a global economy that is completely different from the economy in which European integration got its start in the early post-war period. But there is no doubt that the various national political elites would show natural reticence in the face of new and growing losses of sovereignty to the EU in this field (as in others, if the truth be told).

But it would be worthwhile to reflect upon a few simple figures that evince one of the many European paradoxes. While the total GDP of the EU-15 nations – according to calculations made by Bruegel researchers (Darvas *et al.* 2013, 2) – 'exceeded that of the United States by 15 per cent in 1982, it is expected to be 17 per cent lower in 2017'. Why is this a paradox? Because during this period of time, the EU – from the institutional perspective – achieved fundamental goals, such as the Single Market, the euro and the Eastern enlargement; nevertheless, it showed a constant reduction in total GDP compared to the US.[6]

One additional point: in a united Europe that has not grown to the degree that we might expect given its institutional progresses, the paradox becomes further complicated. There is a system of European enterprises that at first glance, once again in comparison to the United States, does not show such an enormous gap with its American counterparts as can be found in the case of GDP.[7] On the contrary, in more than one ranking we have seen a neck-and-neck race between American and 'European' firms, when the latter are tallied up no longer based on their Member State of origin, but as being common partners of the Union. Another reason to move towards an industrial policy that is genuinely Community based and supranational.

Something has truly changed in the world of economics

This is a twofold change, based on a rediscovery of manufacturing as an immutable source of economic growth, and on a reassessment of the role of industrial policy.

Two changes that we have tried to weave into a single plot, a single narrative, throughout the pages of this book. There is still one point which we would like to call attention to here at the conclusion: we'll call this point, 'The Time of Coincidence'. In the two communities of economists and politicians, a gentle breeze of fresh ideas has started to blow with greater force in recent years. Our goal has been to present some of the basic evidence about the Manufacturing Renaissance–New Industrial Policy binomial, using the two *Economist* debates (2010 and 2011) as our starting point in the Prologue.

We have encountered authoritative economists and important policy-makers along the way, from Europe, the US and beyond. A natural division of labour has always existed between the two groups: the former try to explicate the principles upon which a 'new' industrial policy is based, while the latter should try to implement useful policies that are in line with these principles. The good news, for a change, is that they are all working at practically the same pace: hence our call to a 'Time of Coincidence'.

A quick recap of some of the principle data analysed in this long essay is in order. There were the Communications by the European Commission on 'Industrial Policy' that were released between 2002 and 2014. On the other side of the Atlantic, in a similar governmental move, there was the 'Advanced Manufacturing Partnership' put forward by the Obama Administration. Many national governments from within the EU have launched programmes for restarting (or reinforcing, depending on the case) quality manufacturing, guided in particular by the strategy of 'Europe 2020'. Certainly the phrase 'Industrial Policy' is not always explicitly used: in Germany's case, as we noted specifically in Chapter 1, the title of choice was 'High-Tech Strategy 2020'.[8] Yet all of these programmes, regardless of their labels, tend to promote the 'structural change' that is so dear to Dani Rodrik. The common efforts by the Western industrialized countries have been to push industrial structures in the direction of a new frontier of technological progress.

As concerns the field of theory, we wish to recall the ad hoc reflection that we dedicated in Chapter 1 to the work of Rodrik himself and of the late Alexis Jacquemin (for many years economic adviser to President Jacques Delors at the European Commission in Brussels). Many other influential economists of our times have made their appearances in these pages as well. We should also now cite a handful of Research Centres and/or collective study programmes that merit mention. Among others, we are thinking of:

i   the 'WWWforEurope project' (the WWW stands for 'Welfare, Wealth, Work') directed by Karl Aiginger in Vienna and financed by the European Commission as part of the '7th Framework Programme';

ii   the wide-ranging, excellent work of the Institute for Manufacturing (IfM) at the University of Cambridge, where amongst their research projects there are those carried forth by the 'Babbage Industrial Policy Network' led in part by Ha-Joon Chang, an author whose work has been frequently cited in this book;

iii the policy-oriented research programmes carried out both some of the most influential Brussels-based think-tanks such as Bruegel (e.g. *Manufacturing Europe's future* (Veugelers 2013)) and EPC (e.g. 'Towards a New Industrial Policy for Europe' (Dhéret *et al.* 2014)), and some of the most prestigious management consulting firms such as The Boston Consulting Group (e.g. 'The Shifting Economics of Global Manufacturing' (Sirkin et al.)) and Roland Berger Strategy Consultants (e.g. 'Industry 4.0: The New Industrial Revolution. How Europe will Succeed' (2014));

iv   as another European example, the activity of BusinessEurope (2014), 'the leading advocate for growth and competitiveness at the European level' (see for example its document on the 'Ten Priorities' for the new European Commission), and as an American example, the forward-looking initiative of 'The MIT Task Force on Production and Innovation' which now consists of two reports: the first – *Making in America* – edited by Suzanne Berger (2013),[9] and the second one – *Production in the Innovation Economy* – by Richard M. Locke and Rachel L. Wellhausen (2014);[10]

v   and, halfway between academic research and institutional activity, there is the new 'OECD Flagship', launched by the Paris-based organization in 2010 under the heading 'Perspectives on Global Development'; the title of their recently published report speaks for itself: *Industrial Policy in a Changing World* (OECD 2013).

The examples of governmental, institutional and scientific initiatives for study and research give us the opportunity to move forward in a plethora of directions. John Maynard Keynes (1936), in *The General Theory*, wrote the following, one of the most famous and most cited excerpts of that work:

> The ideas of economists and political philosophers, both when they are right and when they are wrong, are more powerful than is commonly understood. Indeed, the world is ruled by little else. Practical men, who believe themselves to be quite exempt from any intellectual influence, are usually the

slaves of some defunct economist. Madmen in authority, who hear voices in the air, are distilling their frenzy from some academic scribbler of a few years back ... soon or late, it is ideas, not vested interests, which are dangerous for good or evil.

Focusing our attention one final time on the Manufacturing Renaissance/ Industrial Policy binomial, the analyses that we have undertaken in the preceding pages give us the hope that this contemporary moment, this 'Time of Coincidence', may be rich enough and wise enough to sidestep some of the risks that Keynes outlines, transforming the exchange of ideas between 'economists' and 'practical men' into a virtuous circle.

Notes

1 See, for example, Telò (2001).
2 As an example of *political* unions, his fifth category, El-Agraa cited the unification of East and West Germany in 1990.
3 Michele Salvati (2001 rightly argues in this regard:

> No one denies that globalization and the free international circulation of capital require all nations (with the exception of the United State as global hegemony) to adopt very similar macroeconomic policies: a nearly-balanced budget, low inflation and thus monetary policies that adequately pursue this goal, trade balances that create no great worry. But these macroeconomic policies can be achieved by very different economic and social institutions and policies: external pressures are all pushing in the same direction, but – beyond the most simplistic or necessarily uniform macroeconomic setting – national policies continue to shore themselves up on models of capitalism from the recent past, models that are profoundly different from the Anglo Saxon variety.

4 After the Treaty of Amsterdam (Articles 81 and 82), the revised Treaty on the Functioning of the European Union (TFEU) renumbered the Articles 101 and 102.
5 It has elsewhere been noted how the 'political choice of cohesion' represents 'a profound change in the principles that underline European political, economic, and monetary integration' (Leonardi 1995).
6 Given the US=100, the EU-15 GDP was, as stated above, 115 in 1982, then 99 in 1997 and 90 in 2012 (with a forecast of 83 in 2017); the data are expressed in PPP. A related decline is also found, again in the EU-15 vs US comparison carried out by Breugel, in the dynamic of GDP per capita and GDP per employee. The explanation of these poor performances lies in the 'productivity problem', which, if it is going to be properly confronted, requires a transition towards an 'innovation-based economy' (Darvas *et al.* 2013, 2).
7 See, in particular, the analyses carried out in the previous chapters on European Champions (Chapter 2), and on the three international rankings: Competitiveness, Doing Business, FDI (Chapter 4).
8 As we saw in Chapter 1, other notable European examples are France and the UK, while outside the EU we mentioned Japan and other Asian countries as well.
9 '*Making in America* [S. Berger (2013, xiii) writes] started from an idea about what researchers from across MIT could contribute to national and international debates on the role of production in bringing innovation to life in the economy.'
10 Locke and Wellhausen (2014, 1) write: '*To live well, a nation must produce well.* This statement, which opened the MIT *Made in America* study in 1989, is as true today as it was when the book was originally published (Dertouzos, Solow, and Lester 1989).'

References

Berger S. (ed.) (2013) *Making in America: From Innovation to Market*, 'The MIT Task Force on Production and Innovation', Cambridge, MA, MIT Press.

BusinessEurope (2014) 'Ten Priorities to Boost Investment, Growth & Employment. What Companies Expect from the New Commission', October (www.businesseurope.eu).

Darvas Z., Pisani-Ferry J., Wolff G. (2013) 'Europe's Growth Problem (And What to Do About It)', *Bruegel Policy Brief*, 13, April (www.bruegel.org).

Dhéret C., Frontini A., Hedberg A., Morosi M., Pardo R. (2014) 'Towards a New Industrial Policy for Europe', EPC Issue Paper No. 78, European Policy Centre, Brussels, November (www.epc.eu).

Draghi M. (2014), 'Memorial Lecture in Honour of Tommaso Padoa-Schioppa', London, 9 July (www.ecb.europa.eu).

El-Agraa A. M. (2001) *The European Union: Economics and Policies*, 6th edn, Upper Saddle River, NJ, Prentice Hall.

Keynes J.M. (1936) *The General Theory of Employment, Interests, and Money*, New York, Harcourt.

Leonardi R. (1995) *Convergence, Cohesion and Integration in the European Union*, London, Macmillan.

Locke R. M., Wellhausen R. L. (eds) (2014) *Production in the Innovation Economy*, 'The MIT Task Force on Production and Innovation', Cambridge, MA, MIT Press.

OECD (2013) 'Perspectives on Global Development 2013: Industrial Policies in a Changing World', Paris, May (www.oecd.org).

Roland Berger Strategy Consultants (2014), 'Industry 4.0: The New Industrial Revolution. How Europe will Succeed', *Think Act*, March (www.rolandberger.com).

Salvati M. (2001) 'Preface to the Italian Edition' (Bologna, Il Mulino, pp. 7–19) of R. Dore, *Stock Market Capitalism: Welfare Capitalism: Japan and Germany vs the Anglo-Saxons*, Oxford, Oxford University Press, 2000.

Sirkin H. L., Zinzer M., Rose J. (2014) 'The Shifting Economics of Global Manufacturing. How Cost Competitiveness Is Changing Worldwide', The Boston Consulting Group, August (www.bcg.persectives.com).

Telò M. (ed.) (2001) *European Union and New Regionalism: Regional Actors and Global Governance in a Post-Hegemonic Era*, Aldershot, Ashgate.

Veugelers R. (ed.) (2013) 'Manufacturing Europe's Future', *Bruegel Blueprint*, XXI, Brussels (www.bruegel.org).

Appendix I*

EU official documents on industrial policy: an overview

(Brussels, 22 January 2014)
Communication from the Commission to the European Parliament, the Council, the European Economic and Social Committee and the Committee of the Regions, COM (2014)14
For a European Industrial Renaissance
'**Overall, EU industry has proved its resilience in the face of the economic crisis**. It is a world leader in sustainability and returns a EUR 365 billion surplus in the trade of manufactured products (EUR 1 billion a day), generated mainly by a few high- and medium-technology sectors. They include the automotive, machinery and equipment, pharmaceuticals, chemicals, aeronautics, space and creative industries sectors, and high-end goods in many other sectors, including food.'

(Brussels, 10 October 2012)
Communication from the Commission, COM (2012)582
A Stronger European Industry for Growth and Economic Recovery: Industrial Policy Communication Update
'This Communication proposes a partnership between the EU, its Member States and industry to dramatically step up investment into new technologies and give Europe a competitive lead in the new industrial revolution … The Commission proposes to jointly focus investment and innovation **on six priority lines**: advanced manufacturing technologies, key enabling technologies, bio-based products, sustainable industrial and construction policy and raw materials, clean vehicles, smart grids.'

(Brussels, 14 October 2011)
Communication from the Commission, COM (2011)642
Industrial Policy: Reinforcing Competitiveness
'The main drivers of strong economic growth are competitive firms of all sizes.'

(Brussels, 28 October May 2010)
Communication from the Commission, COM (2010)614
An Integrated Industrial Policy for the Globalisation Era: Putting Competitiveness and Sustainability at Centre Stage
'It is a flagship initiative of the **Europe 2020** strategy.'

'This policy paper sets out a strategy for supporting a strong, diversified and competitive industrial base in Europe that offers well-paid jobs while generating less CO2 and using resources more efficiently.'

'Examples include: a more favourable business environment; faster industrial innovation; increased efforts to fight protectionism; support to help industry transform to meet new challenges.'

(Brussels, 9 May 2010)
Report to the President of the European Commission, by Mario Monti
A New Strategy for the Single Market
Ch. 3, section 3.7: 'The Single Market and Industrial Policy' (pp. 86–88)
'The word is no longer taboo. Europe's leaders are discussing the merits, and limits, of an active industrial policy. The return of interest for industrial policy goes parallel with a renewed attention to the importance of manufacturing for Europe's economy and a wide concern for the profound transformation of the European industrial base triggered by the crisis.'

(Brussels, 3 March 2010)
Communication from the Commission (COM (2010)2020)
Europe 2020: A Strategy for Smart, Sustainable and Inclusive Growth
Ch. 2, Flagship Initiative: 'An Industrial Policy for the Globalisation Era' (pp. 15–16)
'The Commission ... will draw up a framework for a modern industrial policy, to support entrepreneurship, to guide and help industry to become fit to meet these challenges, to promote the competitiveness of Europe's primary, manufacturing and service industries and help them seize the opportunities of globalisation and of the green economy.'

(Brussels, 2002–2007)
Communication(s) from the Commission
- 2007 (July): *Mid-term Review of Industrial Policy.*
- 2005 (October): *Implementing the Community Lisbon Programme: A Policy Framework to Strengthen EU Manufacturing – Towards a More Integrated Approach for Industrial Policy.*
- 2004 (April): *Fostering Structural Change – An Industrial Policy for an Enlarged Europe.*
- 2003 (November): *Some Key Issues in Europe's Competitiveness: Towards an Integrated Approach.*
- **2002 (December): *Industrial Policy in an Enlarged Europe.***

'Enlargement will be a major source of opportunities for industry in new and existing Member States alike. It should make a positive contribution to overall industrial competitiveness. The competitiveness of manufacturing industry is a cornerstone of EU's sustainable development strategy. Industrial policy is horizontal in nature and aims at securing framework conditions favourable to industrial competitiveness ... However, it needs to take into account the specific needs and characteristics of individual sectors.'

(Remark: 'Bangemann Communication', Brussels 1990)
Industrial Policy in an Open and Competitive Environment: Guidelines for a Community Approach
European Commission website on 'Industrial Policy': http://ec.europa.eu/enterprise/policies/industrial-competitiveness/industrial-policy/index_en.htm.

Note

* The author would like to thank all of the sources cited in these Appendices – and in the body of this work – for making their material available.

Appendix II.1

Mediobanca's multinationals

Table A.II.1a Overview

Total manufacturing	No. of companies	Net sales 2011 (in € million)		No. of employees	
		Fixed exchange rates	Flexible exchange rates	2002	2011
TRIAD	233	5,529,757	5,927,051	17,045,514	19,141,191
EUROPE	139	2,535,210	2,569,785	8,158,897	9,106,266
US	57	1,956,843	1,981,949	5,669,762	6,136,641
JAPAN	37	1,037,704	1,375,317	3,216,855	3,898,284

Table A.II.1b Net sales by industrial sector (in € million)

	Triad		Europe	
	2002	2011	2002	2011
Oil, energy and mining	16,625	21,439	14,767	15,460
Iron, steel and non-ferrous metals	187,530	316,965	115,935	215,911
Chemicals and pharmaceuticals	630,998	939,013	339,442	516,193
Tyres and cables	63,329	89,779	36,569	49,636
Mechanical engineering:				
Automotive	944,215	1,129,840	413,914	520,961
Aerospace and shipbuilding	173,765	270,542	71,466	111,914
Domestic appliances	43,373	47,115	12,724	11,487
Others engineering	431,023	651,481	234,558	341,397
Electronics	745,221	969,448	151,438	156,115
Building and civil engineering	3,387	2,477	0	0
Cement, glass and other building products	73,118	100,903	69,330	97,153
Paper, printing and publishing	97,103	115,796	58,528	64,638
Food and drinks	330,265	495,949	193,860	258,557
Textiles and clothing	19,717	43,348	11,554	24,937
Other manufacturing industries	123,127	172,537	60,163	80,772
Service industries	153,728	181,760	69,575	70,167
Total	4,036,532	5,548,401	1,853,830	2,535,306

Source: R&S (Ricerche e Studi)–Mediobanca (2013) 'Multinationals: Financial Aggregates', Milan (www.mbres.it).

Appendix II.2

Fortune, 'Global 500: The World's Largest Corporations' (fiscal year 2013) – the EU big five (ranked within countries)

Table A.II.2a Britain: 27 companies[1] and $1,598,958.6 million of total revenues

		500 rank
1	BP	6
2	Tesco	63
3	HSBC Holdings	77
4	Lloyds Banking Group	94
5	Prudential	95
6	Vodafone Group	141
7	Aviva	157
8	Legal and General Group	159
9	Barclays	171
10	Rio Tinto Group[2]	201
11	SSE	215
12	Royal Bank of Scotland Group	255
13	Centrica	263
14	GlaxoSmithKline*	265
15	J. Sainsbury	293
16	Standard Life	374
17	Old Mutual	387
18	Angloamerican[2]	413
19	BT Group	421
20	WM Morrison Supermarkets	435
21	Compass Group	437
22	BAE Systems*	455
23	Astrazeneca*	468
24	Standard Chartered	470
25	International Airlines Group	484
26	Rolls-Royce Holdings*	489
27	British American Tobacco*	499

Notes
* Manufacturing.
1 Plus Unilever ($66,108.6) ranked 140 as company for Britain/Netherlands.
2 Mining.

Table A.II.2b France: 31 companies and $2,078,681.6 million of total revenues

		500 rank
1	Total	11
2	AXA	16
3	Société Gènérale	33
4	BNP Paribas	40
5	GDF Suez	44
6	Carrefour	65
7	Électricité de France	70
8	Crédit Agricole	83
9	Peugeot*	119
10	Groupe BPCE	136
11	Foncière Euris	144
12	Groupe Auchan	149
13	CNP Assurances	175
14	Saint-Gobain*	180
15	Vinci§	188
16	Orange	189
17	Renault*	190
18	Bouygues§	235
19	Sanofi*	238
20	SNCF	253
21	Christian Dior*	289
22	Vivendi	325
23	Air France-KLM Group	351
24	La Poste	364
25	Veolia Environment	376
26	Schneider Electric*	387
27	L'Oréal*	402
28	Danone*	429
29	Alstom*	441
30	Michelin*	448
31	Sodexo	493

Notes
* Manufacturing.
§ Infrastructure, construction.

Table A.II.2c Germany: 28 companies and $2,060,564.3 million of total revenues

		500 rank
1	Volkswagen*	8
2	E.ON	18
3	Daimler*	20
4	Allianz	31
5	Siemens*	58
6	BMW Group*	68
7	BASF*	75
8	Metro	91
9	Munich Re Group	93
10	Deutsche Telekom	99
11	Deutsche Post	110
12	RWE	130
13	Robert Bosch*	155
14	Deutsche Bank	163
15	Bayer*	193
16	Thyssenkrupp*	197
17	Deutsche Bahn	198
18	Continental*	237
19	Lufthansa Group	275
20	Talanx	302
21	Edeka Zentrale	326
22	DZ Ban	335
23	Franz Haniel§	359
24	Landesbank Baden-Württemberg	378
25	Phoenix Pharmahandel	422
26	Energie Baden-Württemberg	440
27	Fresenius*	444
28	TUI	490

Notes
* Manufacturing.
§ Infrastructure, construction.

Table A.II.2d Italy: 9 companies and $728,267.9 million of total revenues

		500 rank
1	ENI	22
2	EXOR Group*[1]	24
3	Assicurazioni Generali	48
4	ENEL	56
5	Intesa Sanpaolo	200
6	UniCredit Group	204
7	Telecom Italia	319
8	Poste Italiane	336
9	Unipol	439

Notes
* Manufacturing.
1 The revenues of Exor Group combine automotive (Fiat and Fiat Industrial) with many other service activities.

Table A.II.2e Spain: 8 companies and $450,282.4 million of total revenues

		500 rank
1	Banco Santander	73
2	Telefónica	109
3	Repsol	126
4	ACS	202
5	Banco Bilbao Vizcaya Argentaria	206
6	Iberdrola	244
7	Gas Natural Fenosa	360
8	Mapfre Group	415

Source: taken from *Fortune* (2014) 'The Global 500: The World's Largest Corporations', 21 July.

Notes
* Manufacturing.

Appendix II.3

European and global M&As: an overview

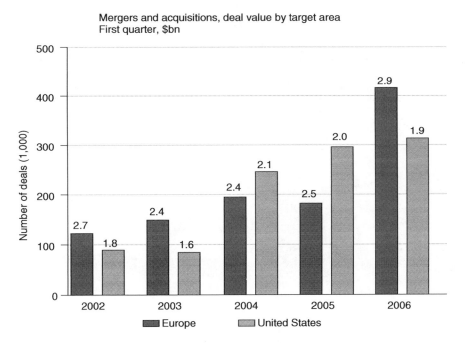

Mergers and acquisitions, deal value by target area
First quarter, $bn

Figure A.II.3a Overtaking (source: *The Economist* (2006) 'Once More Unto the Breach, Dear Client, Once More', 6 April (www.economist.com)).

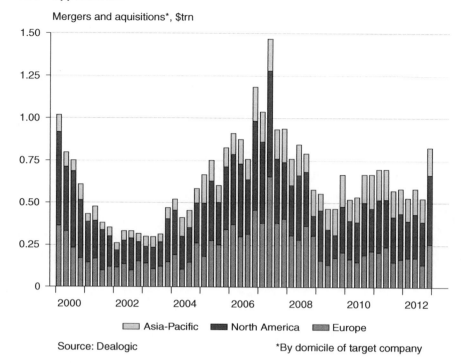

Figure A.II.3b Romance returns? (source: *The Economist* (2013), 'Shall We?' 9 February
(www.economist.com)).

Appendix II.4

SMEs: a European comparison

Table A.II.4a Micro enterprises

	Number of enterprises			Number of employees			Value added		
	Number	*Share*	*EU-27 share*	*Number*	*Share*	*EU-27 share*	*€ billion*	*Share*	*EU-27 share*
Italy	3,491,826	94.4%	92.1%	6,930,947	46.1%	28.7%	185	29.8%	21.1%
France	2,334,664	93.8%	–	4,167,624	28.6%	–	223	26.1%	–
Germany	1,763,465	81.7%	–	4,859,923	18.5%	–	209	15.1%	–
Spain	2,103,390	93.8%	–	4,318,258	39.8%	–	121	27.5%	–
UK	1,495,648	89.4%	–	3,294,670	18.4%	–	177	18.6%	–

Table A.II.4b Small enterprises

	Number of enterprises			Number of employees			Value added		
	Number	*Share*	*EU-27 share*	*Number*	*Share*	*EU-27 share*	*€ billion*	*Share*	*EU-27 share*
Italy	183,198	5.0%	6.6%	3,236,764	21.5%	20.4%	136	21.9%	18.3%
France	128,552	5.2%	–	2,735,962	18.8%	–	149	17.5%	–
Germany	328,593	15.2%	–	6,140,520	23.4%	–	257	18.5%	–
Spain	120,940	5.4%	–	2,297,597	21.2%	–	91	20.6%	–
UK	145,350	8.7%	–	3,227,189	18.0%	–	142	14.9%	–

Table A.II.4c Medium enterprises

	Number of enterprises			Number of employees			Value added		
	Number	Share	EU-27 share	Number	Share	EU-27 share	€ billion	Share	EU-27 share
Italy	19,265	0.5%	1.1%	1,861,089	12.4%	17.3%	101	16.3%	18.3%
France	20,628	0.8%	–	2,204,603	15.2%	–	128	15.0%	–
Germany	55,510	2.6%	–	5,348,282	20.4%	–	280	20.2%	–
Spain	15,484	0.7%	–	1,513,350	13.9%	–	73	16.7%	–
UK	25,727	1.5%	–	2,865,963	16.0%	–	155	16.3%	–

Table A.II.4d SMEs (micro + small + medium)

	Number of enterprises			Number of employees			Value added		
	Number	Share	EU-27 share	Number	Share	EU-27 share	€ billion	Share	EU-27 share
Italy	3,694,288	99.9%	99.8%	12,028,799	80.0%	66.5%	422	68.0%	57.6%
France	2,483,844	99.8%	–	9,108,188	62.6%	–	501	58.5%	–
Germany	2,147,569	99.5%	–	16,348,724	62.2%	–	745	53.8%	–
Spain	2,239,814	99.9%	–	8,129,205	74.9%	–	284	64.8%	–
UK	1,666,725	99.6%	–	9,387,822	52.4%	–	473	49.8%	–

Table A.II.4e Large enterprises

	Number of enterprises			Number of employees			Value added		
	Number	Share	EU-27 share	Number	Share	EU-27 share	€ billion	Share	EU-27 share
Italy	3,196	0.1%	0.2%	3,013,012	20.0%	33.5%	198	32.0%	42.4%
France	4,470	0.2%	–	5,439,018	37.4%	–	355	41.5%	–
Germany	10,758	0.5%	–	9,915,234	37.8%	–	640	46.2%	–
Spain	2,728	0.1%	–	2,731,229	25.1%	–	154	35.2%	–
UK	5,913	0.4%	–	8,524,622	47.6%	–	477	50.2%	–

Table A.II.4f Total

	Number of enterprises			Number of employees			Value added		
	Number	Share	EU-27 share	Number	Share	EU-27 share	€ billion	Share	EU-27 share
Italy	3,697,484	100.0%	100.0%	15,041,81	100.0%	100.0%	620	100.0%	100.0%
France	2,488,314	100.0%	–	14,547,206	100.0%	–	856	100.0%	–
Germany	2,158,327	100.0%	–	26,263,958	100.0%	–	1,385	100.0%	–
Spain	2,242,542	100.0%	–	10,860,434	100.0%	–	439	100.0%	–
UK	1,672,638	100.0%	–	17,912,444	100.0%	–	950	100.0%	–

Source: adapted from the European Commission (2013) 'SBA Fact Sheet for France, Germany, Italy, Spain, and the UK', Brussels, Directorate-General for Enterprises and Industry.

Appendix II.5
Value added by activity as a percentage of total value added

Table A.II.5 Value added by economic activity (% of total value added)

	Agriculture, hunting, forestry, fishing		Industry, including energy		Construction		Trade, transport; accommodation; restaurants; communication		Financial and insurance; real estate; business services		Other service activities	
	2000	2012 or latest available year	2000	2012 or latest available year	2000	2012 or latest available year	2000	2012 or latest available year	2000	2012 or latest available year	2000	2012 or latest available year
Australia	3.8	2.4	20.6	20.5	5.6	7.7	22.5	20.0	28.1	30.7	19.4	18.7
Austria	1.9	1.6	23.7	21.8	7.7	6.8	26.2	25.5	20.7	23.8	19.8	20.5
Belgium	1.3	0.7	21.9	15.9	5.2	5.9	23.1	24.0	26.6	28.5	21.8	24.9
Canada	2.3	–	28.2	–	5.0	–	20.3	–	25.0	–	19.2	–
Chile	5.4	3.6	27.9	27.7	6.6	8.3	19.5	18.4	16.4	20.1	24.3	21.9
Czech Republic	3.6	2.4	30.9	31.0	6.6	6.3	27.1	24.5	15.0	18.3	16.8	17.5
Denmark	2.5	1.4	21.1	17.0	5.5	4.8	24.4	23.7	21.1	25.7	25.4	27.3
Estonia	4.8	4.1	21.6	21.2	5.9	7.8	29.4	26.9	21.6	23.3	16.7	16.7
Finland	3.5	2.8	28.0	19.0	6.3	6.9	21.9	22.5	19.6	23.6	20.6	25.1
France	2.5	2.0	17.8	12.5	5.0	6.3	23.1	22.8	27.5	30.4	24.1	26.0
Germany	1.1	0.8	25.2	25.8	5.3	4.7	20.3	18.6	26.2	27.2	21.9	22.9
Greece	–	3.4	–	14.3	–	2.1	–	28.2	–	26.4	–	25.6
Hungary	5.9	4.7	27.1	26.8	5.3	3.8	21.5	22.9	19.2	21.8	21.0	20.0
Iceland	8.5	8.3	17.2	21.0	9.3	4.4	24.8	20.8	18.5	22.6	21.8	22.9
Ireland	3.6	1.6	28.0	26.3	7.3	1.6	25.0	25.2	21.1	25.4	15.0	19.9
Israel	1.7	1.9	19.0	15.2	5.4	5.7	18.0	16.9	31.1	36.3	24.7	24.1

Italy	2.8	2.0	22.6	18.4	5.1	5.9	26.1	24.8	24.4	28.3	18.9	20.6
Japan	1.5	1.2	24.3	20.5	7.0	5.6	20.7	24.6	15.9	17.0	30.7	31.1
Korea	4.6	2.6	31.6	33.8	6.9	5.8	21.7	18.8	19.3	19.1	15.8	19.7
Luxembourg	0.7	0.3	12.8	6.7	6.5	6.2	23.5	24.2	41.9	44.8	14.7	17.8
Mexico	4.2	3.4	29.4	29.6	6.4	6.6	29.8	28.1	19.0	18.9	12.7	13.5
Netherlands	2.5	1.7	19.1	19.4	5.7	4.9	26.1	23.2	25.6	25.5	21.0	25.3
New Zealand	8.4	–	20.8	–	4.7	–	22.1	–	26.9	–	17.1	–
Norway	2.1	1.2	37.7	36.6	4.0	5.9	21.0	16.1	15.3	18.8	20.0	21.4
Poland	4.9	3.9	23.3	24.6	7.8	7.8	29.2	30.0	18.0	17.2	16.8	16.4
Portugal	3.6	2.3	20.3	18.5	8.2	5.1	26.7	28.7	19.2	23.0	22.0	22.4
Slovak Republic	4.5	3.1	28.8	27.0	7.2	8.2	26.4	26.7	16.6	18.3	16.6	16.7
Slovenia	3.4	2.7	28.1	25.2	6.7	5.9	22.6	24.7	19.8	21.0	19.4	20.5
Spain	4.2	2.5	20.8	17.4	10.3	8.6	28.1	29.5	16.9	20.3	19.6	21.8
Sweden	2.0	1.6	24.2	19.9	4.3	5.3	22.2	23.0	22.5	23.3	24.7	26.9
Switzerland	1.3	0.7	21.2	21.3	5.2	5.5	25.7	26.0	21.3	20.3	25.1	26.2
Turkey	10.8	8.9	24.6	21.8	5.4	4.9	29.1	31.8	19.5	20.2	10.6	12.4
United Kingdom	0.9	0.7	20.8	14.5	6.0	6.0	26.8	24.6	25.4	31.3	20.1	22.8
United States	–	–	–	–	–	–	–	–	–	–	–	–
Euro area	2.4	1.7	22.0	19.3	5.9	5.8	23.8	23.2	24.7	26.9	21.3	23.2
EU-28	2.3	1.7	22.0	19.3	6.0	5.9	24.4	24.0	24.2	26.2	21.2	22.8
OECD	–	–	–	–	–	–	–	–	–	–	–	–
Brazil	–	–	–	–	–	–	–	–	–	–	–	–
China	15.1	10.1	40.4	38.5	5.6	6.8	16.6	16.3	8.3	11.1	14.1	17.1
India	–	–	–	–	–	–	–	–	–	–	–	–
Indonesia	15.6	15.3	40.4	36.8	5.5	10.3	20.8	20.2	8.3	7.2	9.3	10.2
Russian Federation	6.4	3.9	31.1	29.5	6.6	6.5	33.1	28.9	4.6	16.2	18.3	15.1
South Africa	3.3	2.6	29.3	24.4	2.5	4.0	24.3	25.1	18.6	21.5	22.0	22.5

Source: OECD (2014) *OECD Factbook 2014: Economic, Environmental and Social Statistics*, Paris, OECD, 6 May (www.oecd-ilibrary-org).

Appendix II.6

Share in gross value added (GVA)

Table A.II.6 Share in gross value added (GVA) in 2012 and change in shares of GVA between 2000 and 2012 (%)

Sectors	Agriculture, forestry and fishing		Mining and quarrying		Manufacturing		Electricity, gas and water supply		Construction		Market services		Non-market services	
Country (Y1–Y2)	Change	Share	Change	Share	Change	Share	Change	Share	Change	Share	Change	Share	Change	Share
Austria (2000–2012)	-0.3	1.6	0.2	0.5	-1.9	18.2	-0.2	3.0	-0.9	6.8	2.4	49.3	0.7	20.5
Belgium (2000–2012)	-0.6	0.7	-0.1	0.1	-5.9	12.8	0.0	3.1	0.6	5.9	2.8	52.5	3.1	24.9
Bulgaria (2000–2012)	-6.2	6.4	0.5	2.4	2.8	16.7	-0.1	5.4	0.9	5.9	4.1	47.9	-2.0	15.3
Cyprus (2000–2012)	-1.3	2.5	-0.1	0.2	-4.0	5.7	1.0	3.2	-2.9	5.8	2.7	56.4	4.6	26.2
Czech Republic (2000–2012)	-1.2	2.4	-0.1	1.2	-1.2	24.7	1.3	5.1	-0.3	6.3	0.7	42.8	0.8	17.5
Germany (2000–2012)	-0.3	0.8	0.0	0.2	0.1	22.4	0.5	3.2	-0.6	4.7	-0.7	45.7	1.0	22.9
Denmark (2000–2012)	-1.1	1.4	0.6	3.6	-4.3	11.0	-0.3	2.4	-0.7	4.8	3.9	49.4	1.9	27.3
Estonia (2000–2012)	-0.6	4.1	0.2	1.3	-1.7	15.4	1.0	4.5	1.9	7.8	-0.7	50.2	0.0	16.7
Greece (2000–2011)	-3.2	3.4	-0.3	0.3	-1.7	9.2	1.2	3.9	-4.7	2.5	3.1	55.3	5.5	25.5
Spain (2000–2011)	-1.7	2.5	-0.1	0.2	-4.4	13.5	0.6	3.2	-0.2	10.1	3.5	48.6	2.3	21.9
Finland (2000–2012)	-0.7	2.8	0.2	0.4	-10.3	15.4	1.1	3.2	0.6	6.9	4.6	46.1	4.5	25.1
France (2000–2012)	-0.5	2.0	0.0	0.1	-5.3	10.0	0.0	2.4	1.3	6.3	2.6	53.2	1.9	26.0
Hungary (2000–2012)	-1.1	4.7	0.0	0.3	-0.2	22.7	-0.1	3.9	-1.5	3.8	3.9	44.6	-0.9	20.0
Ireland (2000–2012)	-2.0	1.6	-0.2	0.4	-2.5	23.3	1.0	2.6	-5.8	1.6	4.5	50.6	5.0	19.9
Italy (2000–2012)	-0.8	2.0	-0.1	0.4	-4.5	15.6	0.3	2.3	0.8	5.9	2.6	53.1	1.7	20.6
Lithuania (2000–2012)	-2.3	4.0	-0.3	0.4	2.0	20.8	-0.3	3.9	0.0	6.0	5.5	49.5	-4.5	15.5
Luxembourg (2000–2012)	-0.3	0.3	-0.1	0.1	-5.6	5.3	-0.4	1.3	-0.3	6.2	3.6	69.0	3.0	17.8
Latvia (2000–2012)	0.5	5.0	0.5	0.6	0.1	14.5	0.4	4.5	-0.6	6.2	3.4	53.7	-4.2	15.6

Source: European Commission (2013) 'EU Industrial Structure Report: Competing in Global Value Chains', Luxembourg, Publication Office of the European Union.

Appendix III.1

EU and US R&D expenditure

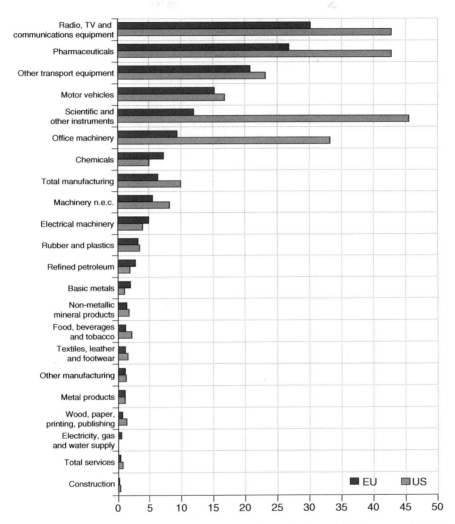

Figure A.III.1 EU and US R&D expenditure as shares of value added in sectors in 2006
(%) (source: European Commission (2011) 'EU Industrial Structure
Report: Trends and Performance', Directorate-General for Enterprise and
Industry, Luxembourg, Publications Office of the European Union).

Note
The EU is represented by 17 countries: Austria, Belgium, Czech Republic, Denmark, Finland,
France, Germany, Greece, Hungary, Ireland, Italy, Netherlands, Poland, Portugal, Spain, Sweden and
the UK. The industries are classified according to ISIC Rev. 3.1.

Appendix III.2
EU-27 revealed comparative advantage

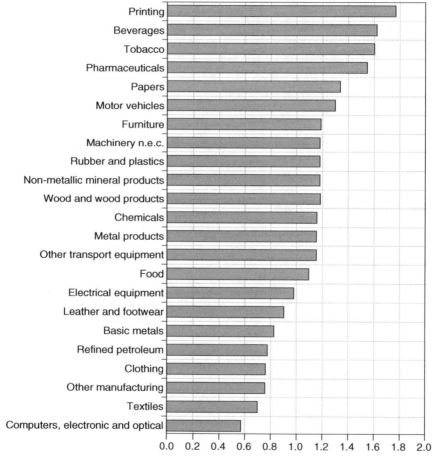

Figure A.III.2 EU-27 RCA index in 2009 (source: European Commission (2011) 'EU Industrial Structure Report: Trends and Performance', Directorate-General for Enterprise and Industry, Luxembourg, Publications Office of the European Union).

Appendix IV

Europe 2020 and the knowledge investment

Table A.IVa Horizon 2020: The EU Framework Programme for Research and Innovation

Structure
- Excellent Science: to promote the research and the policies in actual and emerging technology and science (Regulation No. 1291/2013, Annex I, Part I: 'This Part aims to reinforce and extend the excellence of the Union's science base and to consolidate the ERA [European Research Area] in order to make the Union's research and innovation system more competitive on a global scale').
- Industrial Leadership: to aid the European enterprises to reorganize into a global competition (Regulation No. 1291/2013, Annex I, Part II: 'This Part aims to speed up development of the technologies and innovations that will underpin tomorrow's businesses and help innovative European SMEs to grow into world-leading companies').
- Societal Challenges: to reply to the change of European and world societies (Regulation No. 1291/2013, Annex I, Part II: 'This Part responds directly to the policy priorities and societal challenges that are identified in the Europe 2020 strategy and that aim to stimulate the critical mass of research and innovation efforts needed to achieve the Union's policy goals').

Time of this action
From 1 January 2014 to 31 December 2020

Juridical basis
- Art. 173 para. 1 TUFE
- Art. 182 para. 1 TFUE
- Art. 188 TFUE
- Art. 195 TFUE
- Regulation (EU) of the European Parliament and of the Council:

✓ No. 1287/2013 'establishing a Programme for the Competitiveness of Enterprises and small and medium-sized enterprises (COSME) (2014–2020) and repealing Decision No 1639/2006/EC', 11 December 2013
✓ No. 1290/2013 'laying down rules for participation and dissemination in "Horizon 2020 – the Framework Programme for Research and Innovation (2014–2020)" and repealing Regulation (EC) No 1906/2006, 11 December 2013
✓ No. 1291/2013 'establishing Horizon 2020 – The Framework Programme for Research and Innovation (2014–2020) and repealing Decision No 1982/2006/EC', 11 December 2013
✓ No. 1291/2013 'amending Regulation (EC) No 294/2008 establishing the European Institute of Innovation and Technology', 11 December 2013

continued

Table A.IVa Continued

- Commission Decision (2013/C 373/09) 'establishing the European Research Council', 12 December 2013
- Commission Implementing Decision (2013/779/EU) 'establishing the European Research Council Executive Agency and repealing Decision 2008/37/EC', 17 December 2013

Financial basis (Regulation No. 1291/2013)

Initiative	€ million
I Excellent science	24,441.1
1 European Research Council (ERC)	13,094.8
2 Future and Emerging Technologies (FET)	2,696.3
3 Marie Skłodowska-Curie actions	6,162
4 Research infrastructures	2,488
II Industrial leadership	17,015.5
1 Leadership in enabling and industrial technologies	13,557
2 Access to risk finance	2,842.3
3 Innovation in SMEs	616.2
III Societal challenges	29,679
1 Health, demographic change and well-being	7,471.8
2 Food security, sustainable agriculture and forestry, marine, maritime and inland water research, and the bioeconomy	3,851.4
3 Secure, clean and efficient energy	5,931.2
4 Smart, green and integrated transport	6,339.4
5 Climate action, environment, resource efficiency and raw materials	3,081.1
6 Europe in a changing world – inclusive, innovative and reflective societies	1,309.5
7 Secure societies – protecting freedom and security of Europe and its citizens	1,694.6
IV Spreading excellence and widening participation	816.5
V Science with and for society	462.2
VI Non-nuclear direct actions of the Joint Research Centre (JRC)	1,902.6
VII The European Institute of Innovation and Technology (EIT)	2,711.4
Total fund	77,028.3

Table A.IVb COSME: Programme for the Competitiveness of Enterprises and Small and Medium-sized Enterprises

Juridical basis	Regulation (EU) of the European Parliament and of the Council No. 1287/2013
Time of this action (art. 1)	From 1 January 2014 to 31 December 2020
This programme is dedicated to:	SMEs as defined by Communication 2003/361/CE
General objectives (art. 3)	(a) strengthening the competitiveness and sustainability of the Union's enterprises, particularly SMEs; (b) encouraging entrepreneurial culture and promoting the creation and growth of SMEs.
Specific objectives (art. 4)	(a) to improve access to finance for SMEs in the form of equity and debt; (b) to improve access to markets, particularly inside the Union but also at global level; (c) to improve framework conditions for the competitiveness and sustainability of Union enterprises, particularly SMEs, including in the tourism sector; (d) to promote entrepreneurship and entrepreneurial culture.
Budget 2014–2020	*Total fund*: €2,298,243 million *Indicative allocation for specific objective described by art. 4*: (a) no less than 60% (financial instruments); (b) 21.5%; (c) 11%; (d) 2.5%.

Table A.IVc EIT: The European Institute of Innovation and Technology

Juridical basis	• Regulation (EU) of the European Parliament and of the Council No. 1291/2913 ('Horizon 2020'). • Regulation (EU) of the European Parliament and of the Council No. 1292/2013.
Specific objectives	'[T]o integrate the knowledge triangle of higher education, research and innovation and thus to reinforce the Union's innovation capacity and address societal challenges' (Regulation No. 1291/2013, Part VII, para. 1).
Main activities	(a) transferring and applying higher education, research and innovation activities for new business creation; (b) cutting-edge and innovation-driven research in areas of key economic and societal interest; (c) development of talented, skilled and entrepreneurial people with the aid of education and training; (d) dissemination of best practice and systemic knowledge-sharing; (e) international dimension; (f) enhancing European wide impact through an innovative funding model; (g) linking regional development to European opportunities. (Regulation No. 1291/2013, Part VII, para. 3)
Budget (2014–2020)	€2,711.4 million (Regulation No. 1292/2013 art. 19 para. 1)

Table A.IVd ERASMUS+

Juridical basis

Regulation (EU) No. 1288/2013 of 11 December 2013 'establishing "Erasmus+": the Union programme for education, training, youth and sport'.

Structure of the main actions

1 Education and training:

'education and training at all levels, in a lifelong learning perspective, including school education (Comenius), higher education (Erasmus), international higher education (Erasmus Mundus), vocational education and training (Leonardo da Vinci) and adult learning (Grundtvig)'
(Regulation No. 1288/2013, Ch. I, art. 1, para. 3(a))

Actions of the Programme (art. 6)
- (a) learning mobility of individuals (art. 7);
- (b) cooperation for innovation and the exchange of good practices (art. 8);
- (c) support for policy reform (art. 9);
- (d) Jean Monnet activities (art. 10).

2 Youth

'(Youth in Action), particularly in the context of non-formal and informal learning'.
(Regulation No. 1288/2013, Ch. I, art. 1, para. 3(b))
(Regulation No. 1288/2013, Ch. III):

Actions of the Programme (art. 12)
- (a) learning mobility of individuals (art. 13);
- (b) cooperation for innovation and the exchange of good practices (art. 14);
- (c) support for policy reform (art. 15).

3 Sport

'in particular grassroots sport'.
(Regulation No. 1288/2013, Ch. I, art. 1, para. 3(c))
Communication and dissemination (Regulation No. 1288/2013, Ch. VI, art. 22, para. 4)
- 'Comenius', associated with school education;
- 'Erasmus', associated with all types of higher education within the programme countries;
- 'Erasmus Mundus', associated with all types of higher education activities between the programme countries and partner countries;
- 'Leonardo da Vinci', associated with vocational education and training;
- 'Grundtvig', associated with adult learning.

Total found:
€14,774,524,000 (Regulation No. 1288/2013, Ch. V, art. 18)

Allocation of resources, 2014–2020:

77.5% to education and training:

43.0% to higher education, representing 33.3% of the total budget;

22.0% to vocational education and training, representing 17% of the total budget;

15.0% to school education, representing 11.6% of the total budget;

5.0% to adult learning, representing 3.9% of the total budget;

10.0% to youth;

3.5% to the Student Loan Guarantee Facility;

1.9% to Jean Monnet activities;

1.8% to sport, of which no more than 10% to the activity mentioned under point (b) of art. 17;

3.4% as operating grants to national agencies;

1.9% to cover administrative expenditure.

Entry into force

1 January 2014 (Regulation No. 1288/2013, Ch. XI, art. 38)

Access to the programme:

'Any public or private body active in the fields of education, training, youth and grassroots sport may apply for funding within the Programme.'
(Regulation No. 1288/2013, Ch. XI, art. 23, para. 1)

Country participation (Regulation No. 1288/2013, Ch. XI, art. 24):

(a) the Member States;

(b) the acceding countries, candidate countries and potential candidates benefitting from a pre-accession strategy;

(c) those EFTA countries that are party to the EEA Agreement, in accordance with the provisions of that agreement;

(d) the Swiss Confederation, on the basis of a bilateral agreement to be concluded with that country;

(e) those countries covered by the European neighbourhood policy which have concluded agreements with the Union.

Table A.IVe Connecting Europe Facility

Main objectives
Connecting Europe Facility (CEF) aims to improve the performance of investments in trans-European networks (TENs) to improve the connectivity and competitiveness of European regions and companies.

Juridical basis
Regulation (EU) No. 1316/2013 of 11 December 2013 'establishing the Connecting Europe Facility'.
Regulation (EU) No. 1315/2013 of 11 December 2013 'on Union guidelines for the development of the trans-European transport network'.

Budget and structure
(Regulation (EU) No. 1316/2013, art. 5)
Total funds for the period 2014 to 2020: €33,242,259, 000 in current prices:
• transport sector (railway, inland waterways transport infrastructure, road transport infrastructure, maritime transport infrastructure and motorways of the sea): €26,250,582,000 (of which €11,305,500,000 shall be transferred from the Cohesion Fund);
• telecommunications sector: €1,141,602,000.
• energy sector: €5,850,075,000

Entry into force
1 January 2014

Index

Page numbers in *italics* denote tables, those in **bold** denote figures.

222   *Index*

medium enterprises *208*; *see also* SMEs
(small- and medium-sized enterprises)
'megatrends' 48n15
mergers and acquisitions (M&As), cross-
border 6, 123; *see also* competition
policy; European and global **205–6**; and
'European Champions' 61, 79, 81–2,
83–7; European Commission on
103n31; examples 49n25, 82, 101n15,
103n30; and overview of new European
industrial policy 40; waves 40, 56, 70,
104n33
Merkel, Angela 67, 174
MFF (Multiannual Financial Framework)
127, 155
microeconomic policies 8, 14, 47, *191*; *see
also* macroeconomic policies; and
'European Champions' 60, 74; growing
role of 188–93; and models of
capitalism 111, 116
micro enterprises *207*; *see also* SMEs
(small- and medium-sized enterprises)
Microsoft, takeover of Nokia 82
Millennial Perspective (Maddison) 139
Mittal Steel 82
mixed banking 116
Modern Capitalism (Shonfield) 117, 118
Momigliano, Franco 95
Monetary Union *see* European Monetary
Union (EMU)
Monga, C. 15
Monitor dei Distretti (ISP-Intesa
Sanpaolo) 99
Monti, Mario 48n13
Multiannual Financial Framework (MFF)
127, 155
multinationals (Mediobanca) 65–7, *200*

'National Champions' 6, 32, 62–3, 65, 67,
82, 113, 176; *see also* 'European
Champions'
National Science Foundation (NSF), US
18, 164
Neheider, S. 185n4
'neo-American' capitalism 7, 110, 114,
119, 123
'neo-Colbertism' 8
neoliberalism 119
Netherlands, the 36
New Economy 13, 61, 119, 146; in United
States 68, 118
New Industrial Organization, The
(Jacquemin) 31
New Regionalism 188

non-profit sector 113, 133n1, 134n2
normalization 2, 3
'Normalizing Industrial Policy' (Rodrik) 2,
32
NSF (National Science Foundation), US
18, 164

Obama, Barack 28, 34, 178, 193
OECD (Organisation for Economic
Cooperation and Development) 70, 71,
92; 'global vision' 76, *77*, 78; *Industrial
Policy in a Changing World* 194; *OECD
Factbook* 93–4
Of Markets, Products and Prices (Bruegel
report) 64
oil and gas companies 78, 81
O'Mahony, M. 20
OMT (Outright Monetary Transactions)
177
'One Market, One Money' principle 60,
140, 175
Osservatorio Nazionale Distretti Italiani
100
O'Sullivan, E. 15
Ottaviano, G. 63–4
Owen, G. 15

Padoa-Schioppa, Tommaso 17, 190
Paris summit (2008) 176
patents, indicators of 124–5
Pelkmans, J. 15
personal capitalism 115
Persson, Goran 165n6
pharmaceuticals industry 23, 25, 27, 30,
72, 104n32, 124, 125
Pill, Huw 177
Pisani-Ferry, Jean 60, 64, 101n11, 148
Pisano, Gary 34, 128, 129
planned economies, vs. free-market
economies 111, 114
players *see* Big European Players
'plots': from 1950s 56–8; intertwining
58–62
Polanyi, Karl 112
Pontarollo, E. 100
Porter, R. H. 101n10
Porter, Michael E. 128
'Presidency Conclusions,' European
Council 147, 148, 166n10
privatization 12
Prodi, Romano 3, 16, 24, 27, 42, 48n12,
49n24, 92, 95, 146, 182
productive process 5
protectionism 185